IMAGES
of America

FOREST COUNTY

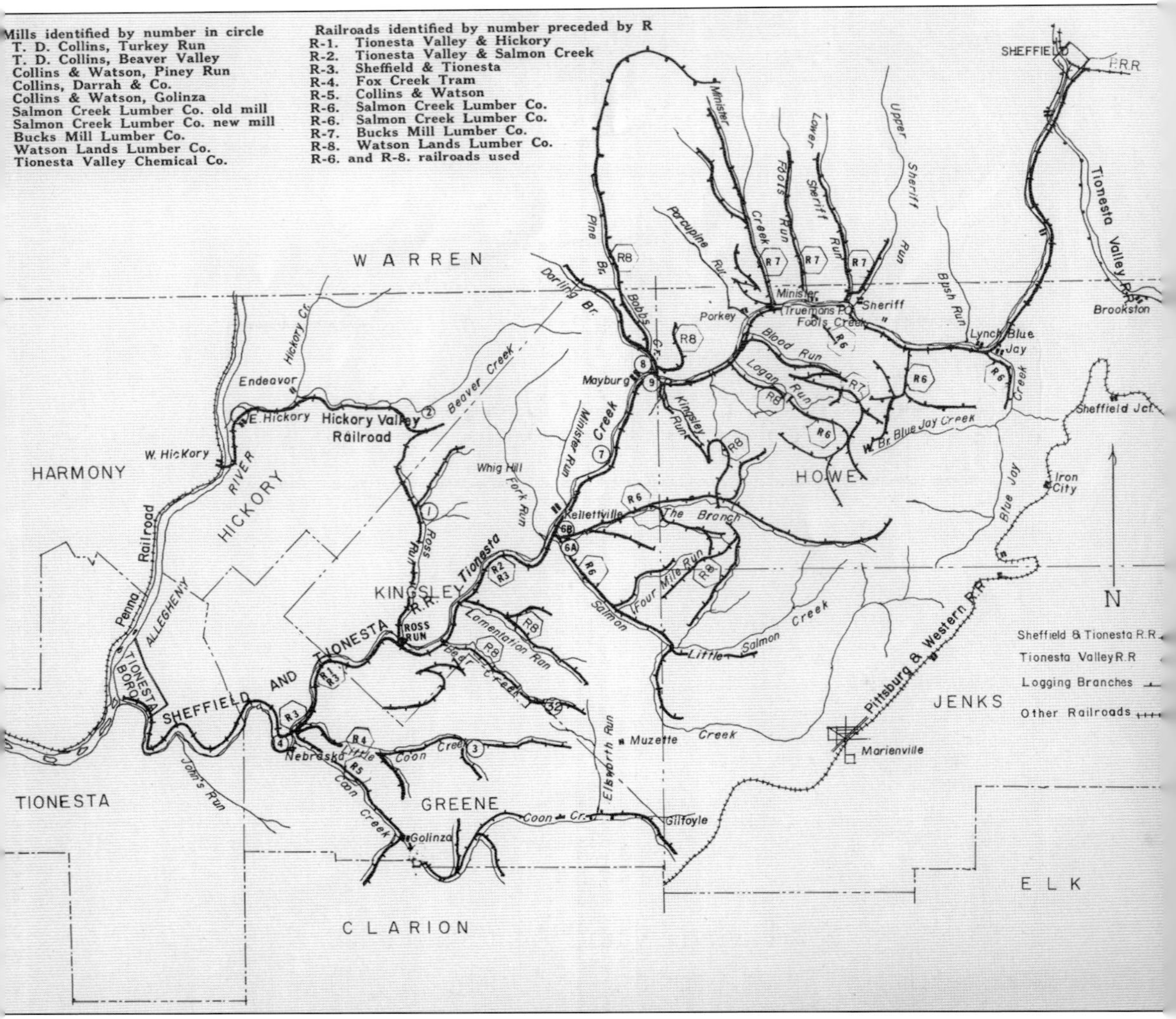

Shown on this c. 1900 map are the mills and railroads operating throughout Forest County at the time and their geographical location in relation to the various waterways. For more efficient mill production and travel, railroads were built along the creeks and rivers, with many communities being established nearby. Most of the railroads and mills have been dismantled, and only traces of their once bustling activity remain today. (Courtesy of the Forest County Historical Society.)

On the Cover: A large tent is pitched for a gathering at "Camp Osocozy" in Balltown, Howe Township. A popular area for recreation, this location had a variety of stunning natural features. The forest was strewn with huge blocks of sandstone and a beautiful waterfall known as Logan Falls. Balltown was named after Israel Ball, who manufactured lumber at his sawmill. Some coal was mined near Balltown, but it was not a long-lived business. (Courtesy of the Forest County Historical Society.)

IMAGES
of America

FOREST COUNTY

Joseph Pavlansky and Paula Hanahan
in association with the
Forest County Historical Society

ARCADIA
PUBLISHING

ISBN 978-1-4671-2619-9

Published by Arcadia Publishing
Charleston, South Carolina

Printed in the United States of America

Library of Congress Control Number: 2016959735

For all general information, please contact Arcadia Publishing:
Telephone 843-853-2070
Fax 843-853-0044
E-mail sales@arcadiapublishing.com
For customer service and orders:
Toll-Free 1-888-313-2665

Visit us on the Internet at www.arcadiapublishing.com

To all the past, present, and future generations of Forest County, Pennsylvania.

CONTENTS

Acknowledgments

We would like to thank Arcadia Publishing for encouraging those interested in their local history to tell their community's story through historical narratives and photographs. We are also appreciative of Caroline Anderson, our title manager, for her professional guidance that enabled us to stay on track.

This book could not have been written without the support and assistance of the Forest County Historical Society, which opened its doors to us with pleasure and gave us access to all the historical photographs and writings they have carefully collected and preserved. We are grateful to the society for all they have done and continue to do to maintain the rich history of Penn's Woods.

To the many past and present historians and enthusiasts who have worked to compile, promote, and share the history of Forest County, we cannot thank you enough. Many thanks also go to Carla Woodside and Dawn Baird of the Sarah Stewart Bovard Memorial Library for their help and cheers.

Fate had a hand in the writing of this book, as the two authors had never met before. Although we live 100 miles apart, a chance encounter brought us together at a time when we both had coincidentally decided to write about Forest County. The scenic wonders of Minister Creek were initially the catalyst that created our connection. We talked about our love for the area and how much it meant to us. Soon after, we decided to write this book together to honor the people and places that had changed our lives forever. With such an expansive library of books, articles, and other historic information on Forest County, we have put together this book to complement those works and inspire a new generation.

Joe would like to specially thank Antonietta "Toni" Iacobacci; his father and mother, Dennis and Bonnie; and sister Shannon for their love and unending support.

Paula is grateful to her loving family and friends for their continuous encouragement and to the peaceful hemlock forest that surrounds her home in Kellettville.

All photographs are courtesy of the Forest County Historical Society.

INTRODUCTION

Visualize the geography of Western Pennsylvania during the 18th and early 19th century, and imagine that you are one of the first pioneers to explore the region. The land, for the most part, is untouched and in perfect balance with its surroundings. The forests are thick with tall trees, wild rock formations, snaking waterways, and various families of animals looking for their next meal. The rolling hills and towering mountains give an unnerving feeling as you bask in the hot sun traversing the wide-open sky. Fresh, uninhibited air whisks past your nostrils and revitalizes your body as the sounds of nature provide a calming feeling despite the inherent danger concealed within the land. Its beauty, you realize, is truly a sight to behold—nature without restraint.

But long before the first settler arrived in what would later be Forest County, Native American tribes called this land home. The historical presence of giant beasts led the Paleo-Indians to this land roughly 10,000 years ago. Some clues of their mysterious lives were left for us to fathom, while others were unearthed along the riverbanks. It is not quite clear which indigenous people chose to dwell here after the earliest natives. However, we do know that centuries later, the Munsee, a subtribe of the Lenape "original people" were sent here to live by the Seneca Nation of the Iroquois Confederacy.

Frequently called the Wolf Tribe, the Munsee had a deep connection to the earth, relying on the sun and stars to guide them along the course of the streams. Keenly adapted to their surroundings, the Munsee planted and hunted in order to survive. They traversed the Allegheny River in canoes made from wood and birch bark, and created footpaths throughout the dense forests. But those seeking new lands would soon threaten their peaceful way of life.

In 1749, the greedy French and British were battling to possess this new frontier. Nine years later, the British finally succeeded in driving out the French, who had attempted to claim territory in the vicinity of West Hickory.

After tensions had settled, a Moravian missionary named David Zeisberger moved to the area and lived amongst the Munsee over a period of four years, and during his time with them, he converted the Indians to Christianity. At the time of his arrival, the Munsee and other displaced Indians were occupying three towns along the Allegheny River that they called Goschgoschunk. Some Indians welcomed the preacher's beliefs, while others revered the Great Spirit. Reverend Zeisberger subsequently left Goschgoschunk in 1770 with a number of Christian Munsee by canoeing down the Allegheny River to Friedenstadt (Town of Peace), to embark on another religious mission.

With the signing of the Treaty of Little Big Tree in 1797, pioneers began to show interest in lands purchased from the Seneca Indians by the Holland Land Company. The very first permanent settlers were the Valentine family. They settled on the west side of the Allegheny River in 1797, across from the present-day Tionesta State Fish Hatchery. After clearing land and planting an apple orchard, they experienced three years of brutal adversity and decided to depart. Another prominent pioneer, Lt. John Range Sr., was gifted a large land warrant as payment for his service in the Revolution. Although the warrant was transferred in 1785, John did not live there until 1816, on a piece of land that is now Tionesta.

Then came a new century, the 1800s, and it was spirited. The forest was characterized by majestic giants, eastern hemlock, American birch, and the gold prize, white pine. It was wild terrain inhabited by panthers, bears, wolves, and deer. Settlers attracted by the promise of prosperity had to be tough to choose this land, and those who survived made some lasting changes.

Eli Holeman came in 1800, and four years later began operating a ferry that shuttled emigrants and militia across the Allegheny River where the Hunter Station Bridge now crosses. In 1805, Poland Hunter chose a large Allegheny River island to farm and build on. From his vision, the Jamieson Lumber and Supply Company and the Tionesta Sand and Gravel Plant operated on the island for many years. After the plants were closed and the building removed, the Sherman Memorial Lighthouse, a 75-foot-tall working beacon, was erected several years later. The pioneering spirit continued throughout the 1800s with John Cook settling in Cooksburg in 1826.

In 1833, Cyrus Blood along with a crew of men and an ox-team sled cut their way through 12 miles of dense wilderness to the site of his future home in what is now Marienville. Blood's ambition as a young surveyor in Western Pennsylvania was to found a county. On a tract of land purchased from the Holland Land Company, he built a log cabin where he and his family happily settled. After several years of organization, Blood's dream was realized as he was named founder of Forest County in 1848.

With more people settling in the area and realizing the potential of the land, the lumbering industry was beginning to gain momentum. Lumber mills were popping up all along Tionesta Creek. Lumber rafts, many of which were 300 feet long and 50 feet wide, floated down this major tributary of the Allegheny River, taking logs and shingles to markets in Pittsburgh and other cities along the Ohio River.

During the mid-1800s, various sawmills were established throughout Forest County, many of which relied heavily on water power from rivers and creeks. Rivermen worked to float lumber down the creeks to the Allegheny and Clarion Rivers. Prized stands of eastern pine flourished along the streams. Piles of logs awaited spring thaws and heavy rains to carry them to the rivers, where they would be lashed together for their journey, sometimes to markets as far away as New Orleans. Once the lumber was delivered, some pilots walked hundreds of miles back to Forest County.

By 1900, the county reached its peak population with 11,039 residents. Local businesses thrived, and towns sprang up around Marienville, West Hickory, and Tionesta. Businesses included millinery shops, jewelers, barbers, harness shops, drugstores, wagon shops, and general stores. Coal mines and oil wells did exist in the county; however, they were greatly overshadowed by the lumber industry, as well as tanneries and chemical plants. In order to maximize production, lumber companies began to build railroads and purchased special locomotives that could navigate the hills and turns leading in and out of the forest. The lumber industry remained steady until it felt the effects of the Great Depression. By the mid-1900s, many of the mills had closed or moved from the area.

Throughout the latter part of the 1900s and onward through the 21st century, many improvements were completed on aging buildings, homes, bridges, and businesses. However, this did not take away from the charm and classic feel of the communities and their traditions. Forest County survives today mainly as a magnet for those seeking beauty, recreation, and adventure within the unbound wilds of a location on the precipice of perfection.

One

Tionesta Township, Tionesta Borough, and Green Township

The name Tionesta is of Native American origin; however, its exact meaning can only be speculated. Tionesta Township lies in the southwest corner of Forest County. It surrounds Tionesta Borough, a separate municipality and place of the county seat, formed in 1866. The Allegheny River flows southward through Tionesta, hemming in the Allegheny National Forest along the way. By the mid-1800s, oil and lumber commerce were gaining momentum, shaping Tionesta into the hub of activity. It became the meeting place for fleets of lumber headed downriver and flocks of people en route to Elm Street. Anything from wagons to jewelry could be found in town. Green Township is just east of Tionesta Township. Tionesta Creek, impounded as Tionesta Lake, cuts across the township as it flows west toward the Allegheny. The small communities of Guitonville, Golinza, Kiser Corners, and Nebraska are all part of Green Township.

By 1940, lumbering had decimated the forest and the townships went from a hum to a whisper. As the forest slowly recovered, campers, fishermen, and hunters filled the woods and waterways. Tionesta and Green Townships are now home to approximately 1,800 full-time residents; however, many nonresidents have historically come from miles around to enjoy the pleasures of a great escape in the forest or at their "camp."

People today are privileged to have this treasured land because of a man named Howard Zahniser. Zahniser grew up in Tionesta, hiking the Allegheny National Forest and canoeing the Allegheny River. He is noted as being the unwavering author of the Wilderness Act of 1964, which permanently protects millions of acres of federal public lands across the United States for the benefit of all people and wildlife forever. It took over 60 drafts and eight years before Pres. Lyndon B. Johnson signed the Wilderness Act into law. Sadly, Zahniser passed away just four months before the law was signed. He is buried in Riverside Cemetery in Tionesta.

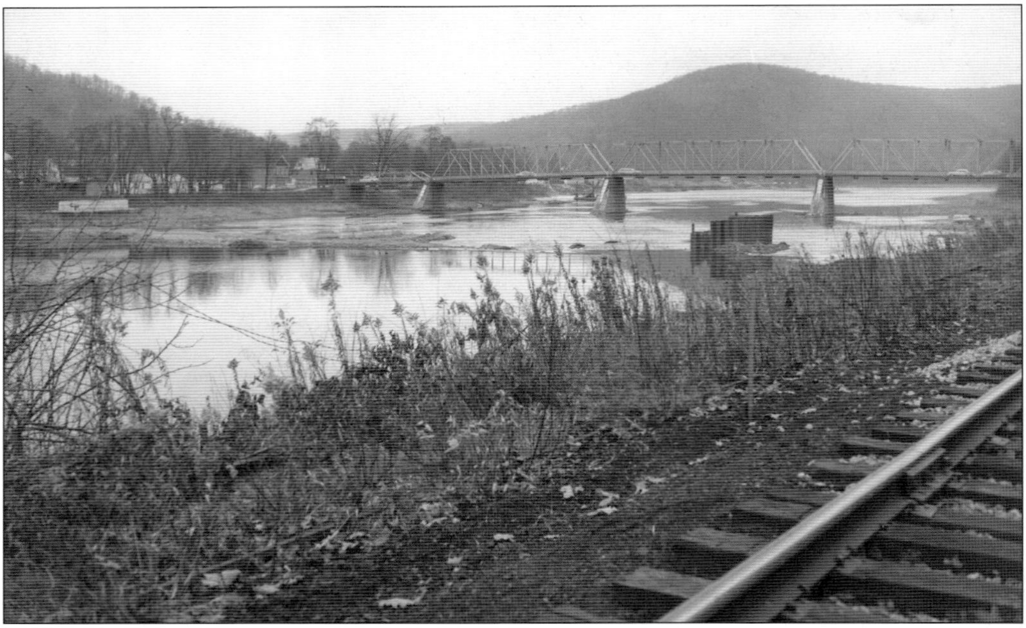

The steel bridge crossing the Allegheny River in Tionesta had been in operation since 1905 and was in need of being replaced. Officials began planning for a new bridge in 1957, with construction commencing on April 24, 1960, and the project being complete in September 1961. This photograph was taken during the early months of construction and shows the old bridge still standing.

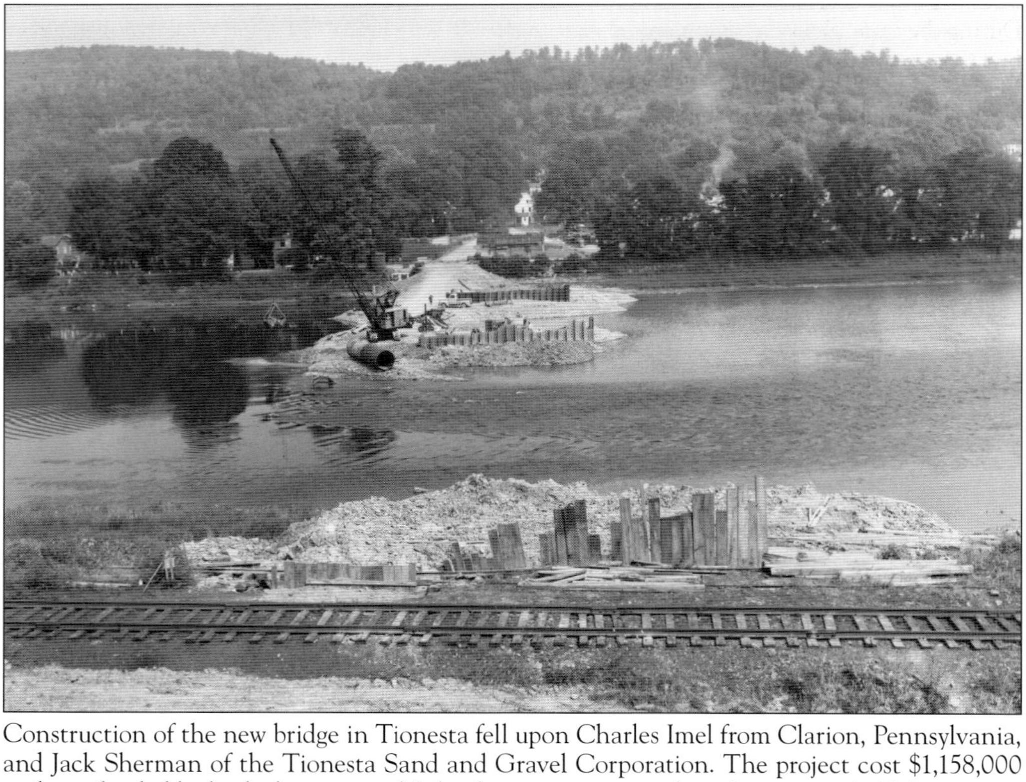

Construction of the new bridge in Tionesta fell upon Charles Imel from Clarion, Pennsylvania, and Jack Sherman of the Tionesta Sand and Gravel Corporation. The project cost $1,158,000 and was funded by both the state and federal governments, with each covering half the cost.

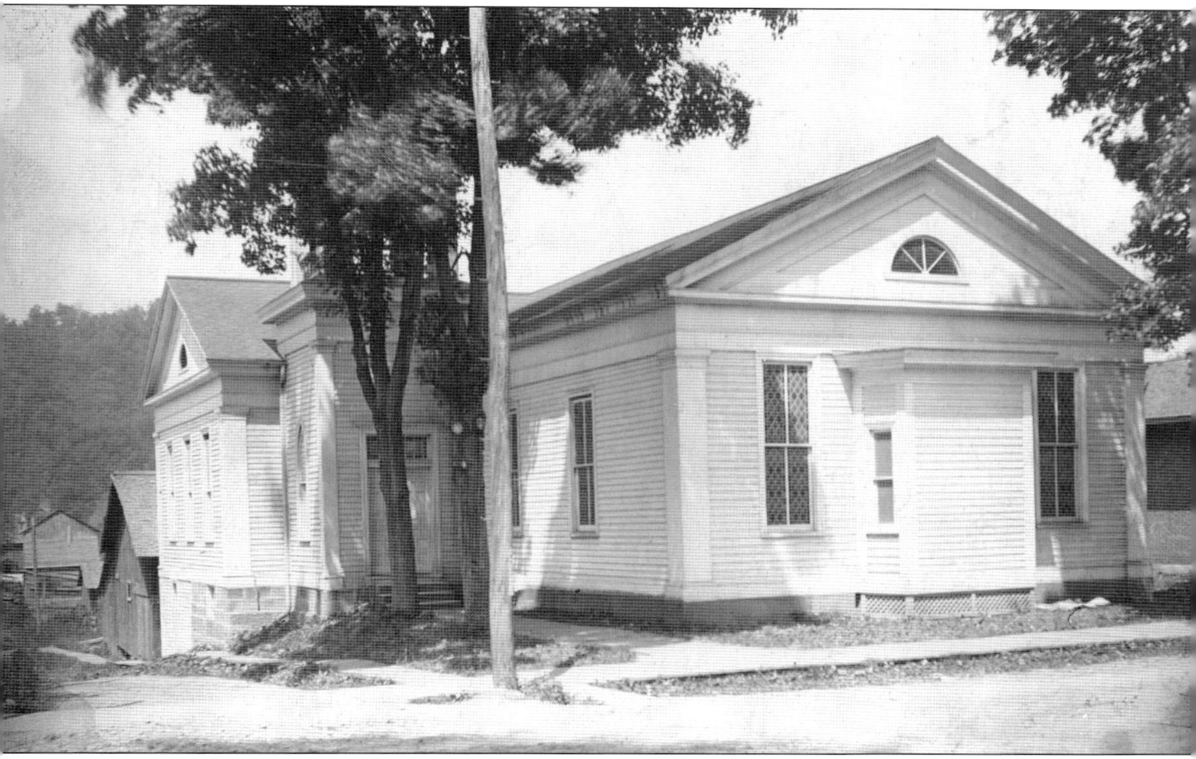

During the early 1800s, Presbyterianism was a faith without a home in Tionesta as many worshipers had to combine with the local Methodist church for services. In 1853, thanks to land donated by Margaret May, Seldon May, and Benjamin May, a Presbyterian church was built for $1,647.32, with services starting on December 10, 1853, under the name Constitutional Presbyterian Church.

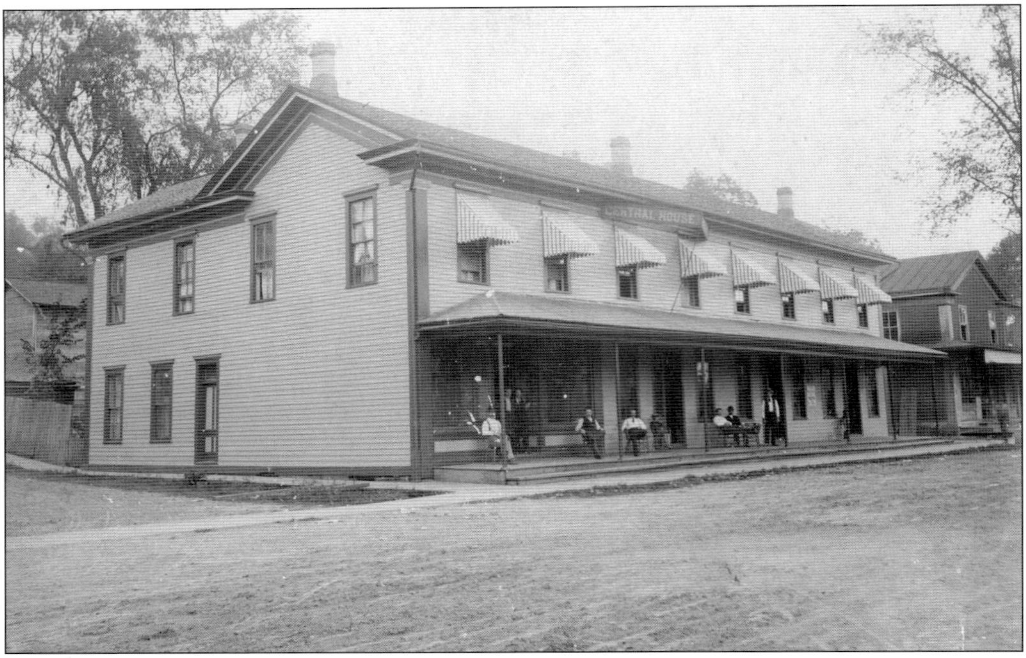

Around 1868, George Sawyer built the Central House Hotel on Elm Street in Tionesta, and later expanded the building in 1874. Not only a hotel, it was also used for various offices, a saloon, showcase rooms for traveling salesmen, a public parlor, and more. In 1943, the building and all its contents were sold at an auction, leaving the vacant lot to become the resting place for Cropp Dairy Products in 1948.

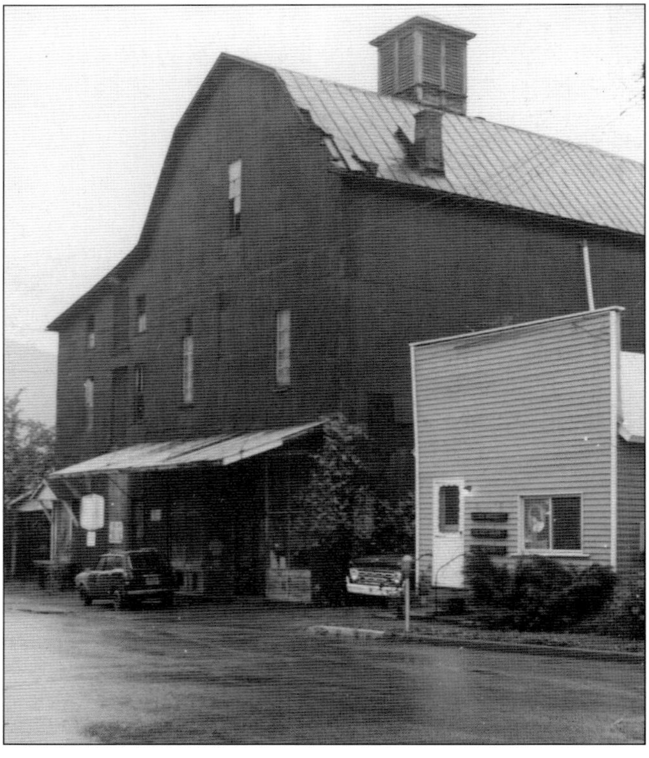

In 1904, Charles Lanson and Freeman Lanson opened a gristmill in Tionesta, but later sold it to Jerry Adams, Archie Clark, and C.A. Childs in 1918. Having sold the company in 1947, Herman Motzer, Karl Flowers, and Paul Tannler bought the building and renamed it the Farmers Feed & Supply Company. After the decline of the milling industry, the business began offering a wide variety of farm and hardware supplies, along with products from the Pennsylvania Farm Bureau Cooperative Association.

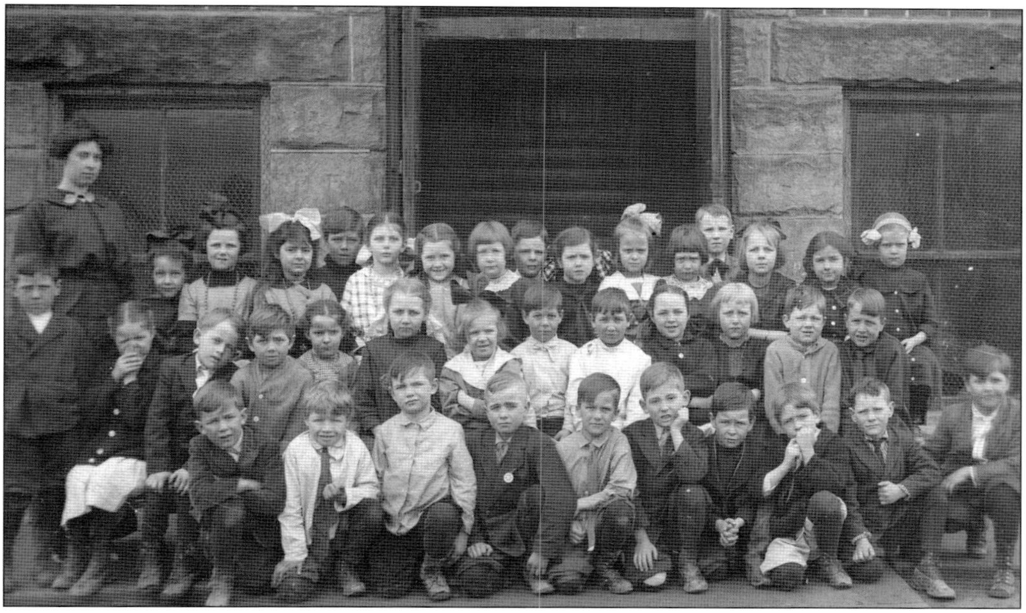

The Tionesta educational system developed through the efforts of local church leaders. Classes were held in various private houses until a public building was erected about 1938. A more modern school was built in 1885 and graduated two students in 1897. Shown are schoolchildren dressed in their best clothing at the Tionesta School around 1914.

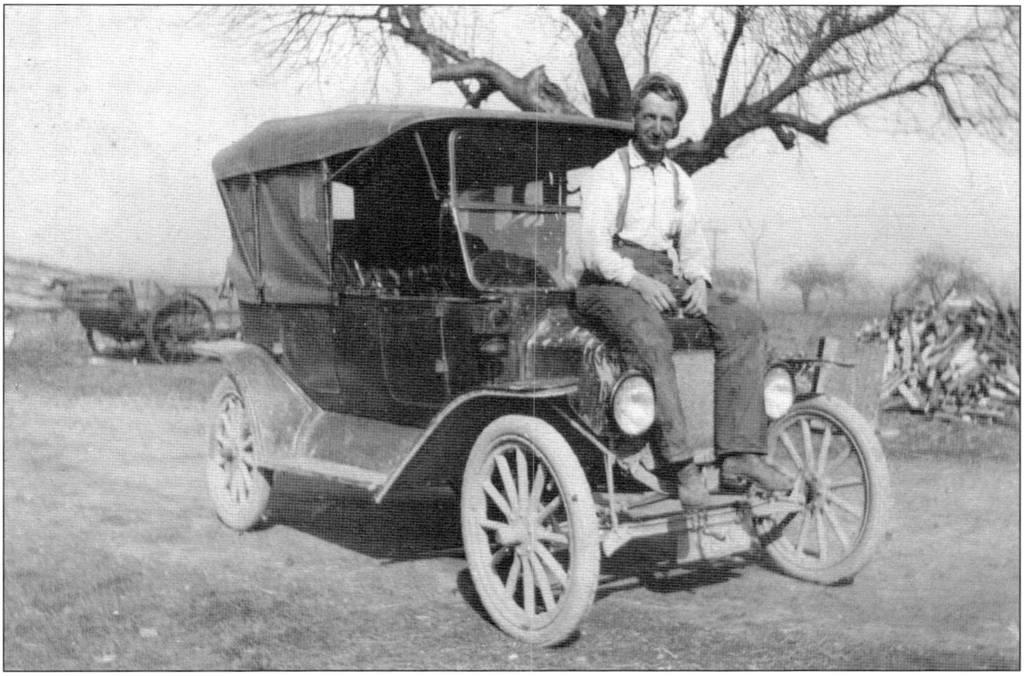

There are a few automobile references in Forest County's archives. In 1908, the first road was paved in Tionesta Borough. Ralph Cook owned the first automobile agency in Tionesta in 1912. Frank Brown worked all over the world, came home, and bought a Studebaker. Harry Potter, a woods foreman for Collins Pine, purchased a seven-passenger Buick in 1919. This smiling gentleman and his ride are unidentified.

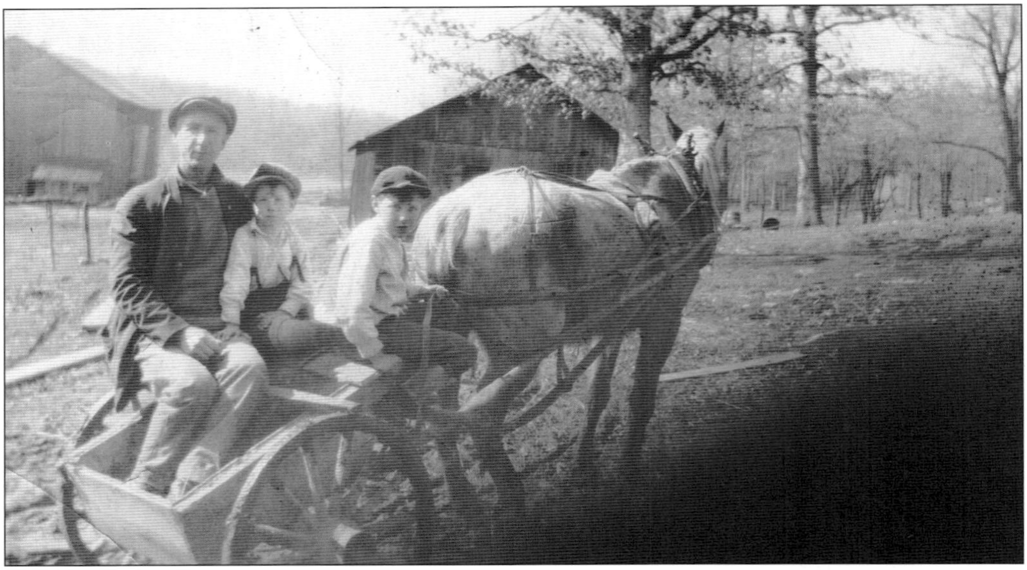

Due to his service in the Revolutionary War, Lt. John Range Sr. was issued a land warrant for 258 acres between Squirrel Creek and Tubbs Run. In 1816, the Range family established a house, farm, and apple orchard on their land. As the population quickly grew in Forest County, farmlands began to spring up all over the countryside. From left to right are Forest County residents John Weant, Miles Taylor, and Paul Taylor at a farm in Tionesta.

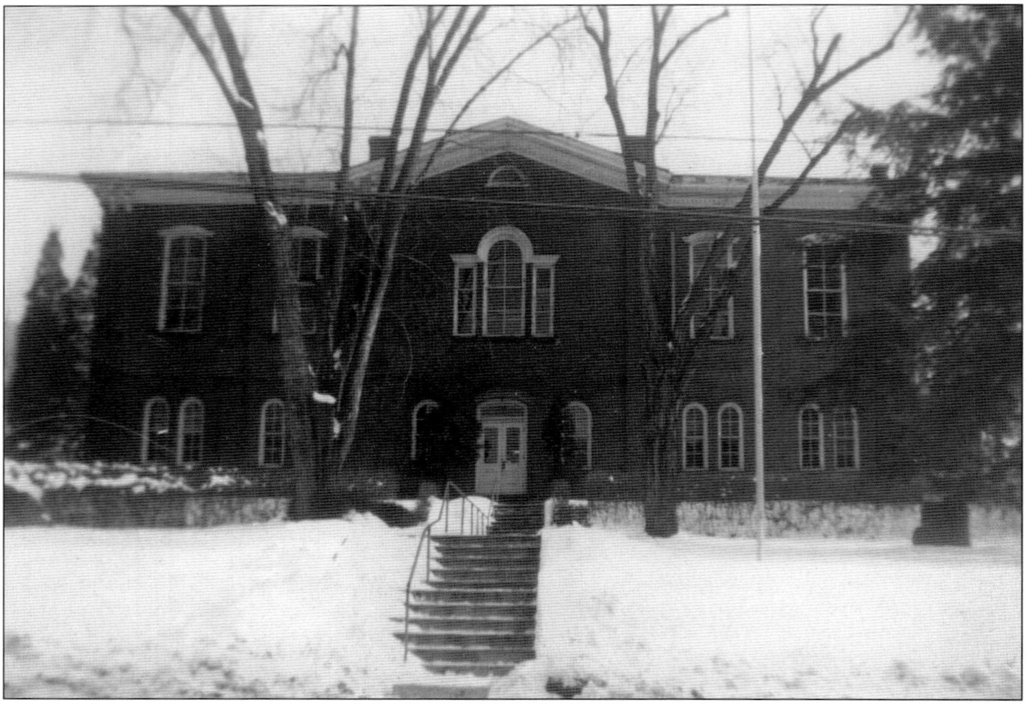

As Forest County grew, the court and county records were moved in April 1867 from Marienville to a larger, temporary building in Tionesta. In early 1868, construction on the first brick building in the county had begun and was finished on July 30, 1870. The Forest County Courthouse cost $24,715 to build.

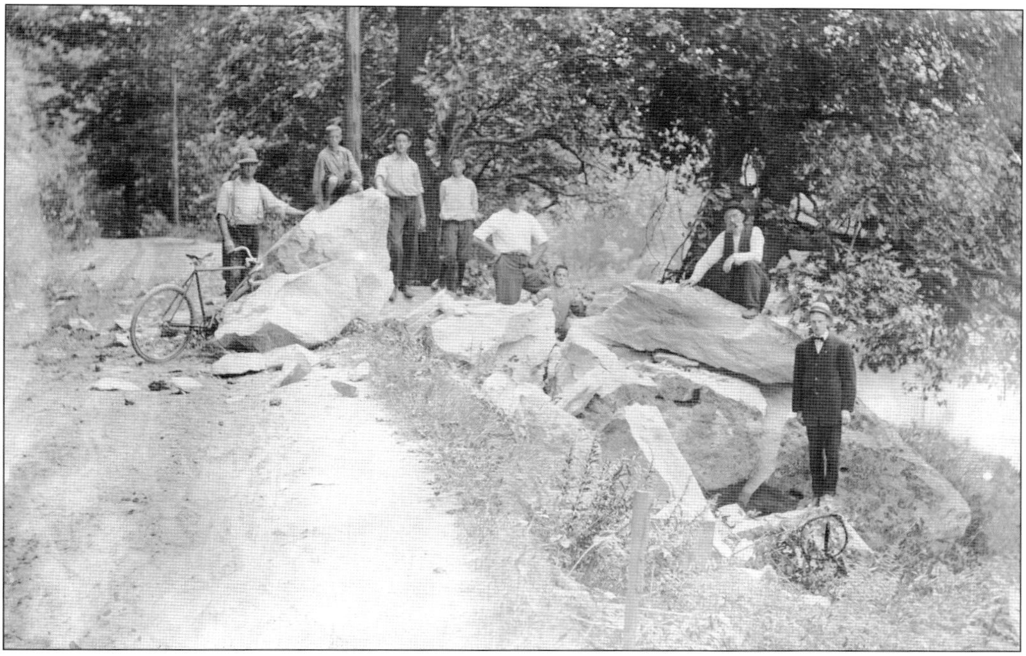

About 17,000 years ago, the entire region of Tionesta was under ice—and even longer before that, the ocean. When the glaciers started to melt, leaving behind large boulders like those pictured, large animals, commonly found in tundra regions, migrated into the area to find food. Paleo-Indians, looking for their own food, followed those animals into the region and settled for a time.

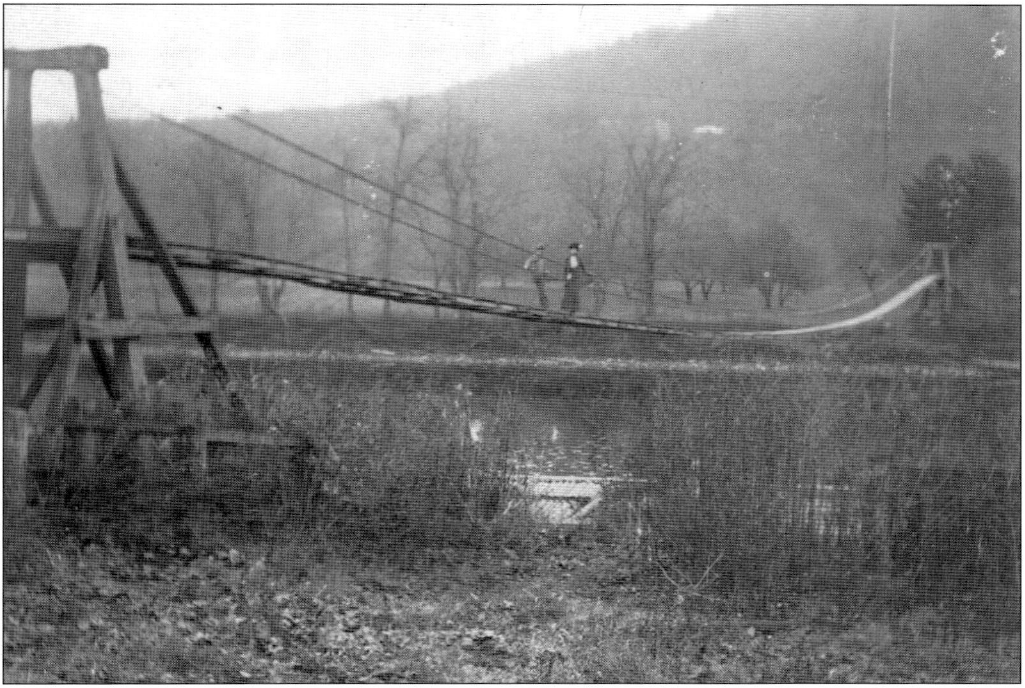

Due to the many creeks in Forest County, residents built swinging bridges to more easily cross from one side to the other. The bridges were relatively low in cost and were made with wood supplied by local mills. Shown in this 1906 photograph is a swinging bridge in Tionesta.

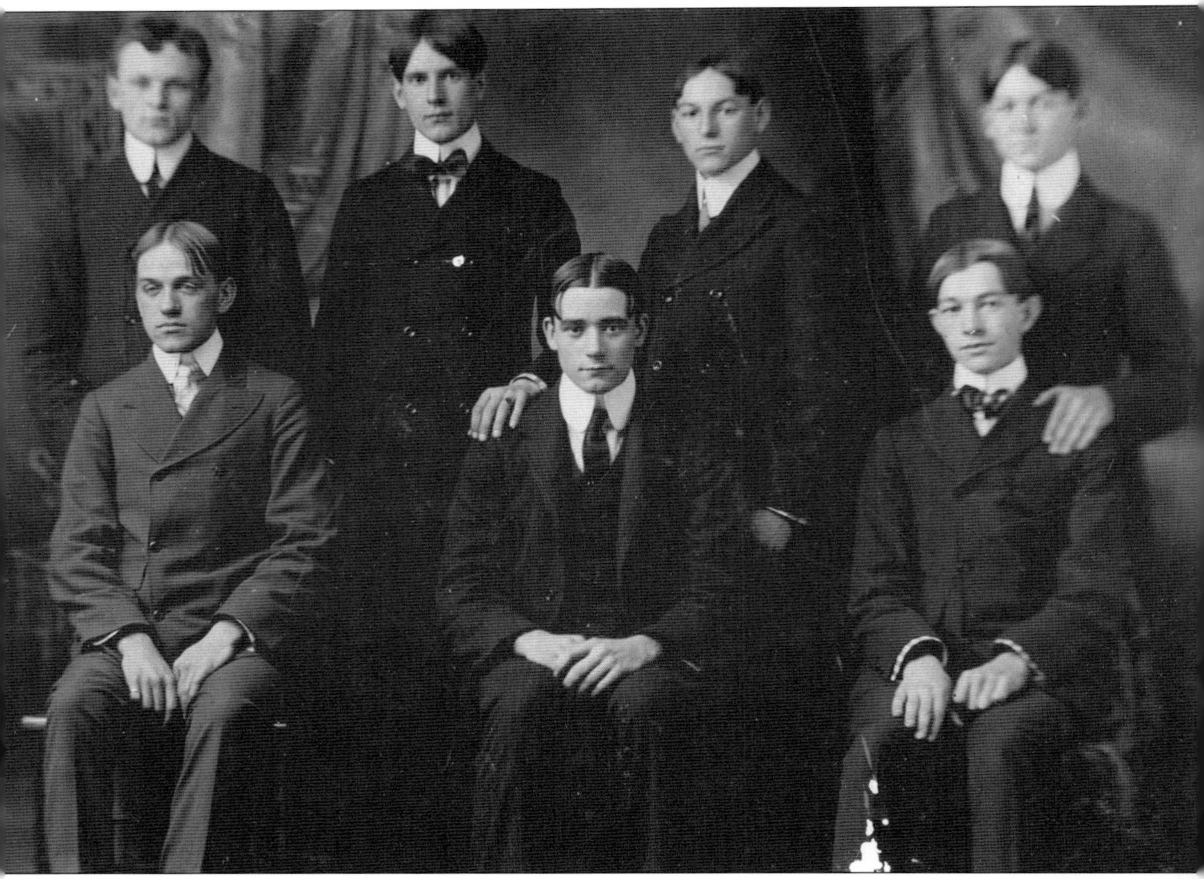

Many families that settled in Tionesta and the Forest County area had early members who became entrepreneurs and solidified their names in history through the businesses they started. This undated photograph shows, from left to right, (sitting) Paul Clark, Gordon Haslett, and Louie Swanson; (standing) Carl Neuk, Archie Holman, Charles Jamieson, and John Lawrence.

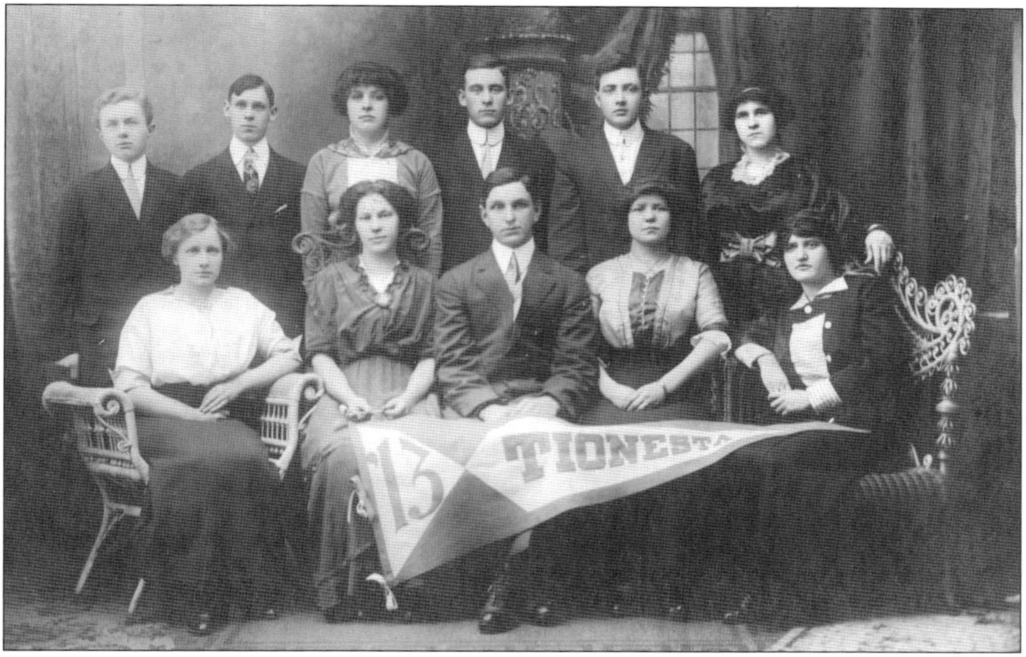

Shown is the 1913 Tionesta High School graduating class. From left to right are (first row) teacher Ruth Diamond, Alice Decker, Irvin Kelly, Mildred Thompson, and Gwendolyn Hill; (second row) Arley Dreyer, Arthur Zuver, Ruth Foreman, Robert Sigworth, Arthur Carson, and Edna Rodda.

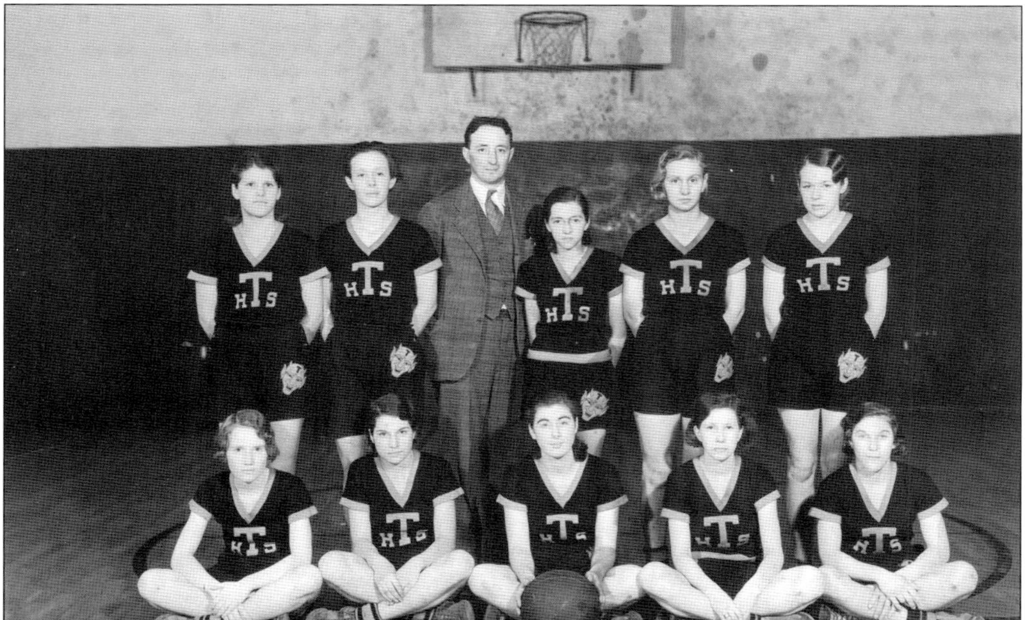

Pictured is the 1931–1932 Tionesta High School girls' basketball team. From left to right are (first row) Lucille Thomas, Louise Mascaro, Betty Amsler, Lois Carpenter, and Marian Cook; (second row) Psakye Stanford, Lucille Matha, Harold Seigworth, Grace Johnstone, Lenora Blum, and Francis Hood.

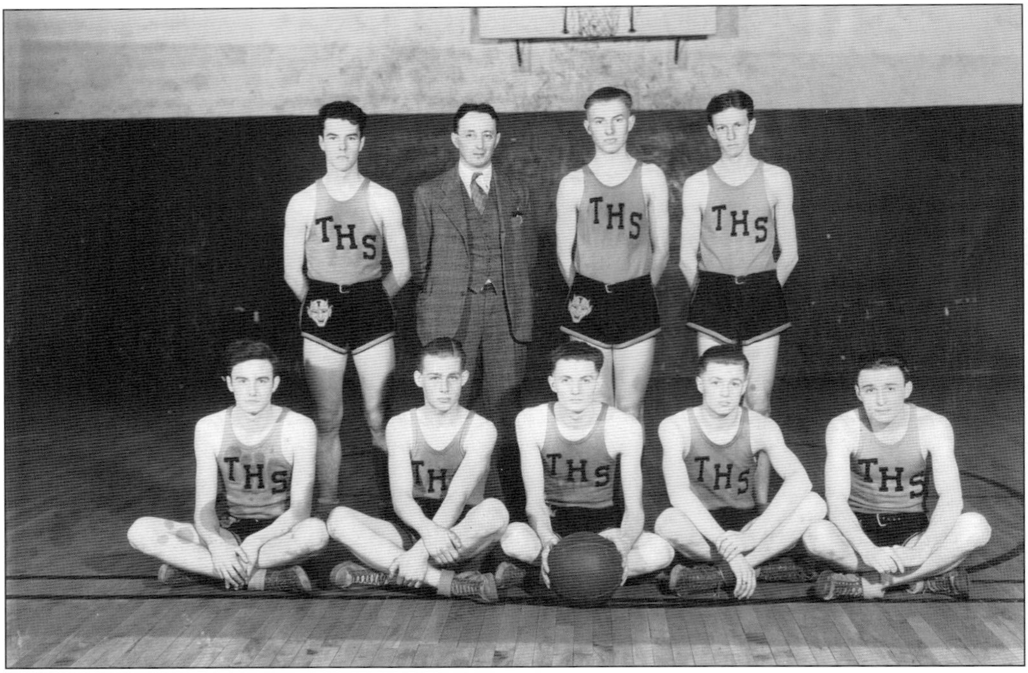

High school sports were a welcome relief from the Great Depression. Shown is the 1931–1932 Tionesta High School boys' basketball team. From left to right are (first row) Chuck Cross, Arner Haslet, Laverne Pears, Walter Pears, and Woodie Shriver; (second row) Chuck Clark, coach Harold Seigworth, Joe Bium, and Francis Confer.

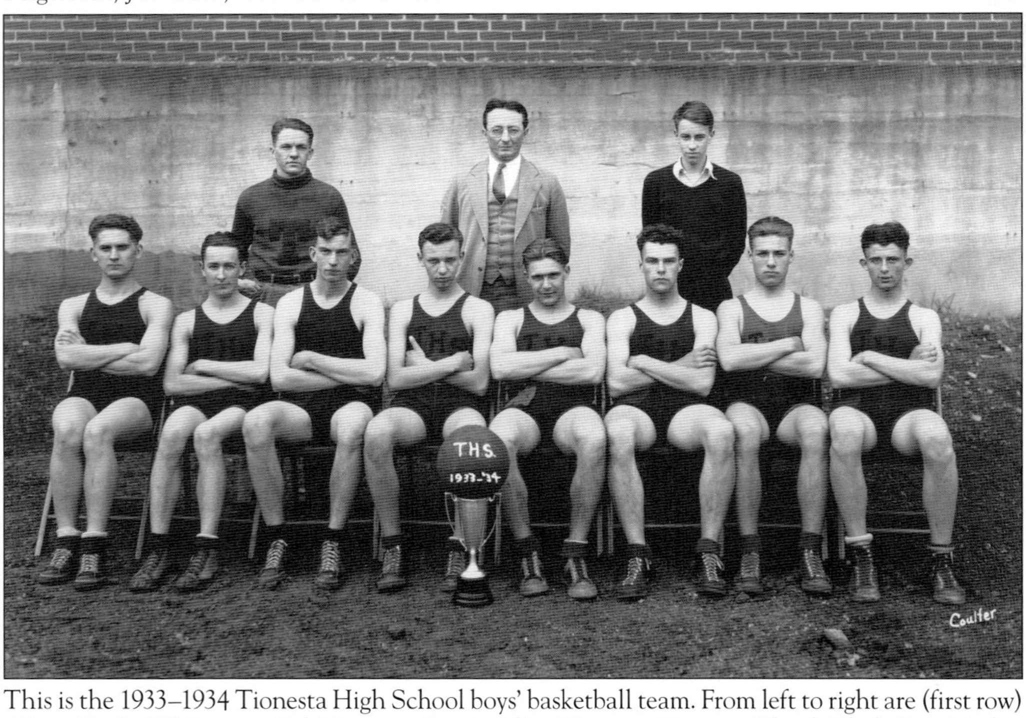

This is the 1933–1934 Tionesta High School boys' basketball team. From left to right are (first row) Albert Koch, Bill Starner, Bob Harman, Randy Allio, Clarence Kinnear, Chuck Clark, Sam Haslet, and Art Coville; (second row) Russell Wilson, Harold Stigworth, and Delmar Jamieson.

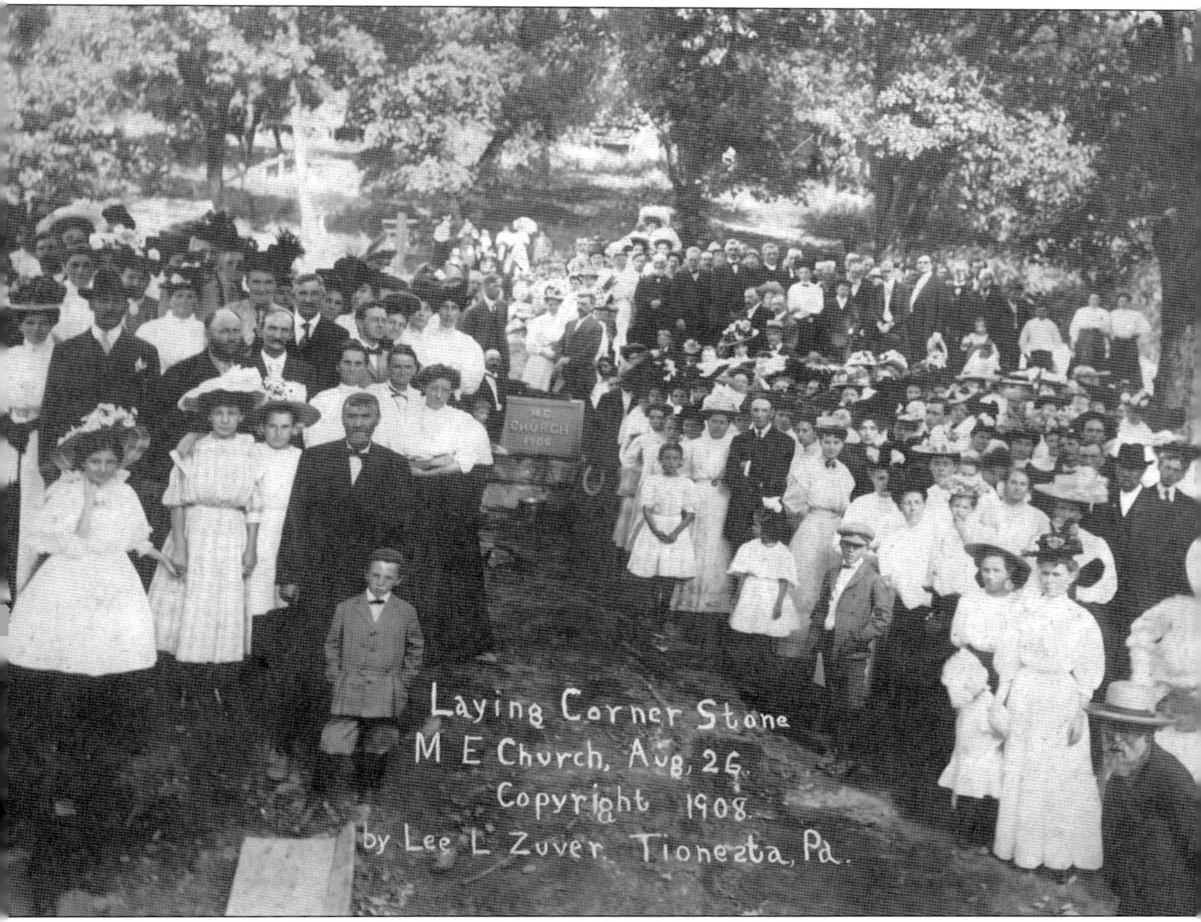

Through the generous donations of Truman Doud "Teddy" Collins, George Watson, and Frank Kreitler, the Methodist church on Elm Street in Tionesta was constructed in 1908. The laying of the cornerstone took place on August 26, 1908, while the dedication ceremony took place on April 11, 1909, Easter Sunday.

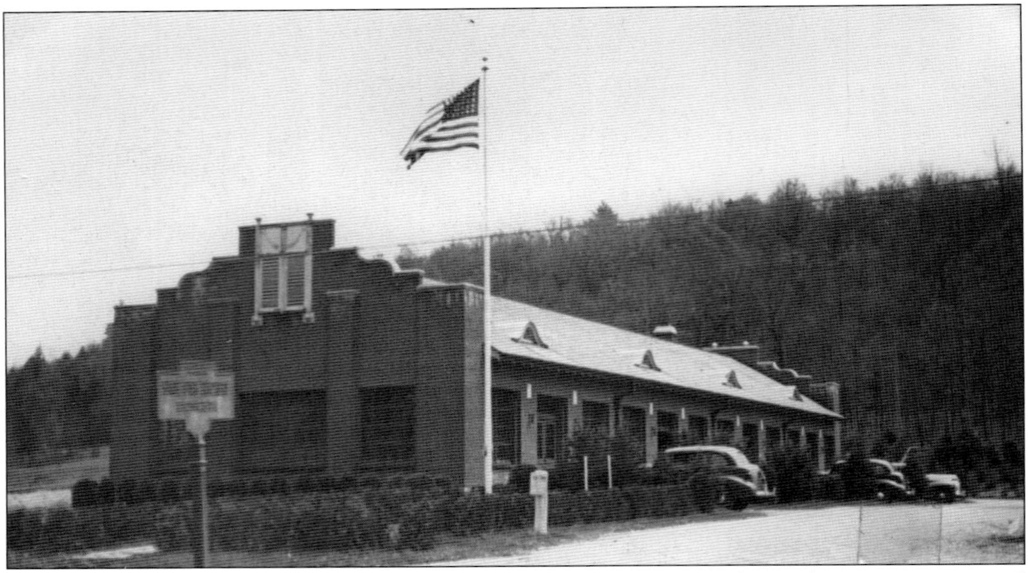

Located on a 378-acre tract in Tionesta Borough, the Tionesta State Fish Hatchery was constructed in 1928. It is in the beautiful woodlands of Forest County near Tubbs Run, which supplies water to the hatchery. Muskellunge, walleye, and steelhead are raised at the facility, which provides stock for streams throughout Northwestern Pennsylvania. The hatchery is owned by the Commonwealth of Pennsylvania and is operated by the Pennsylvania Fish and Boat Commission.

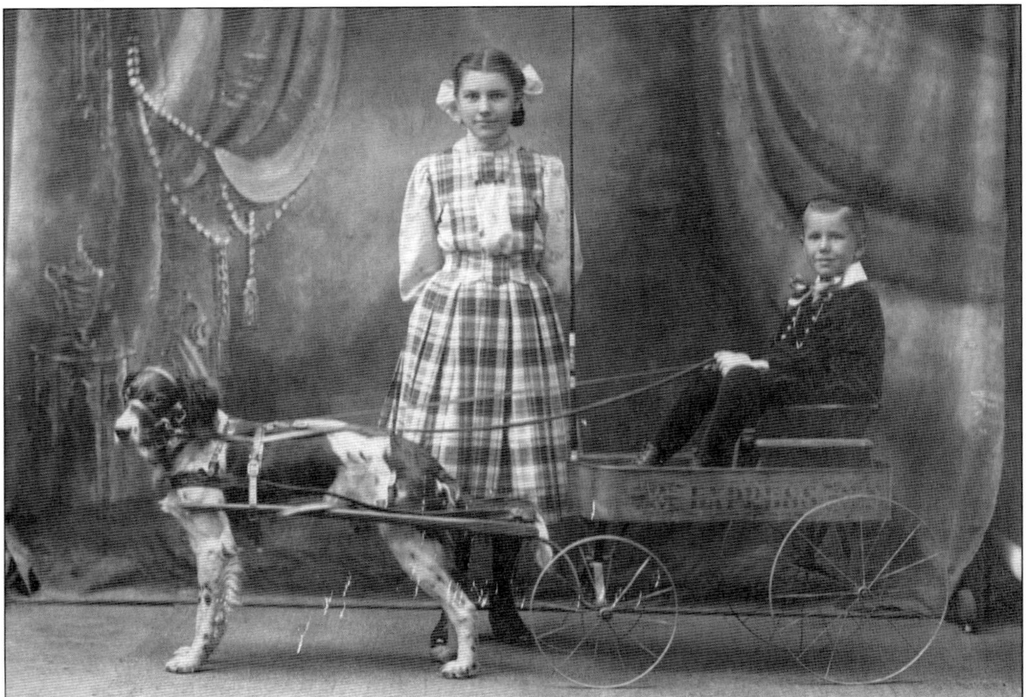

In 1904, brothers Charles Lanson and Freeman Lanson opened the gristmill on Bridge Street in Tionesta. The mill was sold in 1918 and again in 1926, when it was renamed the Tionesta Milling Company. Charles's children Elva May Lanson (left) and Freeman Arthur Lanson pose for a photograph in Tionesta in 1906.

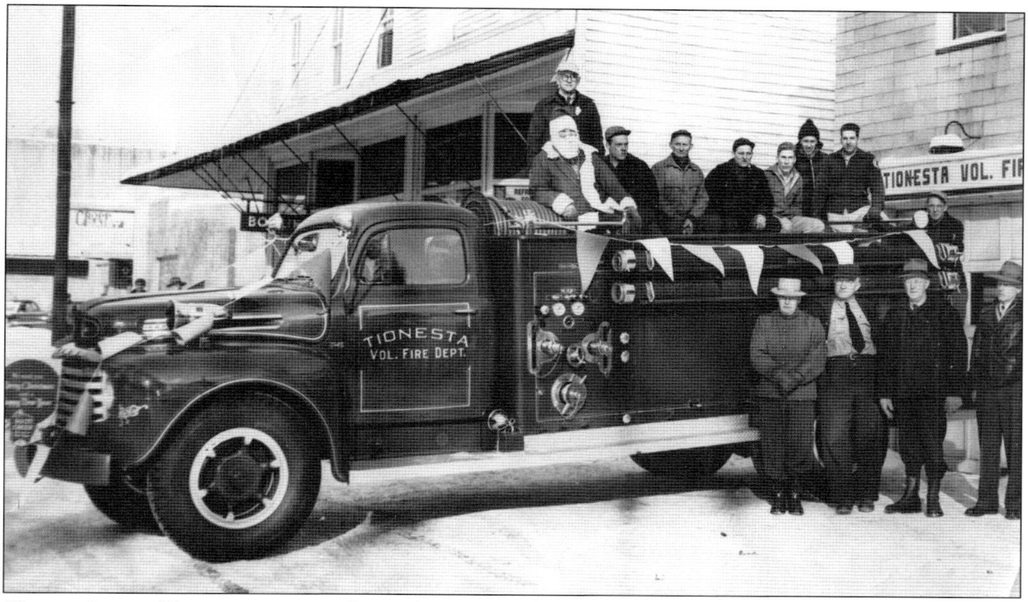

Shown during Christmastime in the 1950s are members of the Tionesta Volunteer Fire Department and various community members. The truck shown is the fire department's first modern truck, which was purchased on December 26, 1950, and had a carrying capacity of 750 gallons of water.

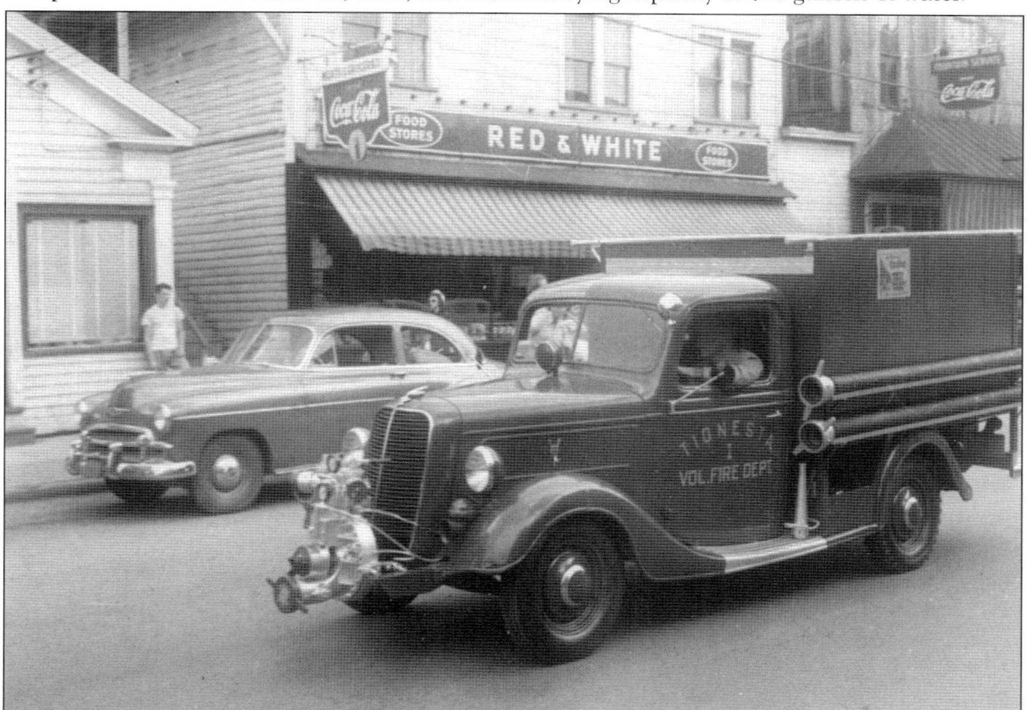

Tionesta's firefighting history dates back to November 1873 when citizens, along with members of council, came together to form the north ward and south ward firefighting companies. The two units remained ill equipped and only completed the minimal amount of training until 1949, when the Tionesta Volunteer Fire Company was formed and more money and training was loaned for a better-organized department.

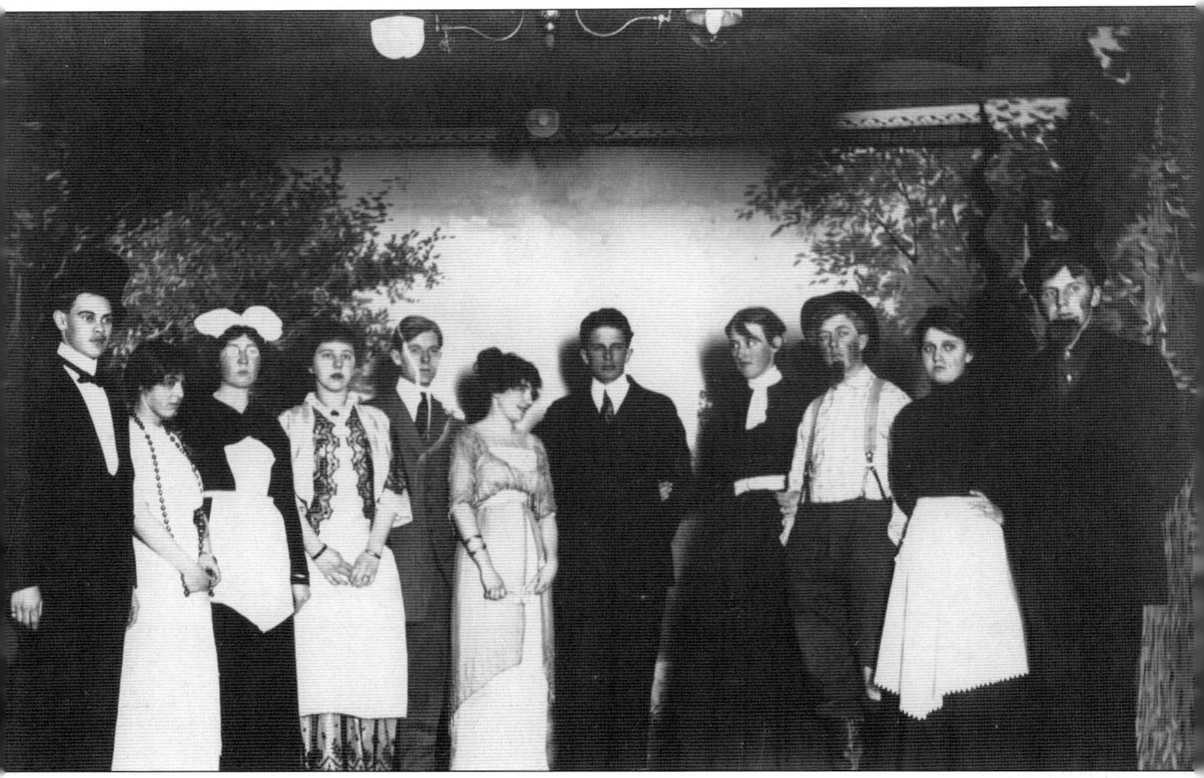

Cast members of the Tionesta School senior class play pose on stage in costume for a photograph in 1916. From left to right are Fred Zuver, Beulah Amsler, Goldie Mealy, Mae Osten, Walter Sigworth, Margaret Bowman, Owen Kiser, Elsie Wolcott, Leslie Carson, Hellen Marie Smith, and Gilbert Killmer.

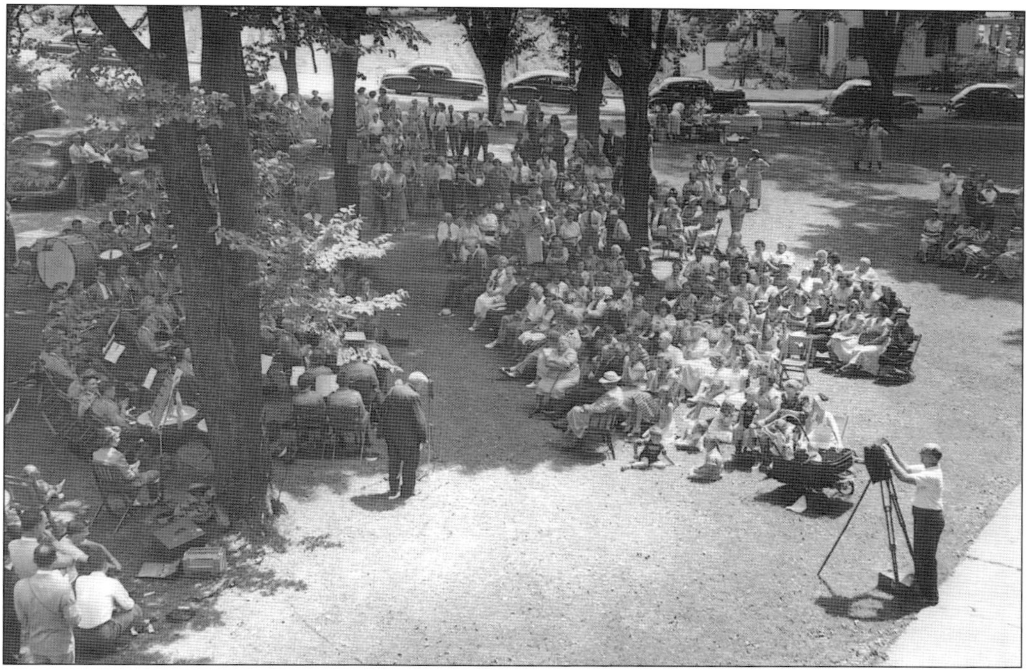

Dr. Forrest Bovard was born in Tionesta on July 14, 1874, and was the son of George and Sarah Stewart Bovard. Following his graduation from the Jefferson Medical School in Philadelphia, Forrest came back to Tionesta in 1899 to open a medical office. In honor of his service to the community, the residents of Tionesta held a Dr. Bovard Day in July 1949.

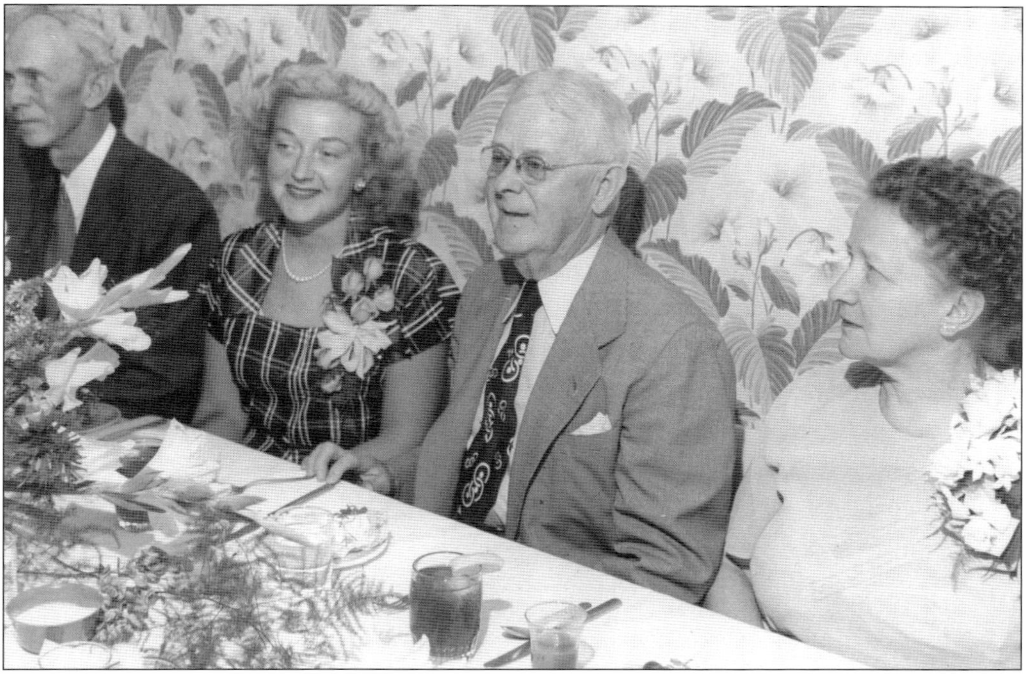

Shown during a dinner celebration at the July 1949 Dr. Bovard Day are, from left to right, his brother Roy Bovard, daughter Alice Bovard, Dr. Forrest Bovard, and his wife, Ruth Bovard. The current library in Tionesta, Sarah Stewart Bovard Memorial Library, is named after Bovard's mother.

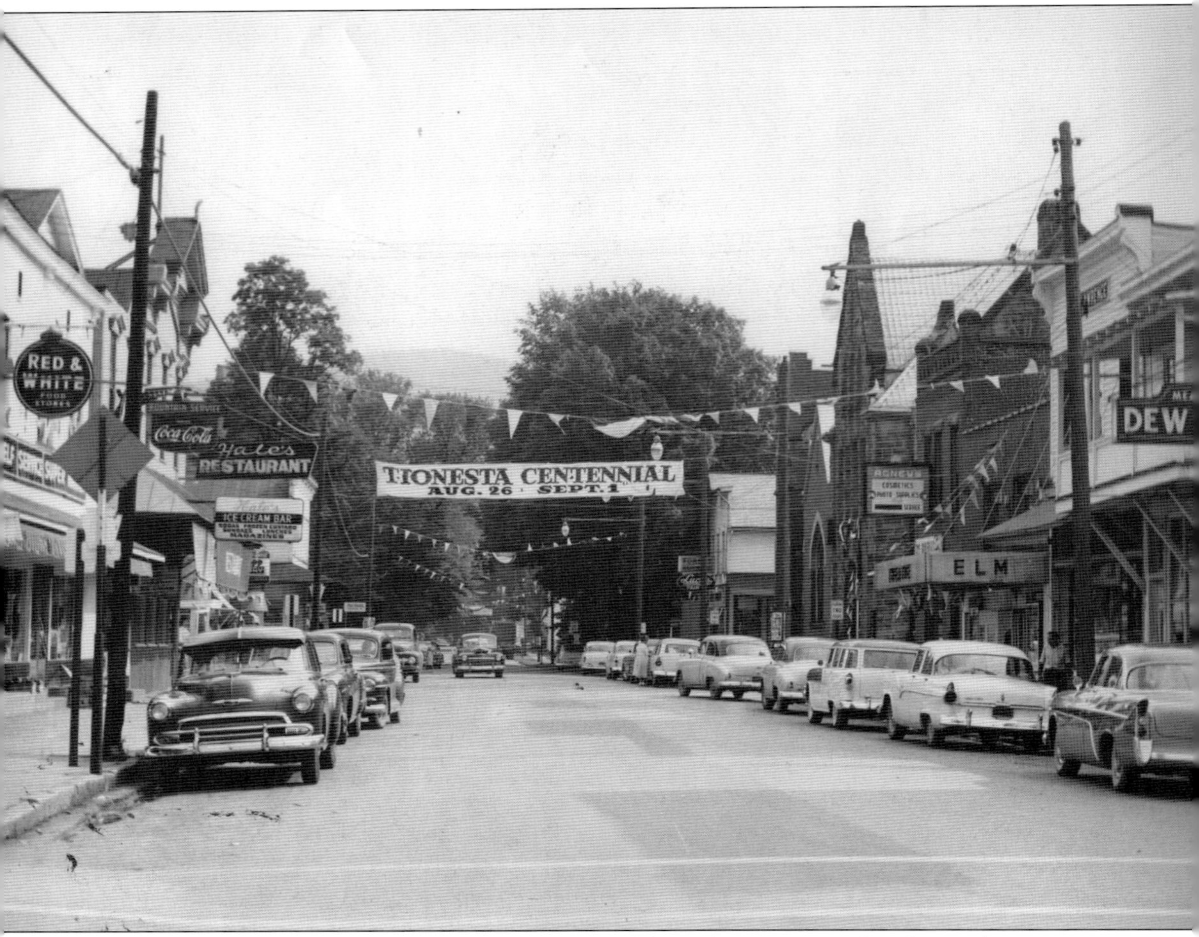

From August 26 to September 1, 1956, Tionesta celebrated its centennial with parades, pageants, historical displays, concerts, and more. The highlight of the celebration was a historical pageant called Out of the Forest, which presented the history of the Indians, early white settlers, the rough pioneer life, industry, and local military history.

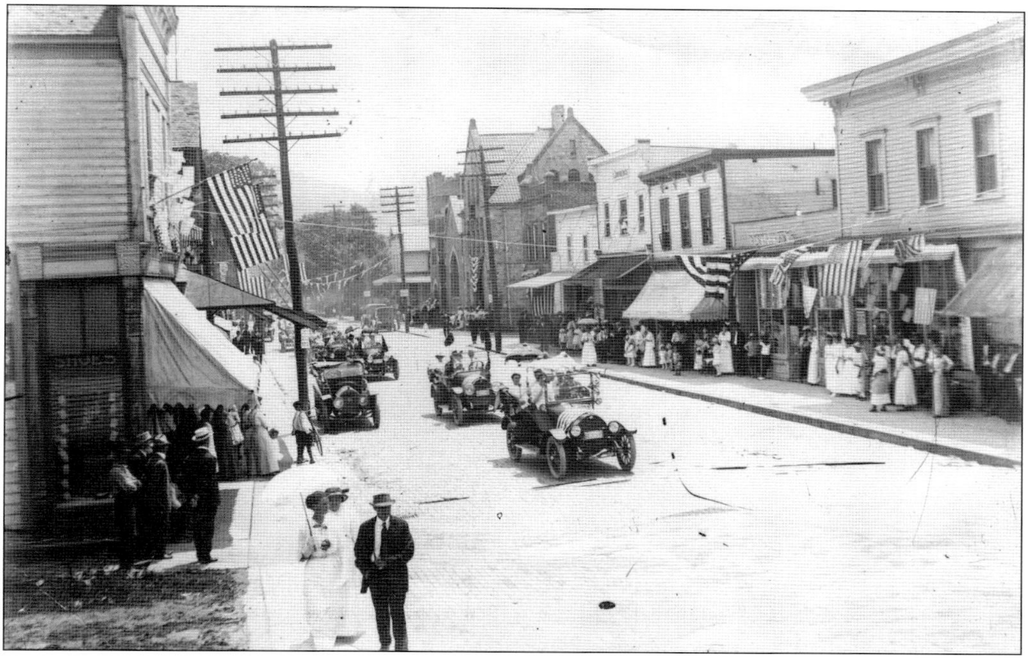

In 1856, the Village of Tionesta became a borough and contained a large business district along the Allegheny River, which was convenient to the workers arriving on rafts. With the advent of various modes of transportation and a population moving farther away from the river, businesses began to spring up along Elm Street in Tionesta around 1906. This c. 1915 photograph shows a parade along Elm Street promoting woman's suffrage.

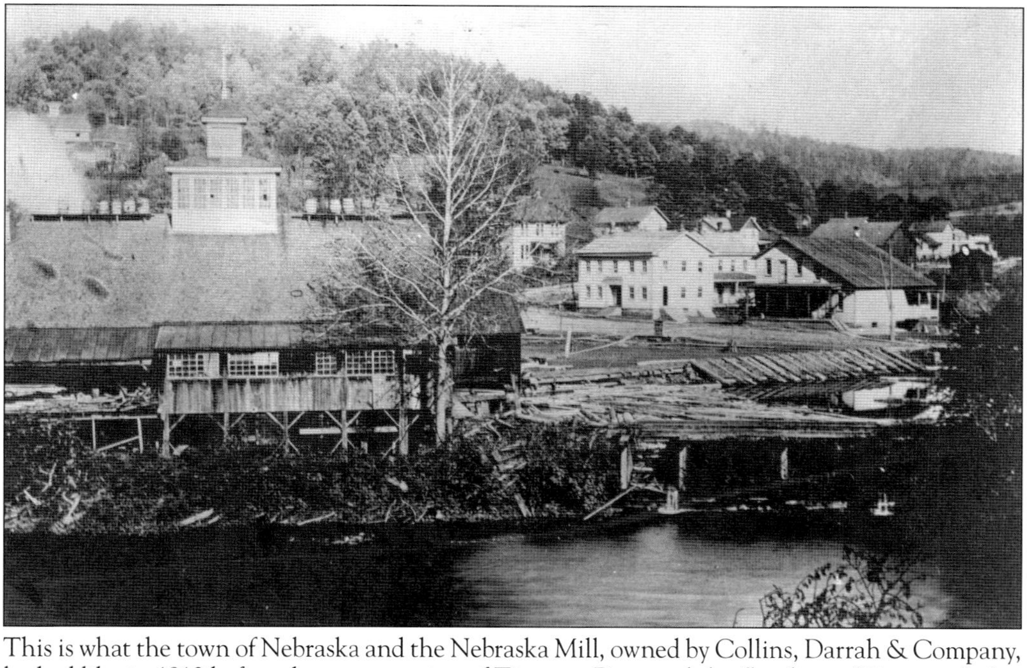

This is what the town of Nebraska and the Nebraska Mill, owned by Collins, Darrah & Company, looked like in 1910 before the construction of Tionesta Dam and the flooding of Tionesta Lake. Although not mandatory, the government urged all residents of Nebraska to evacuate by November 13, 1940, or risk being caught in the flood.

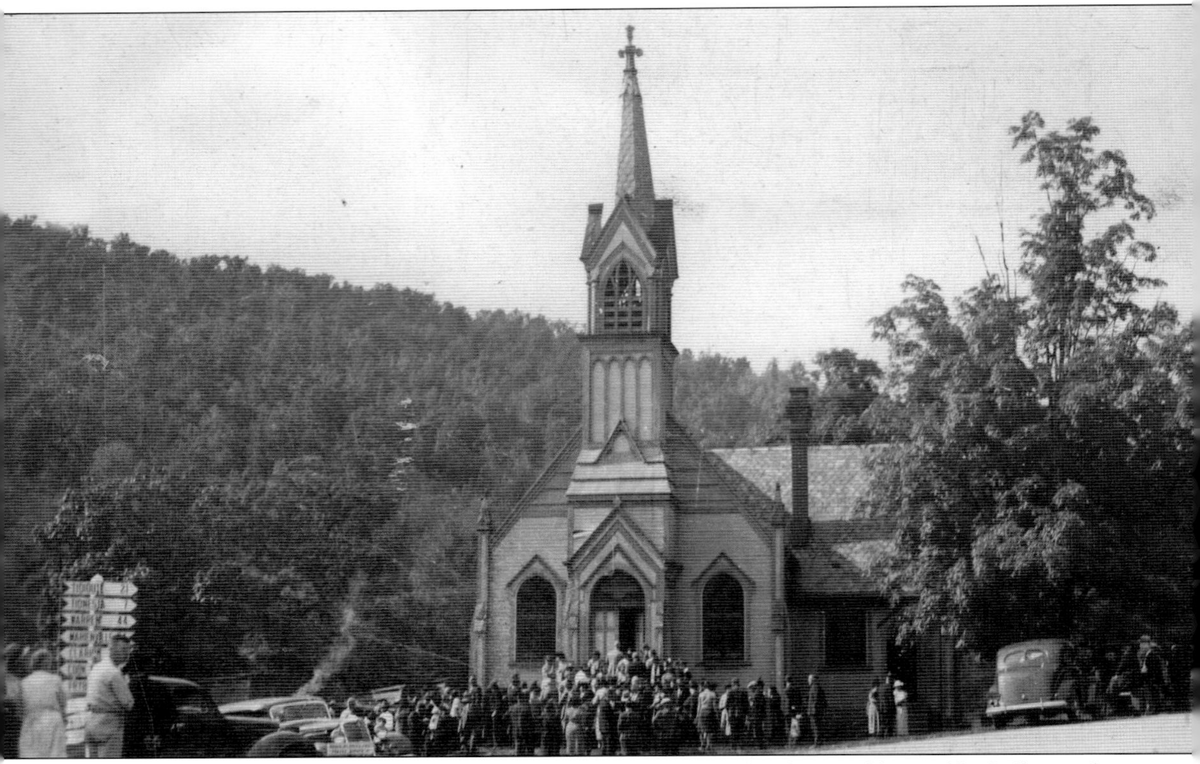

Nebraska Methodist Episcopal Church was built in 1889 on land owned by Teddy Collins, who also financed the cost of its construction. During its years of operation, many activities flourished in the church such as church socials; "class meetings," which took place after the Sunday service so members could gather for prayer meetings or discussions; and staged plays produced by the town residents. When Nebraska was scheduled to be flooded in 1940 to create Tionesta Lake, the church was sold to the Presbyterian church of Grove City, Pennsylvania, and dismantled piece by piece.

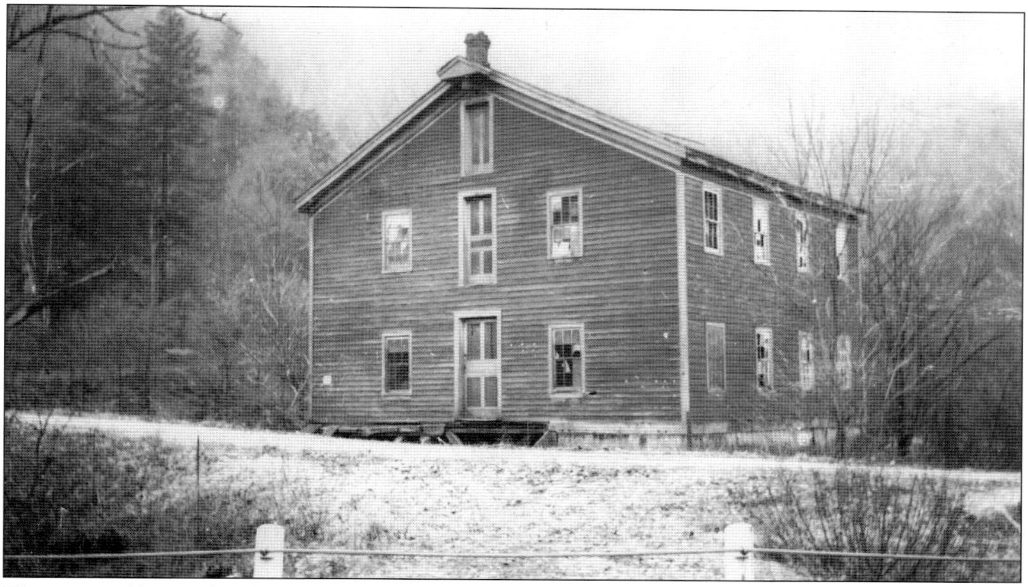

The gristmill in Nebraska was used to grind a variety of grains into cracked corn, cornmeal, and flour. The Ford and Lacy families who purchased the land in the 1830s built the mill sometime between 1840 and 1850. At that time, the area was known as Ford and Lacy Mills or Lacytown. Caroline Ford and George Lacy later changed the name to Nebraska after their visit to the state of Nebraska.

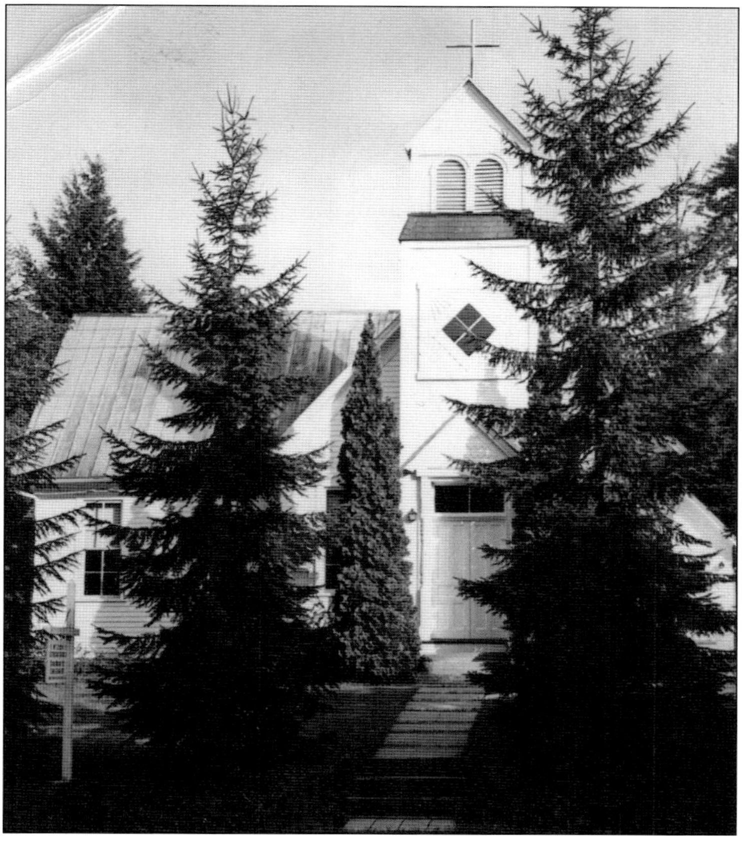

Pictured here is Mount Zion Lutheran Church on German Hill Road in Greene Township on July 24, 1959. German Hill Road, sometimes called Dutch Hill, is about eight miles long and lies between Tionesta Creek and the Allegheny River, extending from Tionesta Township through Green Township and into Kingsley Township. The road gets its name from the German pioneers who began settling in the area in 1842.

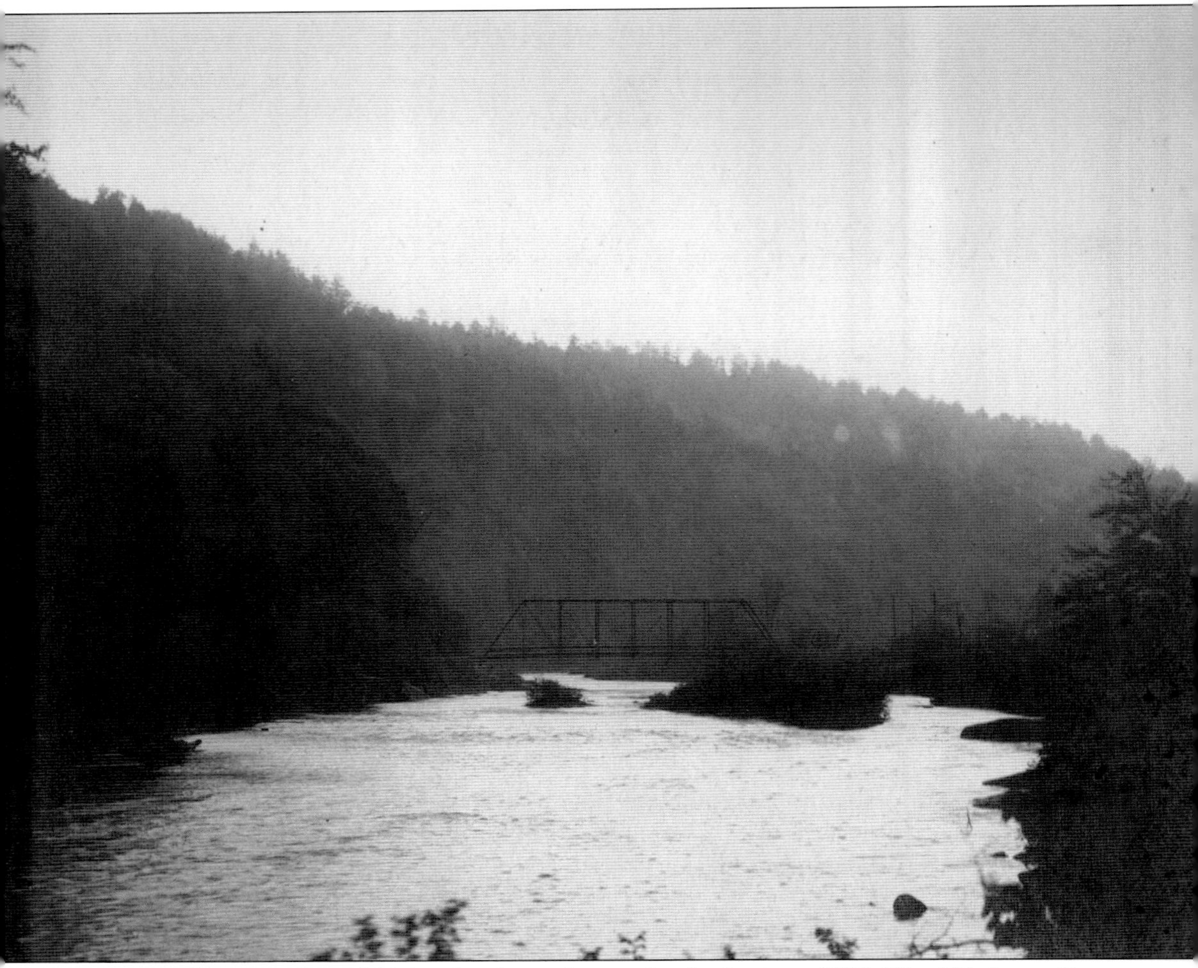

Pictured here is the old Nebraska through truss bridge built in 1873. The US Army Corps of Engineers in Pittsburgh received daily measurements taken with an elaborate water-depth measuring device that was attached to the middle of the bridge. The instrument was fashioned from copper chains, weights, and pulleys. These measurements were later used in the design of the Tionesta Dam. The bridge was replaced in 1932, and today it is often covered by water backed up by the dam.

Two

Hickory Township and Harmony Township

Harmony Township occupies the northwest corner of Forest County with the Allegheny River forming the eastern boundary of the township. West Hickory Creek is a principal stream that flows south through Harmony Township into the Allegheny. West Hickory is the only township in Forest County that is entirely west of the river. The unincorporated communities of West Hickory are Fagundus, Neilltown, Trunkeyville, and Stewart Run. Fagundus was a prominent business center until 1874, when a fire destroyed the entire village. Neilltown (originally known as Neillsburg) is one of the older settlements in Harmony, established in 1855 by Capt. William T. Neill. West Hickory had standard- and narrow-gauge railroads, a large bridge that traversed the Allegheny, and a tannery. Leather and lumber headed out on trains destined for world markets. In 1867, oil fever struck, but it was short lived. The lumber company of Wheeler & Dusenbury was responsible for much of the economic life in this village. A 15,000-barrel oil well that was tapped in 1870 created some stir in Trunkeyville. That year, the Nestle and Peterson Store and the Ventures Hotel opened for business. Like Neilltown, Stewart Run was settled early on when George Siggins cleared some land in 1801. A few years later, Siggins built a sawmill at a different location in Harmony before settling in West Hickory.

Hickory Township, incorporated in 1866, is also located in the northwest region of Forest County with the Allegheny River forming its western boundary. East Hickory, Church Hill, Endeavor, Little Hickory, Queen, and Yellow Hammer are all villages within Hickory Township. Early settler Daniel Harrington wrote that this area was an "old and pretty river village." Lumbering has been carried on here since the pioneer days. Industrial Timber and Lumber Company (formerly Endeavor Lumber Company) operates today in what was originally the site of the Wheeler & Dusenbury Company of Endeavor. Pennsylvania State Route 666 winds and climbs through Hickory Township in line with Beaver Run, adorned by a beautiful stand of hemlocks on either side.

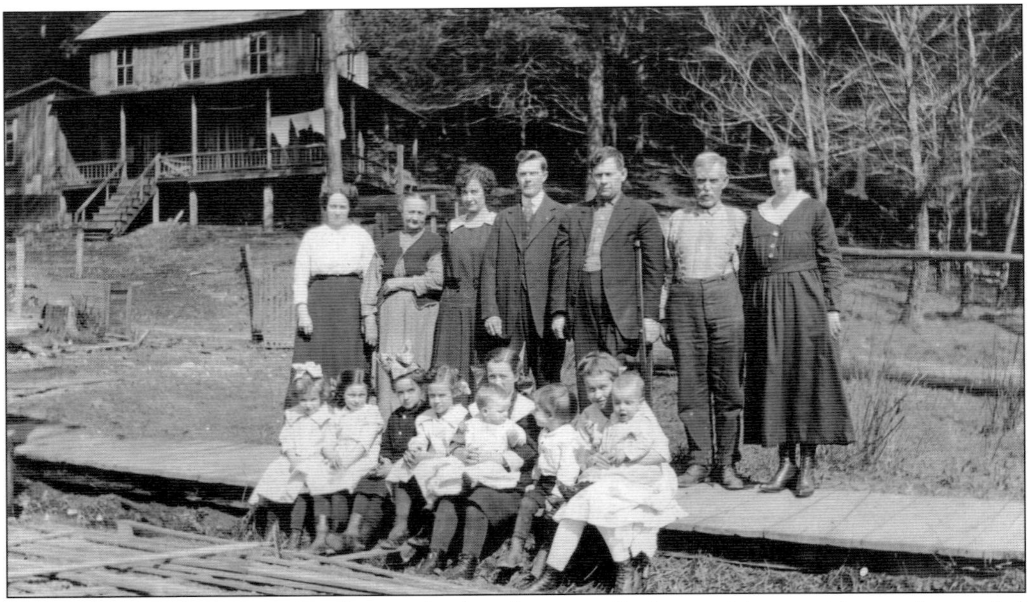

Shown here is the White family outside their home in Endeavor. Many residents who settled in the area worked for the Wheeler & Dusenbury Lumber Company. As production increased in the pine and hemlock mills, opportunities for laborers improved, and the population of the community grew. Nelson Wheeler was a generous soul who provided stability and prosperity to the residents of East Hickory, West Hickory, and Endeavor. The quaint community had a schoolhouse, a kindergarten, and a beautiful white church, which Nelson Wheeler and his wife helped to organize.

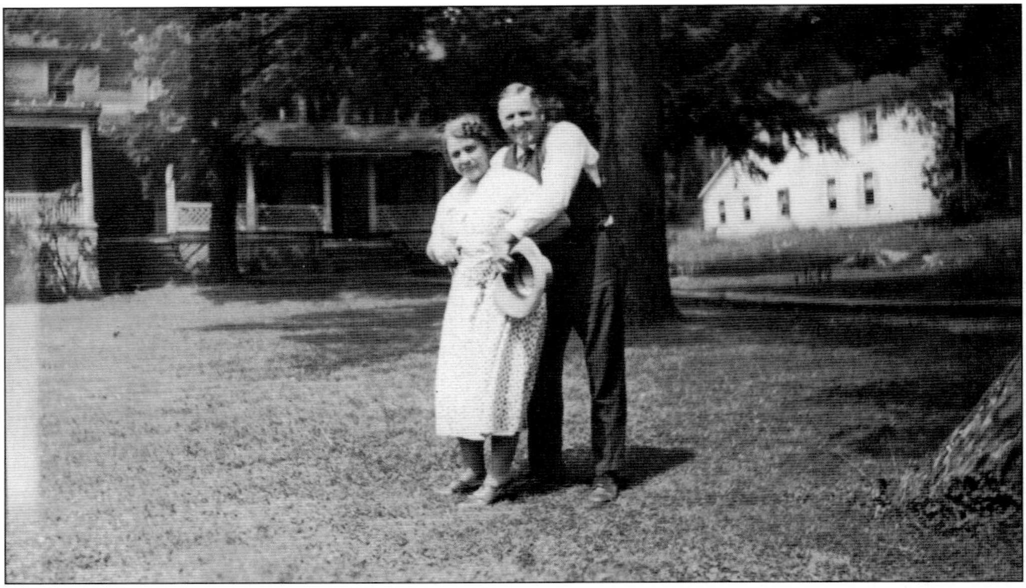

The Endeavor Presbyterian Church had its origins in the white schoolhouse in October 1893 when a Presbyterian Sunday School began to teach classes. On January 24, 1896, the Christian Endeavor Society formed with efforts toward building a place of worship. Their hard work came to fruition on February 6, 1898, when the Endeavor Presbyterian Church was formally dedicated. Shown are Rev. and Mrs. William Thomas.

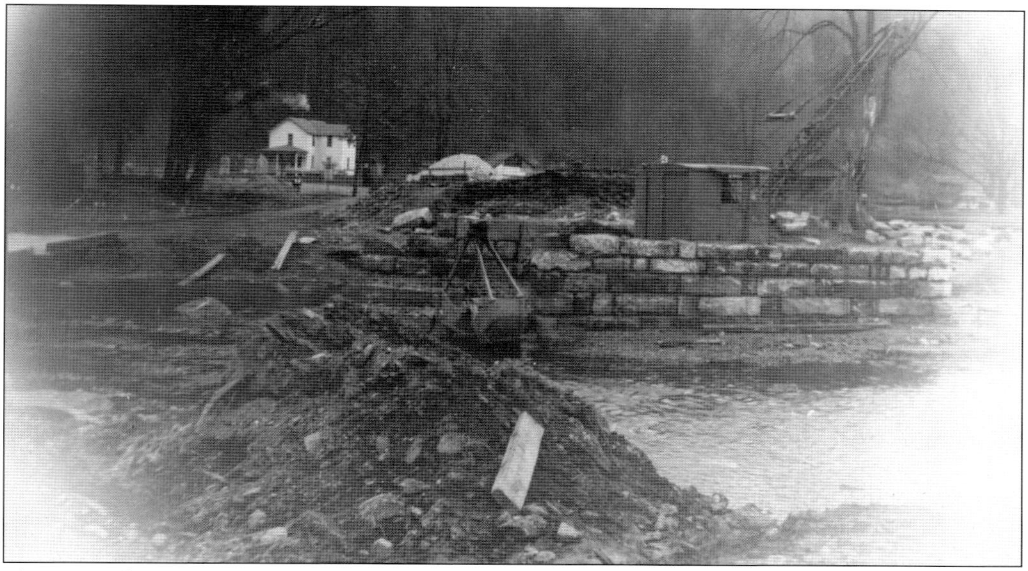

Shown in this c. 1919 photograph is a bridge being constructed over the East Hickory Creek in the upper region of Endeavor. On March 11, 1964, an ice gorge on the East Hickory Creek broke apart and caused the flooding of East Hickory and surrounding areas. The white building in the background is the William Howe house.

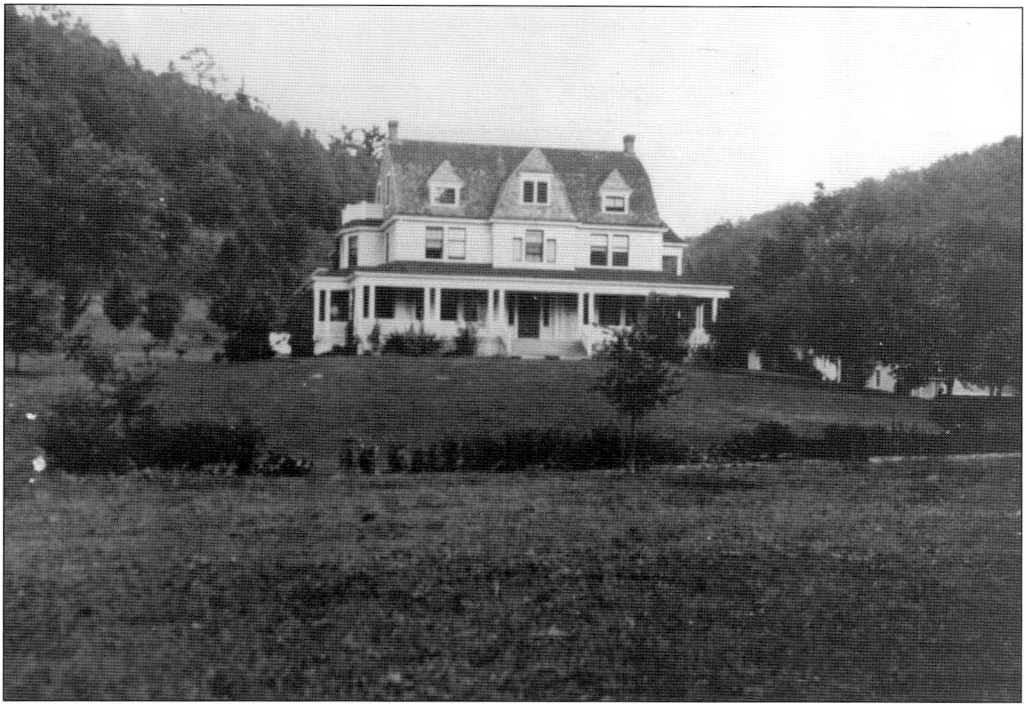

Nelson Wheeler had his start in the Endeavor lumber industry in 1871 when Hamilton Stow turned over management of the Wheeler & Dusenbury Lumber Company. Wheeler also served as Forest County commissioner in 1866 and Pennsylvania representative in 1878. Shown is Nelson Wheeler's house, Bonnie Brae, in Endeavor.

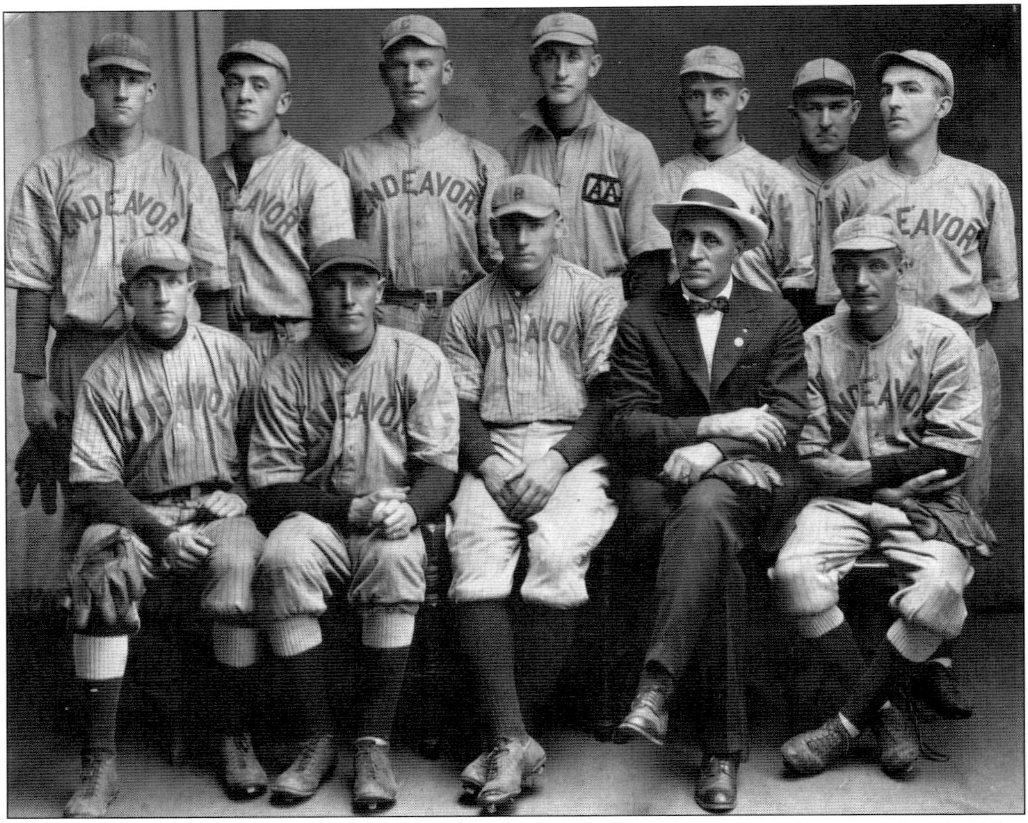

Pictured in 1920 are Endeavor baseball players, from left to right, (first row) Doc Richards, Glen Shaw, Charles Hartzell, Ira Fox, and Earl Bemis; (second row) Travio Erikson, Merle Fox, Bill Smith, Lee Thompson, Gelen McCullough, Archie Hepler, and Walter Strause.

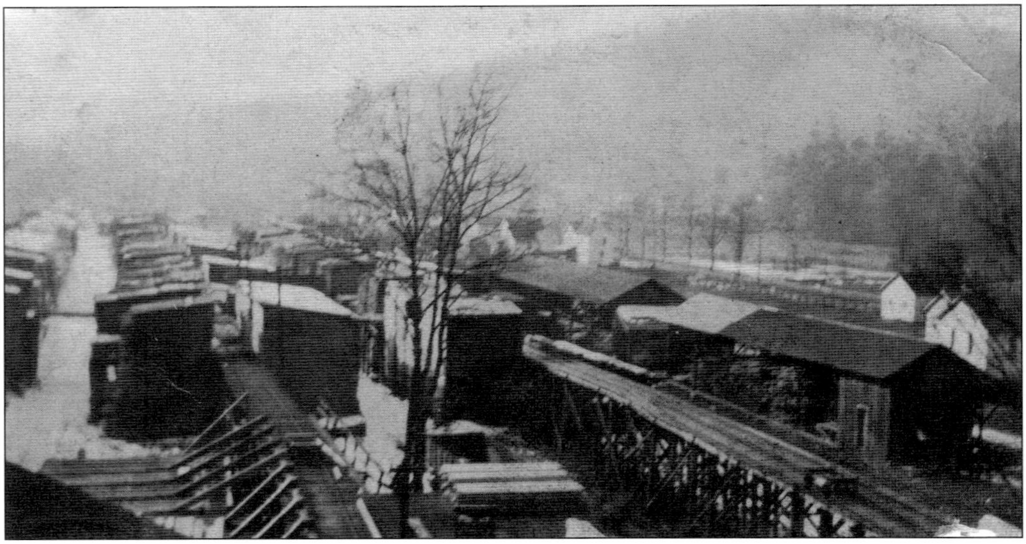

On June 10, 1897, a post office was established in Endeavor with William Stiles as the first postmaster. Stiles came to Endeavor in 1892, and also owned a general store in the area.

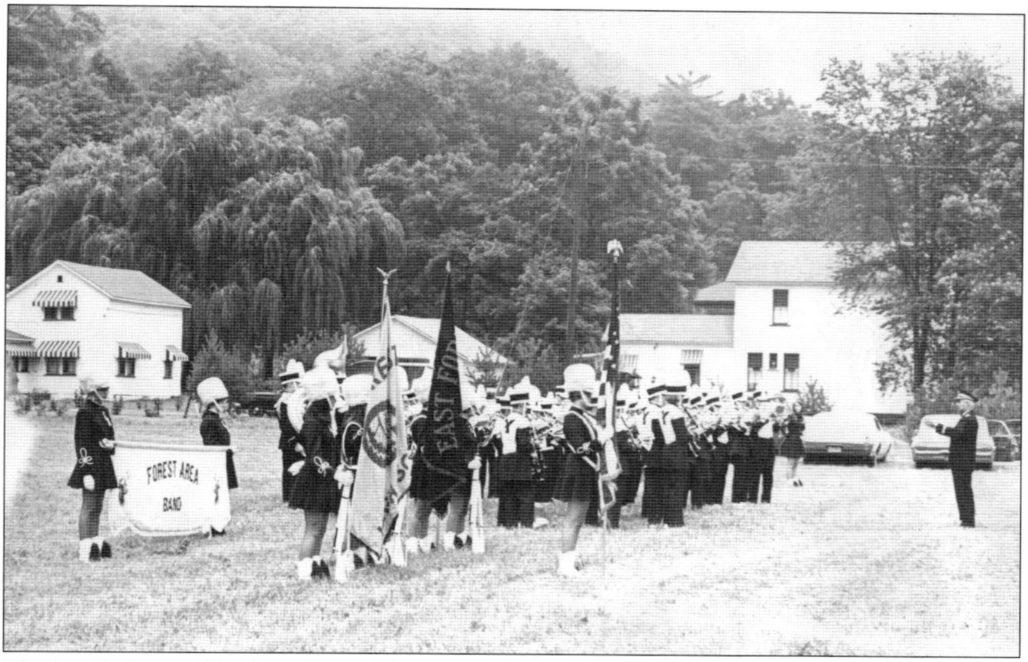

The first Endeavor Old Home Day celebration took place on August 2, 1969, to invite former residents back to their "old home," while others celebrated the past and present of the community. Pictured is the Forest Area Band, led by band director Standish Huffman. The band, which consisted of members from all parts of Forest County, played to a crowd of over 300 people that day.

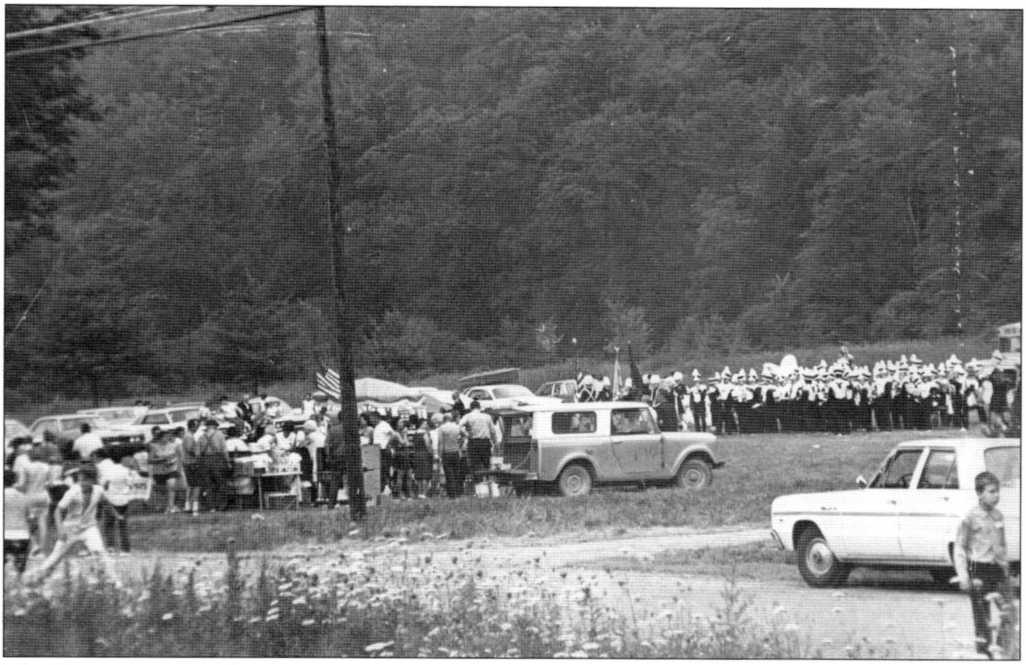

The Forest Area Band is getting ready to present its concert to a crowd attending the first annual Endeavor Old Home Day. A rainstorm during the concert caused many to flee to the community building while others braved the wet conditions. Though the event was planned for only a few hundred people, the committee estimated that over 1,000 attended the celebration.

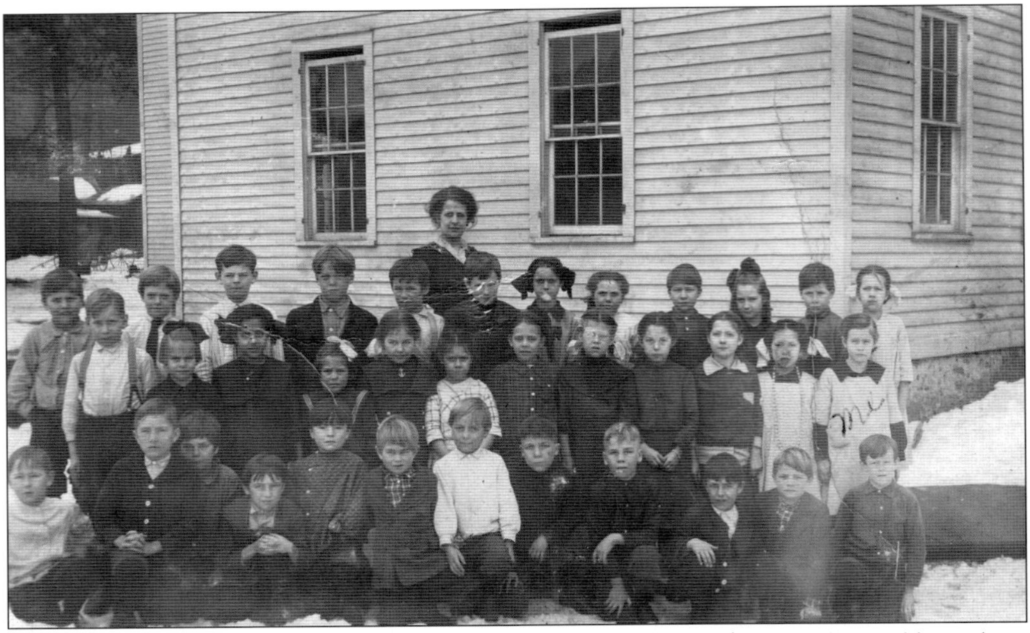

In August 1881, a two-story schoolhouse was built in Endeavor for $900, with an addition later added on July 2, 1896. After a fire destroyed the school in 1925, a Hickory Township–Endeavor School was built and opened in 1926. Pictured are schoolchildren at the old schoolhouse in January 1914.

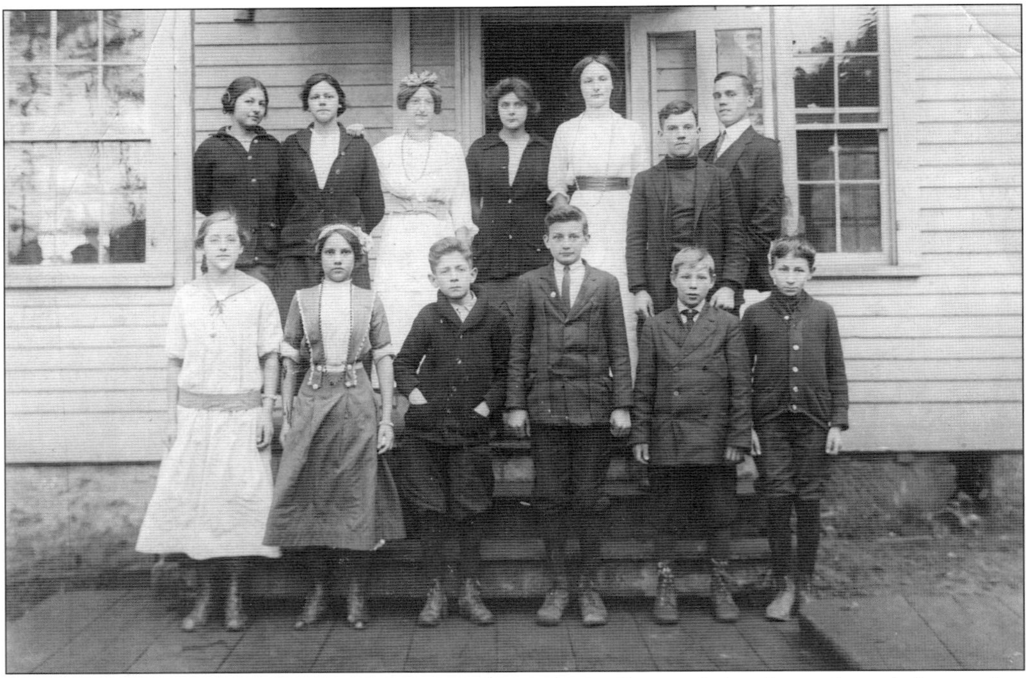

Shown in this 1912 eighth-grade photograph at the Endeavor School are, from left to right, (first row) Mary Brown, May Kiffer, Ray Fox, Galen McCullough, Ernest Gesin, and Jack Mintz; (second row) Olive Jones, Helen Church, Ida Ball, Ethel Hall, Lela Taft, Herman Taft, and Neil Kunselman.

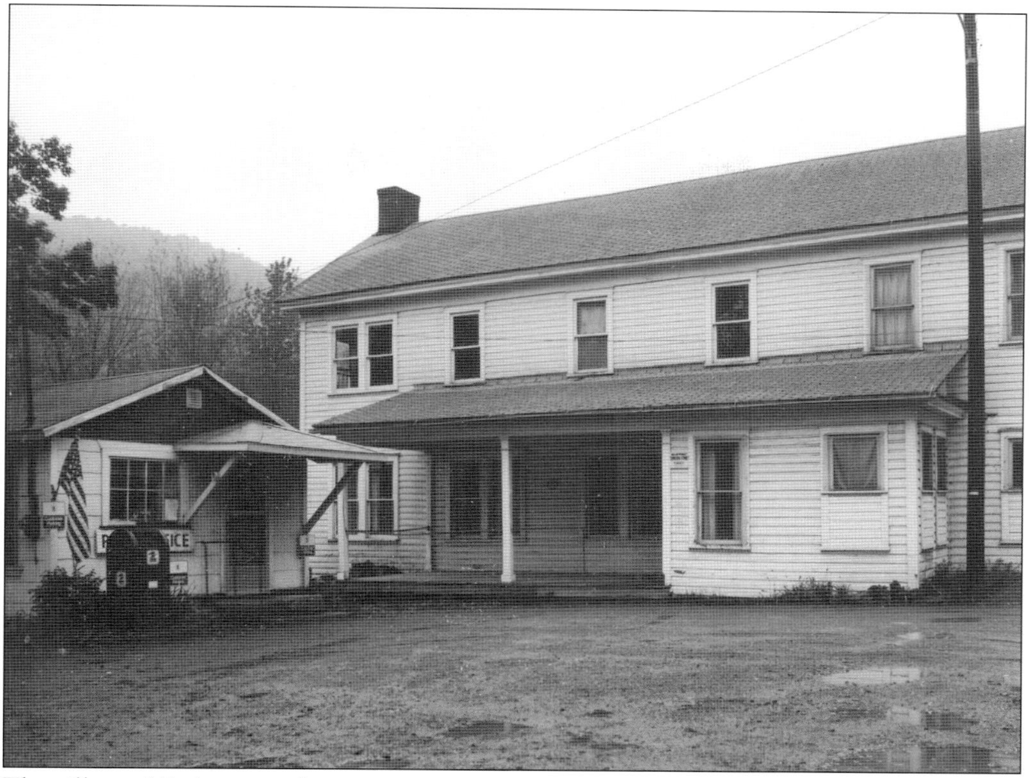

The village of Endeavor took its name from the Christian Endeavor Society of Portland, Maine, which, through the local Methodist and Presbyterian churches, had a strong influence in the area. Pictured are the Endeavor Post Office (left), which was established June 10, 1897, and the community house (right).

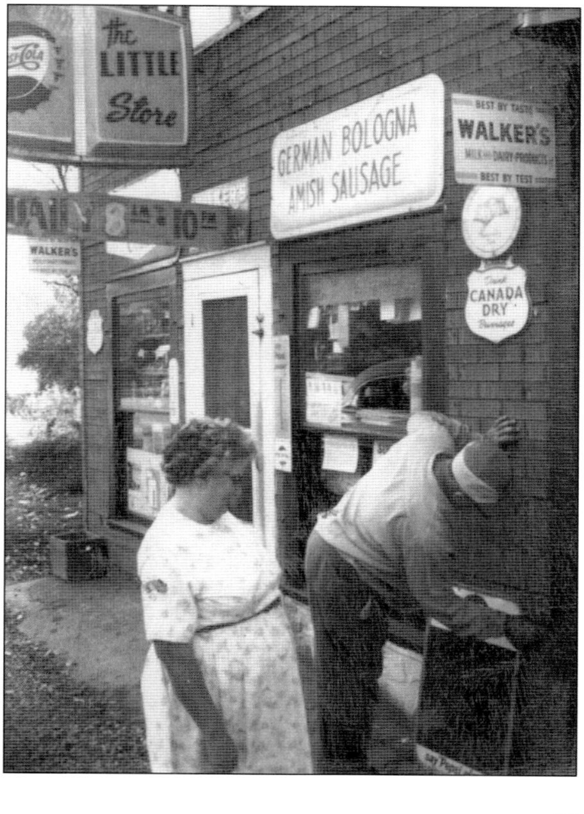

Grant George made everyone feel welcome when they visited his grocery store. A US Army veteran, George and his wife, Marilyn, purchased the store in 1969 and called it the Little Store. Located on Route 62 in East Hickory, people would come from miles around specifically for the thick smoked bacon and the homemade ice cream in waffle cones.

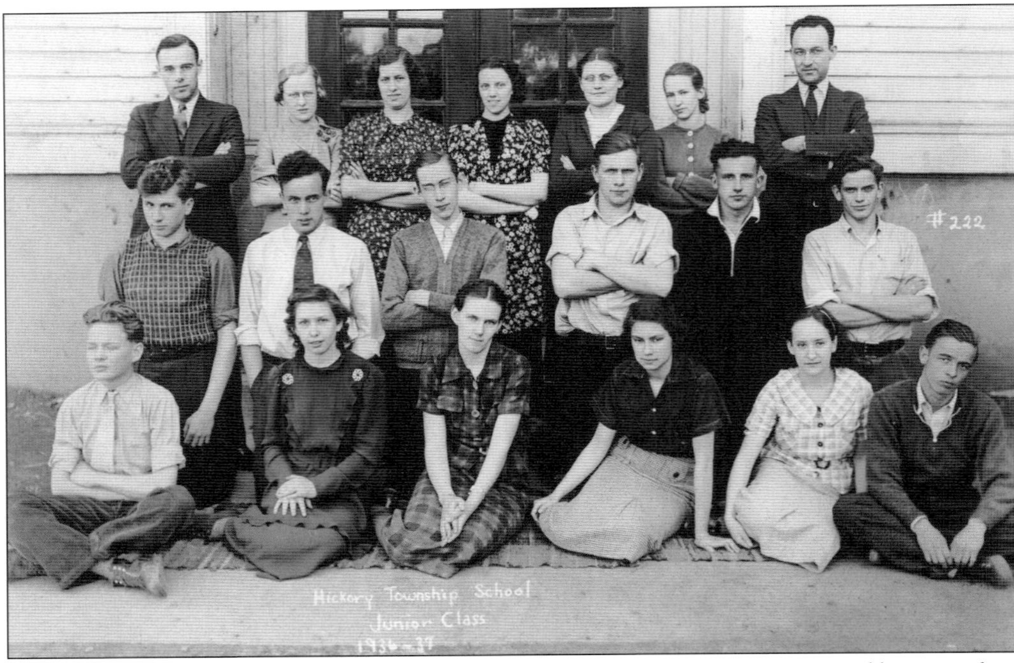

Members of the Hickory Township High School junior class of 1935–1936 pictured here are, from left to right, (first row) Jean Ziegler, Mary Caligiuri, Zellebelle Barber, Flora Mae Thompson, Pauline Kisabeth, and Earl Kennedy; (second row) Bob Black, Lewis Wright, John Thompson, Willis Stover, Howard Fenstermaker, and Wayne Howe; (third row) William Coleman, Geraline Satley, Iris Littlefield, Phyllis Giles, Doriss Mooney, Helena Jackson, and Karl Flowers.

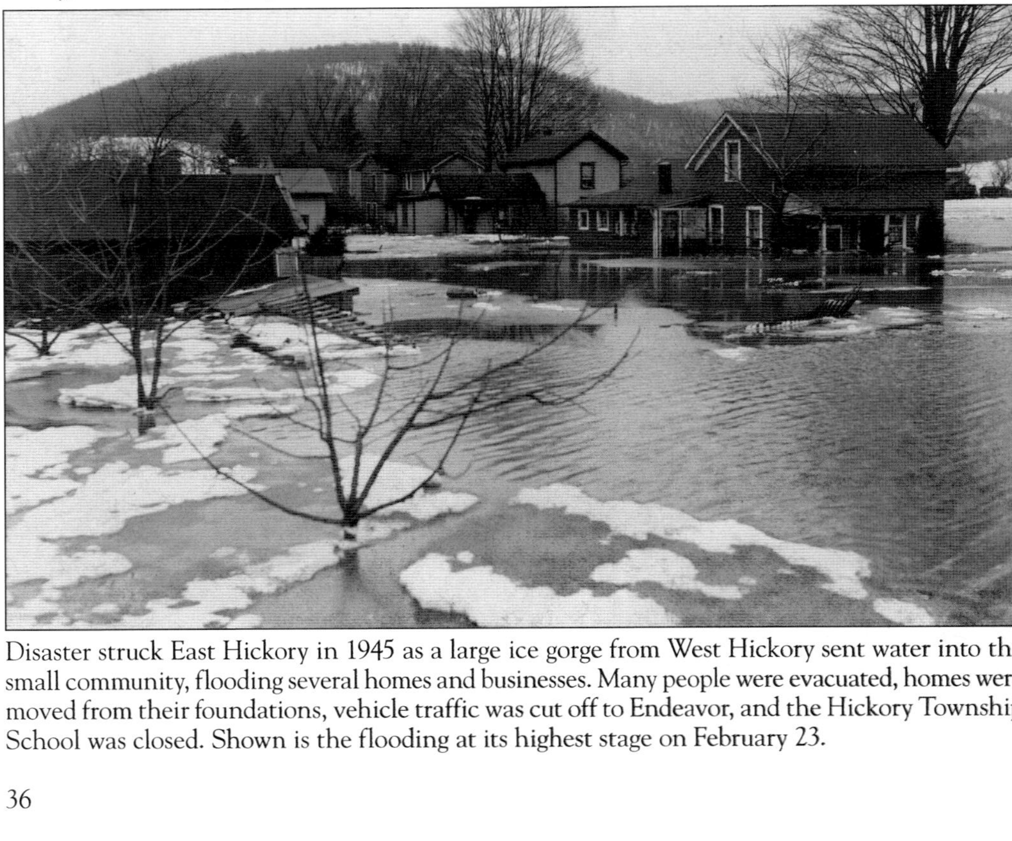

Disaster struck East Hickory in 1945 as a large ice gorge from West Hickory sent water into the small community, flooding several homes and businesses. Many people were evacuated, homes were moved from their foundations, vehicle traffic was cut off to Endeavor, and the Hickory Township School was closed. Shown is the flooding at its highest stage on February 23.

Pictured is Edward Mealy with his shotgun tucked under his arm and a dog at his side somewhere in the village of Yellow Hammer. The small settlement in the wilds of the Allegheny National Forest is near the mountain Fool's Knob and the valley named Dark Hollow. The village of Yellow Hammer is within the township of Hickory. Edward Mealy (1850–1924) was married to Mary Lydia (Bean) Mealy.

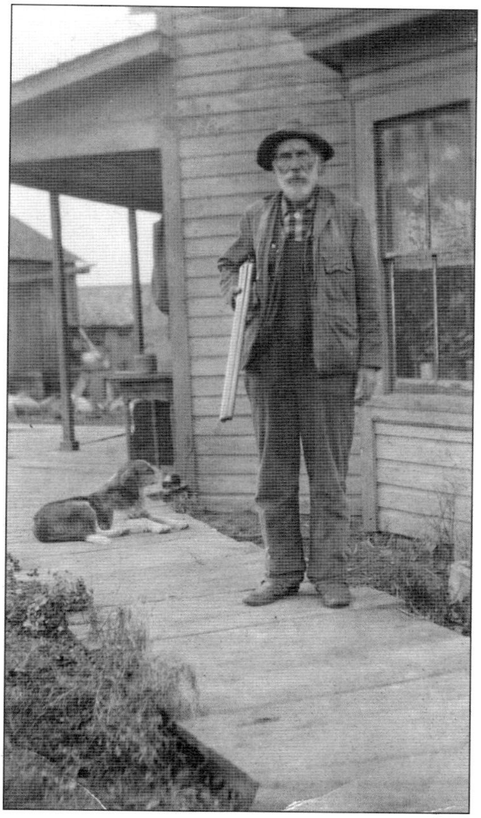

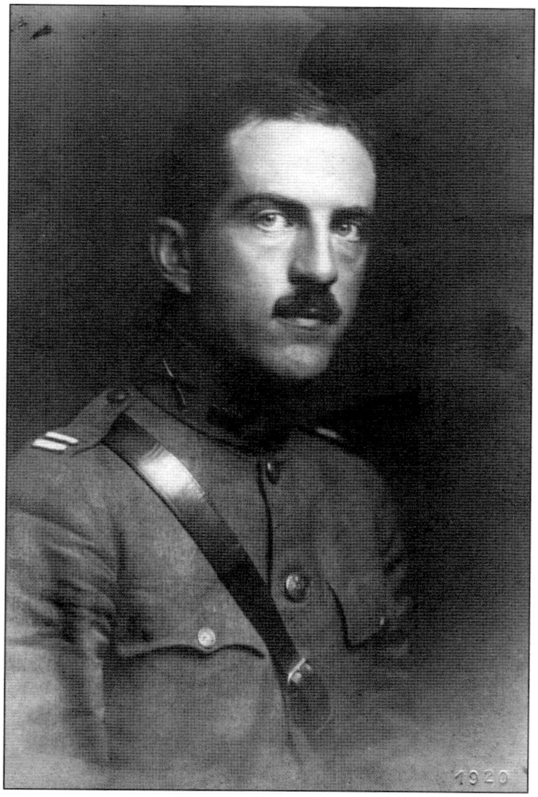

Alexander Royal Wheeler was a graduate of Yale and Oxford Universities, saw combat in World War I, and served seven consecutive terms as Forest County's Republican in the state House of Representatives. He and his wife, Mary Alice (Siggins) Wheeler, and their family were highly regarded for their genuine devotion to the townspeople of Endeavor and their employees, and for their appreciation of forest conservation. By gifting 20 acres of virgin timber and selling another 100 acres to the federal government, the Wheeler family protected 120 acres of old-growth forest forever.

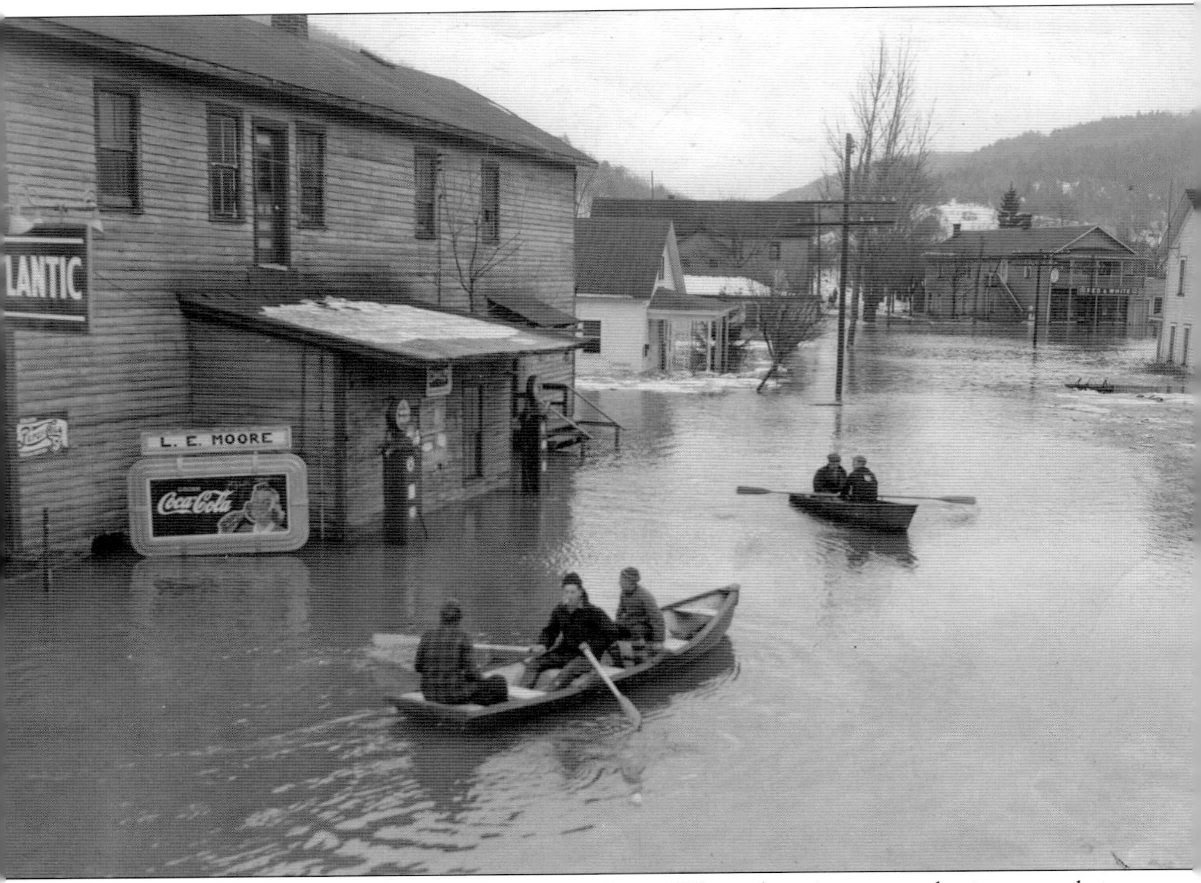

Flooding has long plagued Forest County residents. When the winter snow begins to melt in February and March, the water rushes toward the many rivers and creeks, causing levels to rise significantly. This picture shows flooding in East Hickory on February 23, 1945.

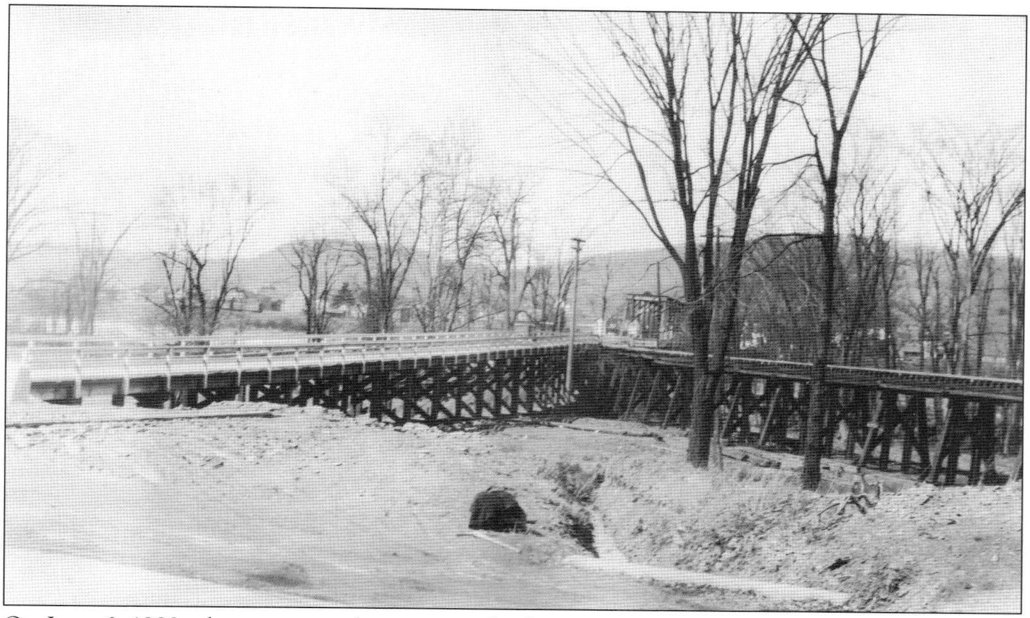

On June 6, 1883, plans were made to erect a bridge at West Hickory in Harmony Township to cross the Allegheny River. Between 1883 and 1887, several wooden structures were built, along with the bridge, which remained until 1896. By late summer 1896, the Hickory Bridge Company had erected a steel truss bridge to replace the wooden bridge. The wood from the original bridge was used to build the rail structure on the right.

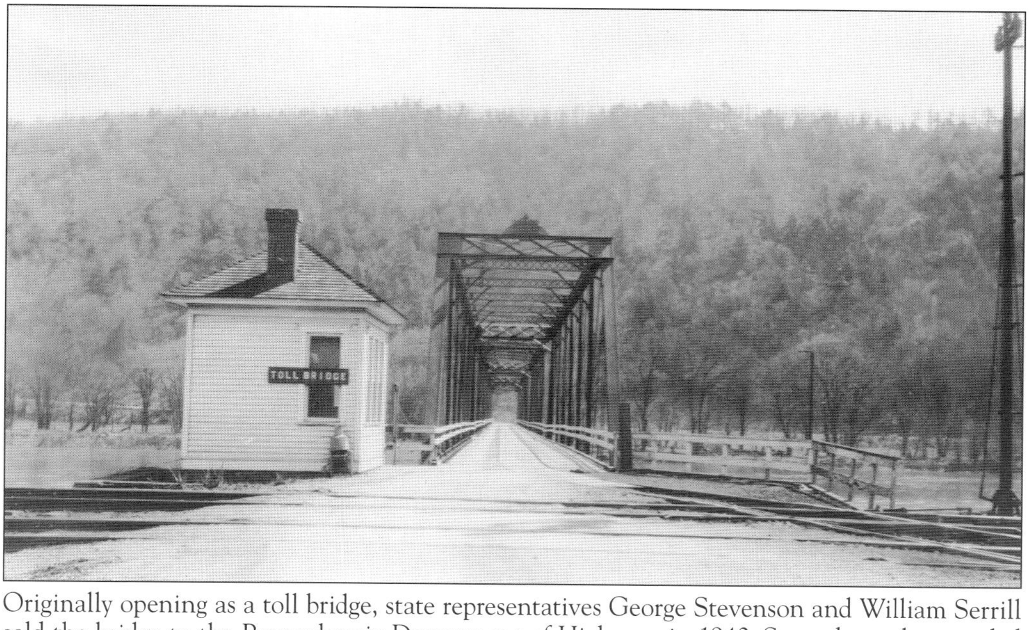

Originally opening as a toll bridge, state representatives George Stevenson and William Serrill sold the bridge to the Pennsylvania Department of Highways in 1940. Several people attended the ceremony at West Hickory's community center building in 1940 to celebrate the bridge changing to toll-free.

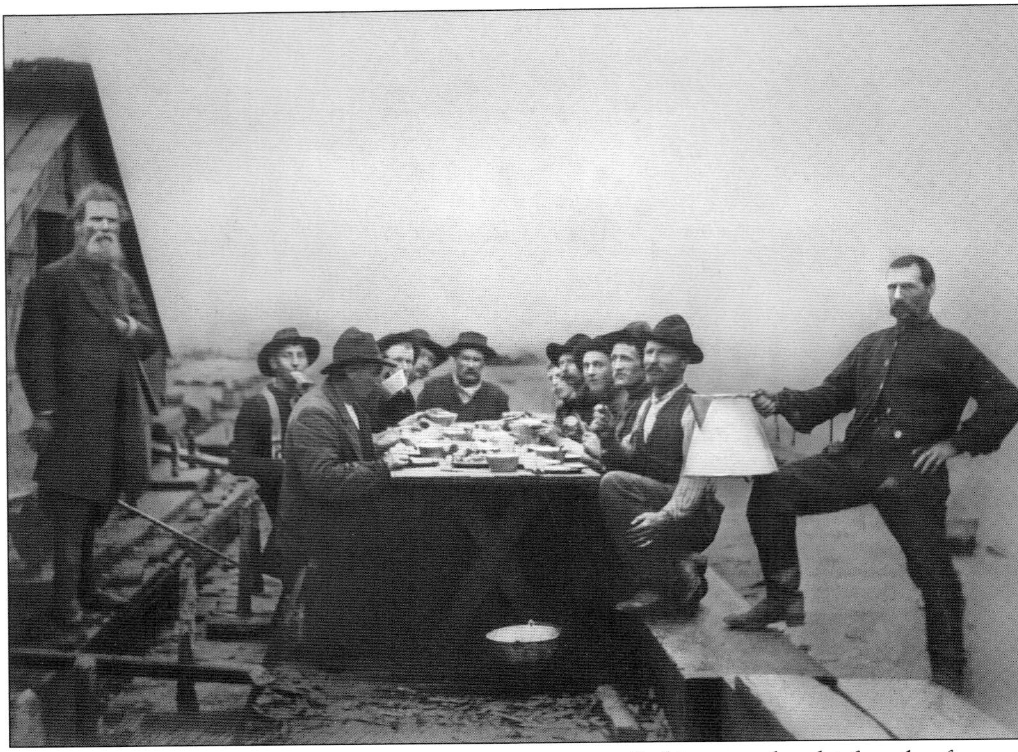

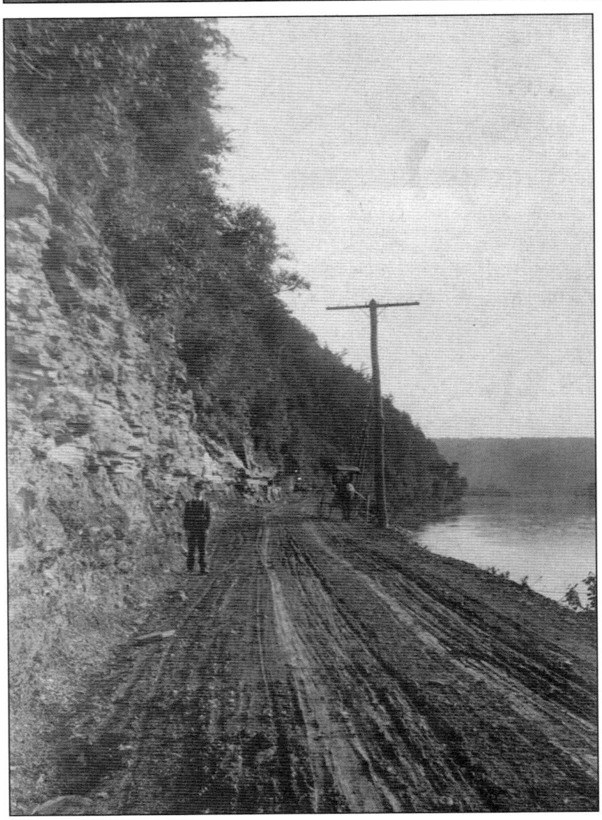

Rafting was the chief mode of transporting lumber before railroads were available. While the timber rafts lay along the shore awaiting the spring thaw and rains, which provided the water highways to Pittsburgh, a crew of raftsmen in Clarington feast before embarking on their turbulent journey. Rafts were also launched from Cooksburg, Nebraska, and West Hickory.

Shown is a view of US Route 62 along the Allegheny River in the late 1800s known as "the Narrows." Frank Secrist maintained the roadways of Forest County until 1931, when the Pennsylvania State Highway Department was established to maintain township roads.

Three

Kingsley Township and Howe Township

Kingsley Township is located in the center of Forest County. Villages within the township include Starr, Crystal Springs, Whig Hill, Kellettville, Newtown, Mayburg, and Muzett. Fourteen streams run through the township's verdant valleys. The area was named after Ebenezer Kingsley of New York. Historical, colorful accounts illustrate his hunting ability and credit him with naming several streams in Forest County, choosing names that reflected his experiences: he killed a bear near Bear Creek, shot a salmon in Salmon Creek, and heard mournful cries near Lamentation Run (these are but a few). Many early settlers in Whig Hill were farmers. Mayburg was named in honor of the May family who managed oil wells in the area. Successful sawmills, railroads, and a wood chemical plant operated there until 1943. Gypsies visited the buzzing town of Kellettville annually, as did vaudeville performer Lillian Mae Mansfield, whose tent show was wiped out by a "cyclone" in 1916. Sightseers lined the streets of Kellettville for the Fourth of July parade and fireworks. Today, campers and residents are treated to Independence Day festivities hosted by the Scherer family, owners of Cougar Bob's Kellettville Tavern (once a schoolhouse), where "You're Nobody until You've Kissed the Moose." The Weller family has hosted the Allegheny Mountain Championship Rodeo since 1980 at the Flying W Ranch. Civilian Conservation Corps (CCC) Camp ANF (Allegheny National Forest)-2 was located in Kellettville in 1936. The company put down a gravel road from Mayburg to Heart's Content.

The Allegheny National Forest covers 99 percent of Howe Township, which also includes the county's highest peak at 1,954 feet. Fourteen communities are contained within Howe Township. Balltown was the oil town, with 60 wells that produced 8,000 barrels per day. Brookston had the tanning and lumber industries. Watson Farm had a combination of oil and lumber businesses. Truemans had a store that supplied all the woodsmen's needs. The smaller lumber mills that operated near Tionesta Creek were in Minister, Blue Jay, and Porkey, with the Pennsylvania & Western Railroad making a connection at Pigeon, Iron City, and Sheffield Junction.

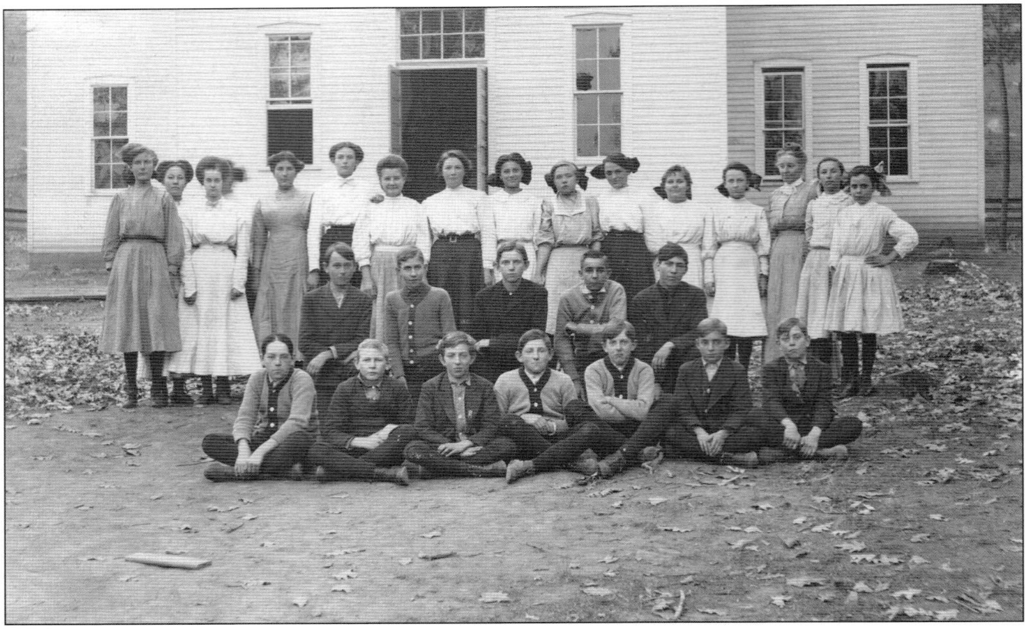

Pictured are schoolchildren in front the Kellettville School during the early 1900s. The grade school and high school students had their own buildings, with the grade school being a two-story structure. The high school burned down in 1913 and was replaced the same year. In 1926, both buildings succumbed to a fire.

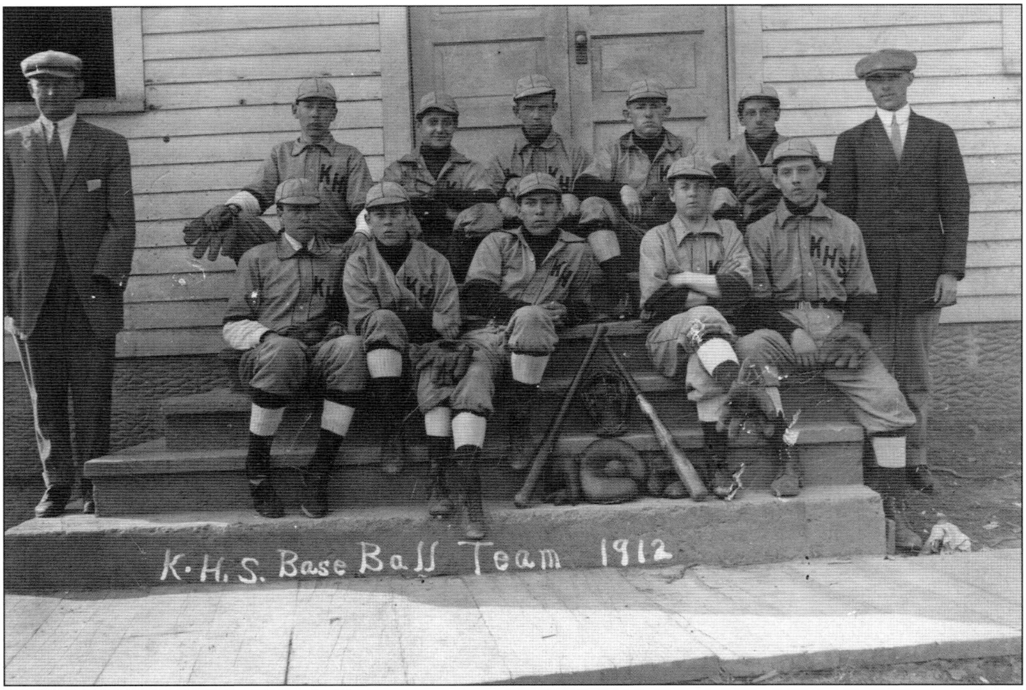

This photograph shows players from the Kellettville High School baseball team in 1912. Sitting on the steps are, from left to right, (first row) Clair Smather, Reed Detar, Rollin Carbaugh, Dewey Detar, and Glenn Graham; (second row) Warren Jones, William Watson, James Flynn, Orrie Kinch, and Andy Babonick. Standing are professors Jack Frost (left) and William Keister.

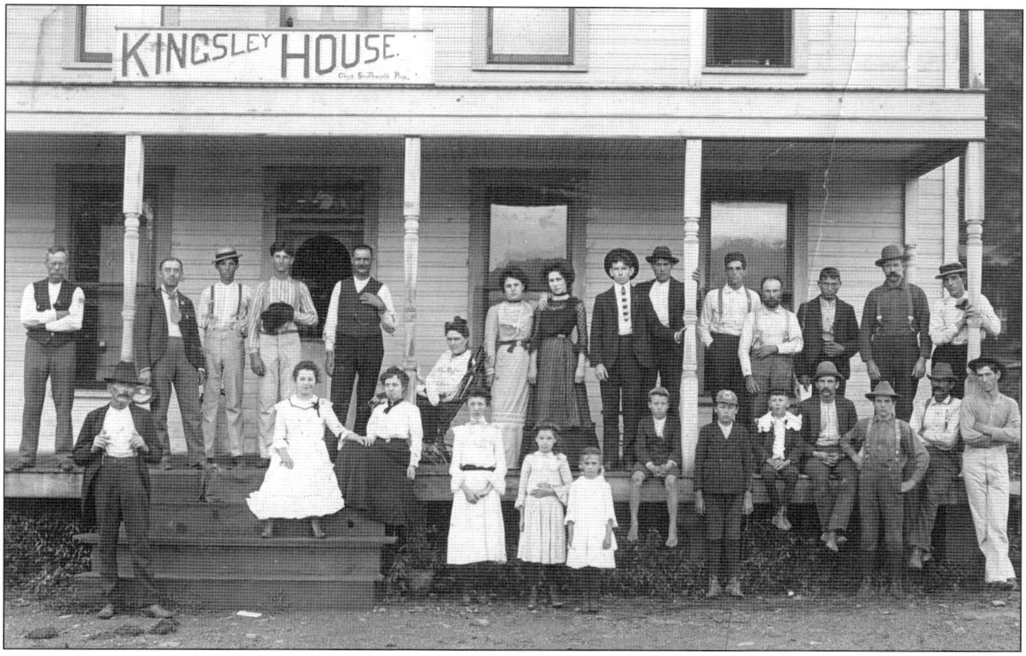

Kingsley Township was named after one of the earliest settlers of Tionesta, Ebenezer Kingsley. Pictured here is the Kingsley House, a four-story hotel in Kellettville. This establishment, as well as many others in Kellettville, was shut down when the town was abandoned by 1942 due to flooding caused by the building of the Tionesta Dam. At one time, Kingsley Township was a lively, booming area. There were a variety of industries, including a tannery, a wheel hub factory, two sawmills, and a wood-kiln factory. There were also several local businesses such as the Kingsley House, Kribbs and Ray Livery, Watson and Company general store, Frank Harkless's drugstore, and William Silze's jewelry store.

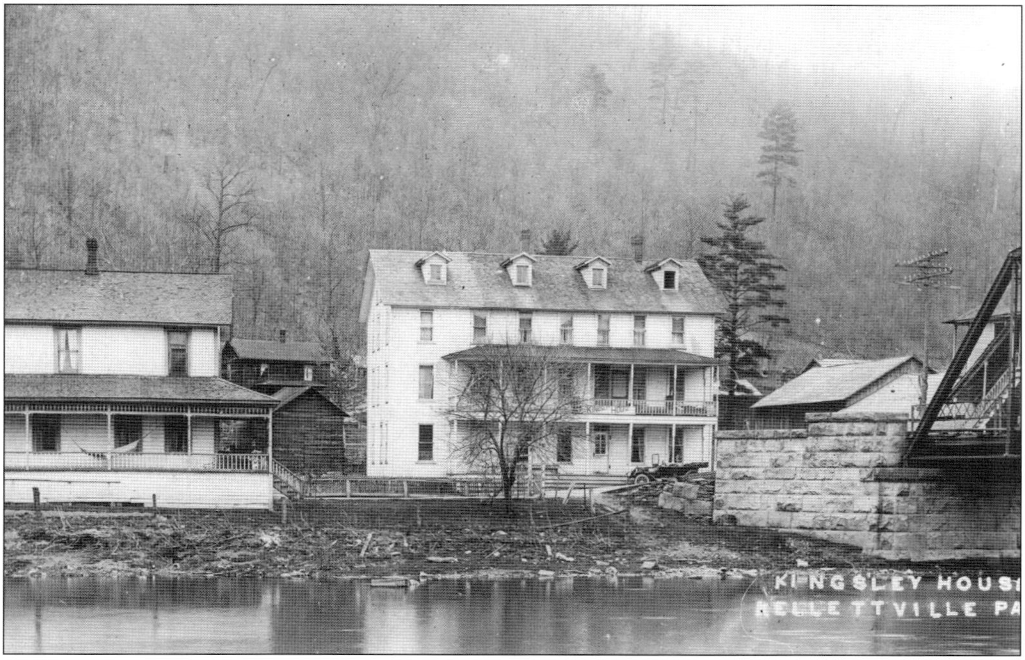

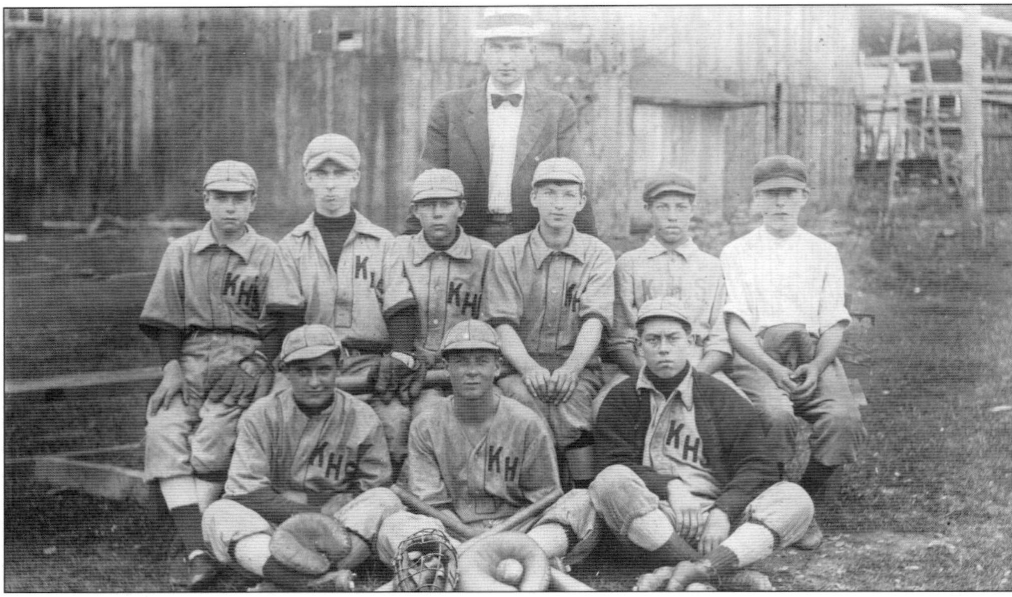

In the early 1900s, Kellettville was a bustling town that continued to grow. Folks there enjoyed many types of recreation such as hunting, fishing, and, when the long-awaited warmth of spring came, playing baseball. With only nine players, this Kellettville High School baseball team did not get much of a break when taking the field.

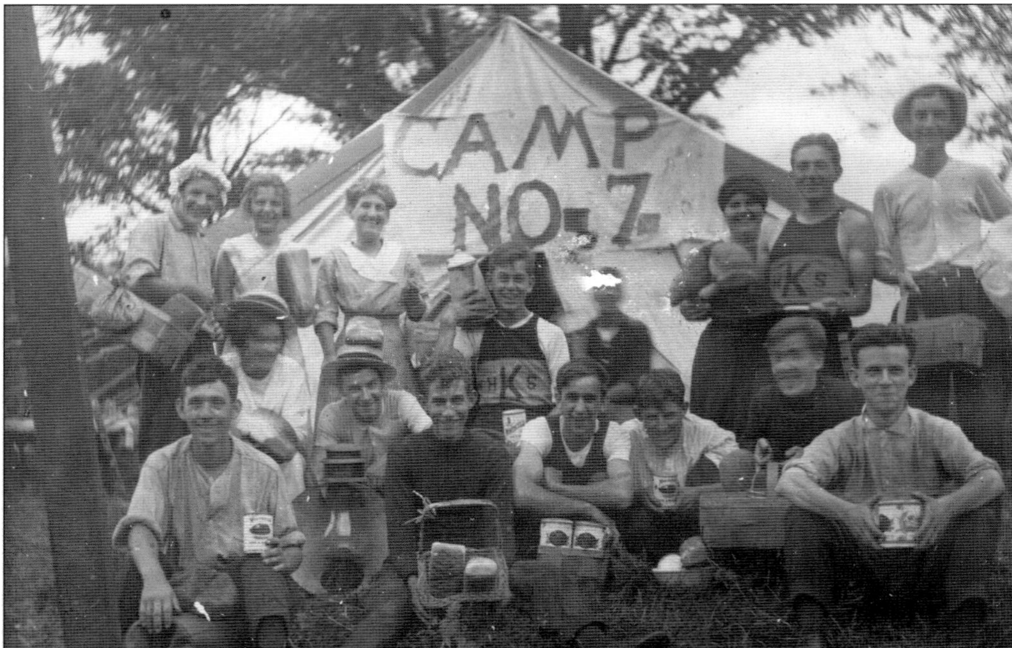

Kellettville contained three churches before the town was abandoned in 1943 due to the building of the Tionesta Dam. The churches were St. Ann's Catholic Church established by Father Winkler, the Free Methodist Church established by Rev. D.B. Tobey, and the Methodist church established by Rev. S.B. Torrey and financed by Teddy Collins. Shown are helpers and children at the camp of Kellettville Sunday school in June 1914.

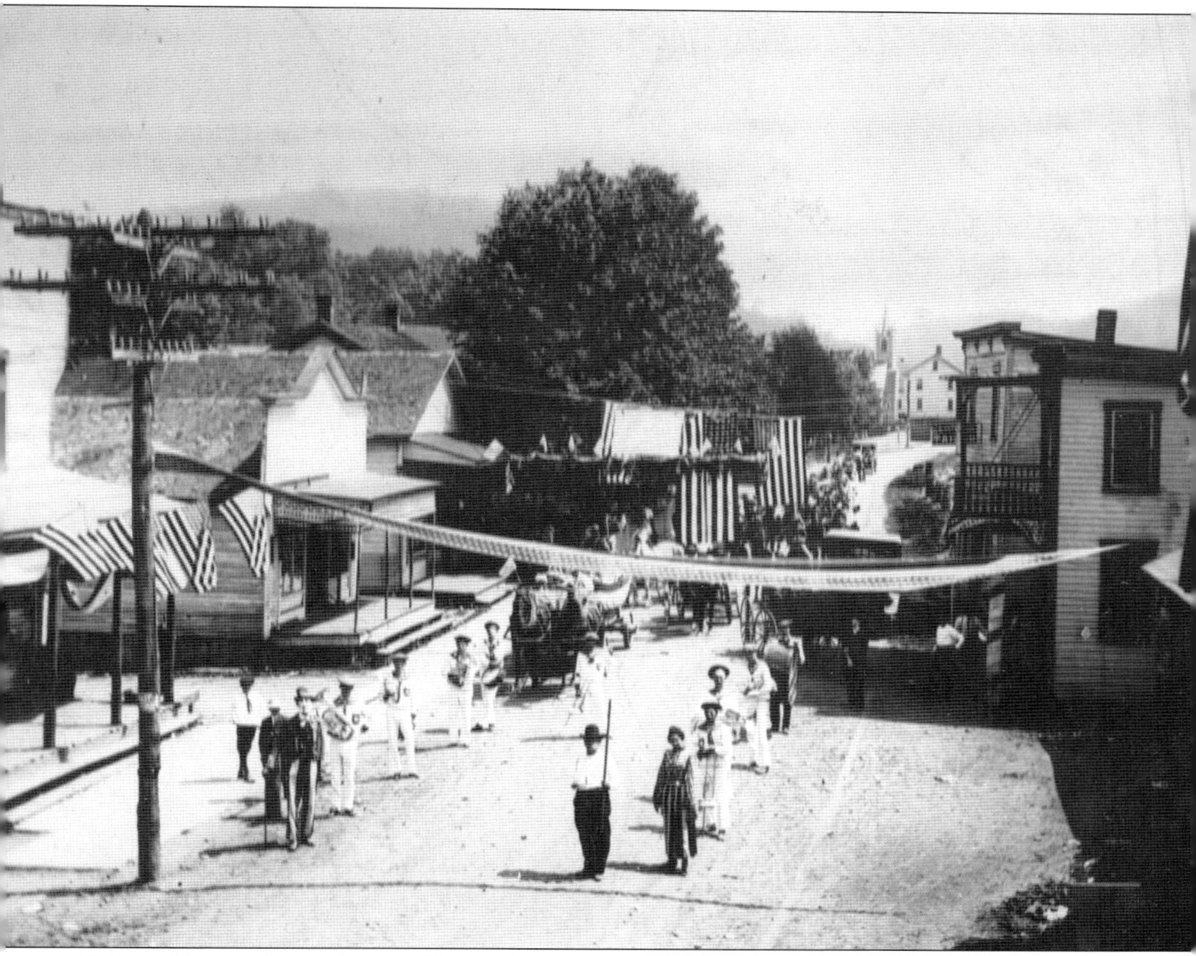

Kellettville once boasted over 1,300 residents, a wood factory, two sawmills, and a tannery. Due to the completion of the Tionesta Lake and Dam in 1940, residents were forced to abandon the town in 1943. This image shows Main Street in Kellettville as it looked on July 4, 1909, during a parade.

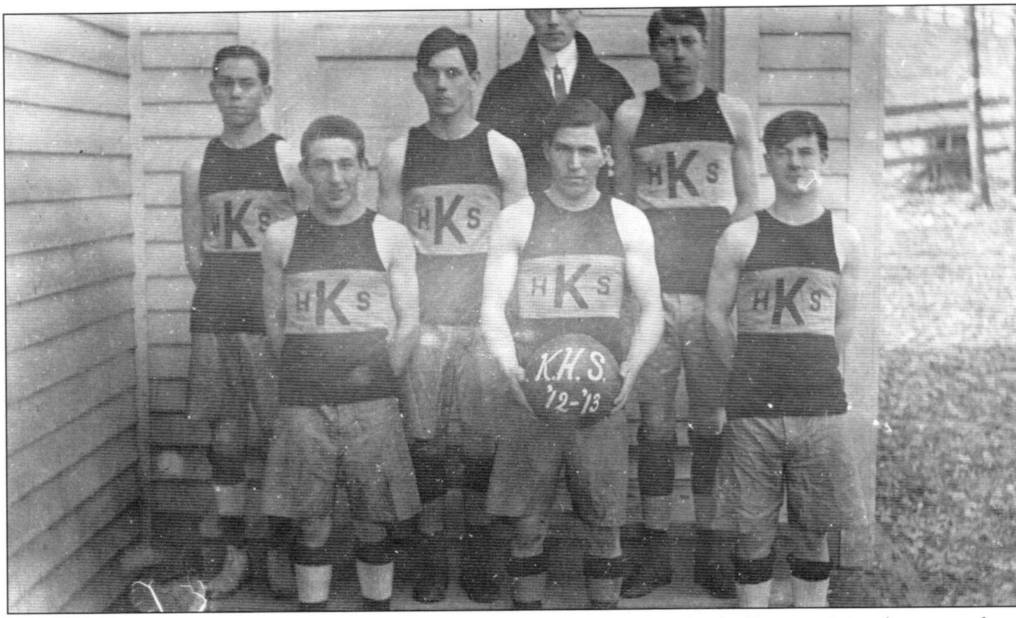

Pictured here is the 1912–1913 Kellettville High School boys' basketball team. Members are, from left to right, (first row) Jake Carbaugh, Rolland Carbaugh, and Dewey Detar; (second row) Reed Detar, Glenn Graham, and Clair Smathers. The coach is unidentified.

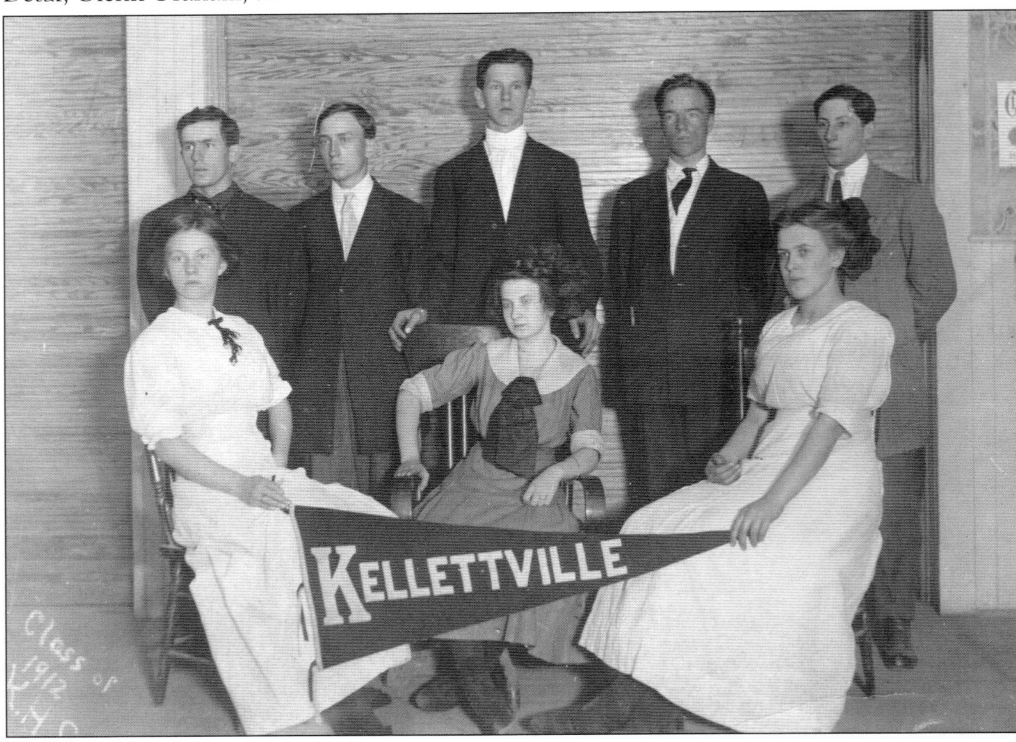

Shown here is the Kellettville High School class of 1912 as they proudly display their school banner for all to see. Dressed in their best are, from left to right, (first row) Anna Lease, Pearl Detar, and Margaret Lorom; (second row) Walter Wilson, Glen Reche, Julian Robbins, Alvin Sallade, and Sherman Butler.

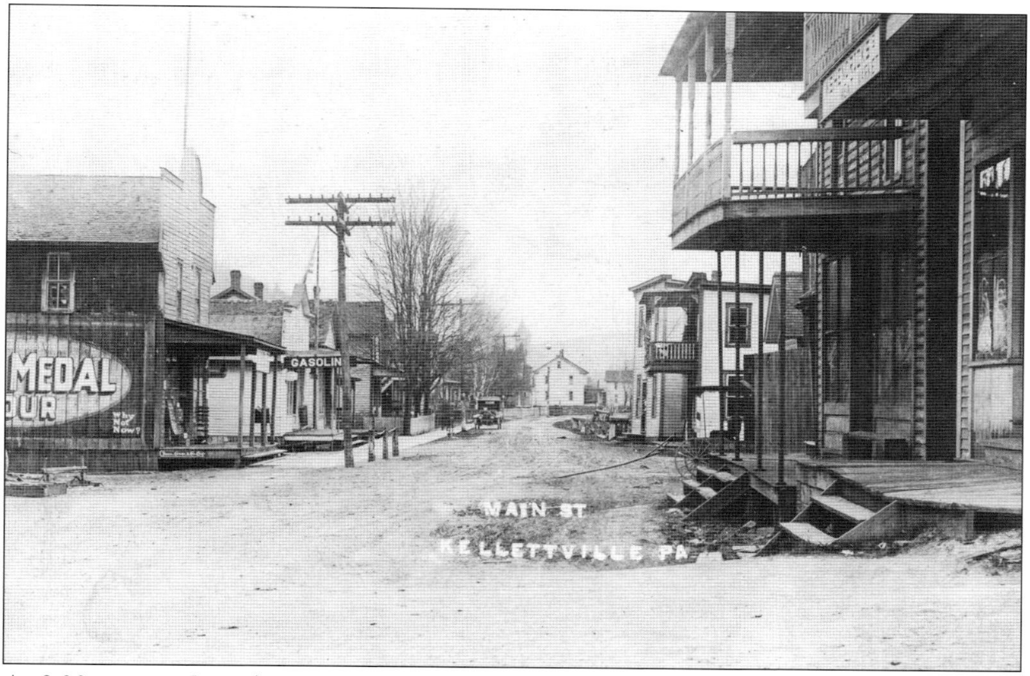

At 2:00 a.m. on Saturday, September 7, 1919, a fire broke out in the Kribbs and Ray Livery, which quickly spread throughout Kellettville. The damage was so extensive that the entire town was on the verge of being destroyed. Forming a bucket brigade, townsfolk worked together and extinguished the flames by late afternoon. Shown in this photograph is Main Street in Kellettville shortly before the disaster.

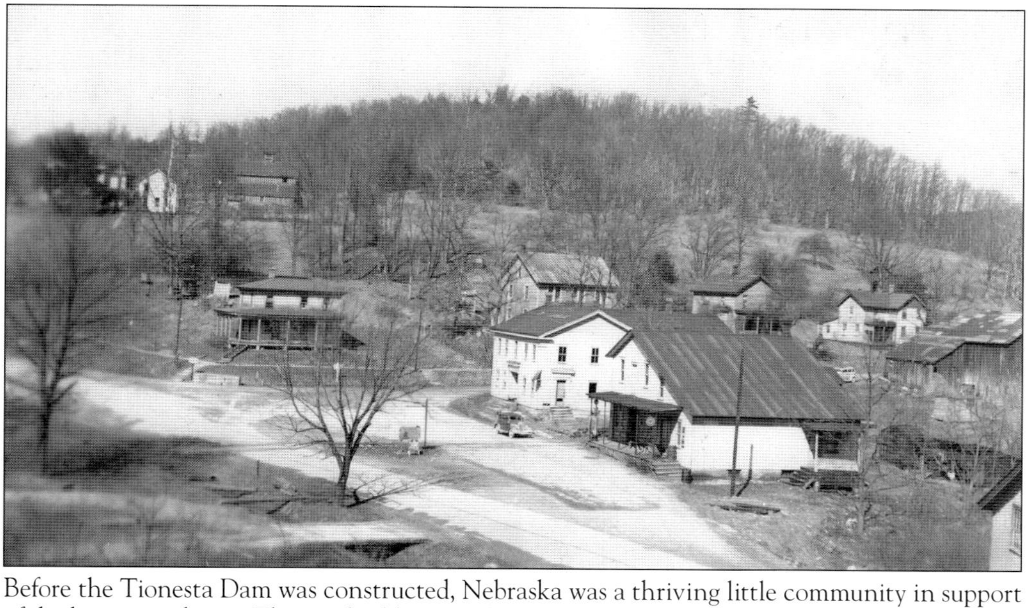

Before the Tionesta Dam was constructed, Nebraska was a thriving little community in support of the logging industry. The two buildings in the center of this photograph are the Salmon Creek Mercantile company store (foreground) and the Thompson Hotel.

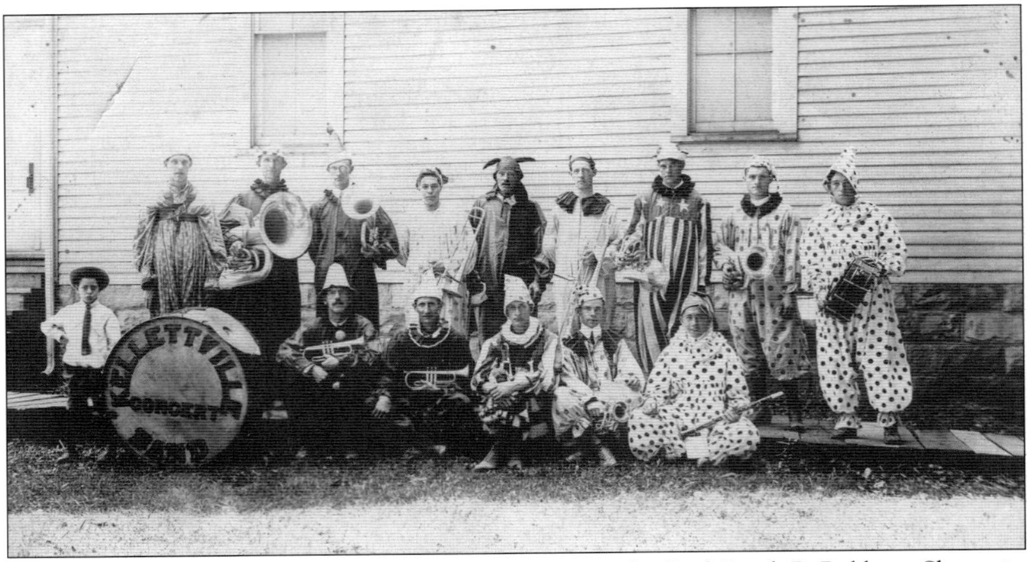

The Kellettville Concert Band organized around 1906 under Prof. Frank B. Robbins. Shown in this undated photograph is the band in full costume during a celebration in Kellettville. Parades, holiday celebrations, jubilees, and festivals were all common occurrences that brought the small community together and drew in residents from the surrounding area.

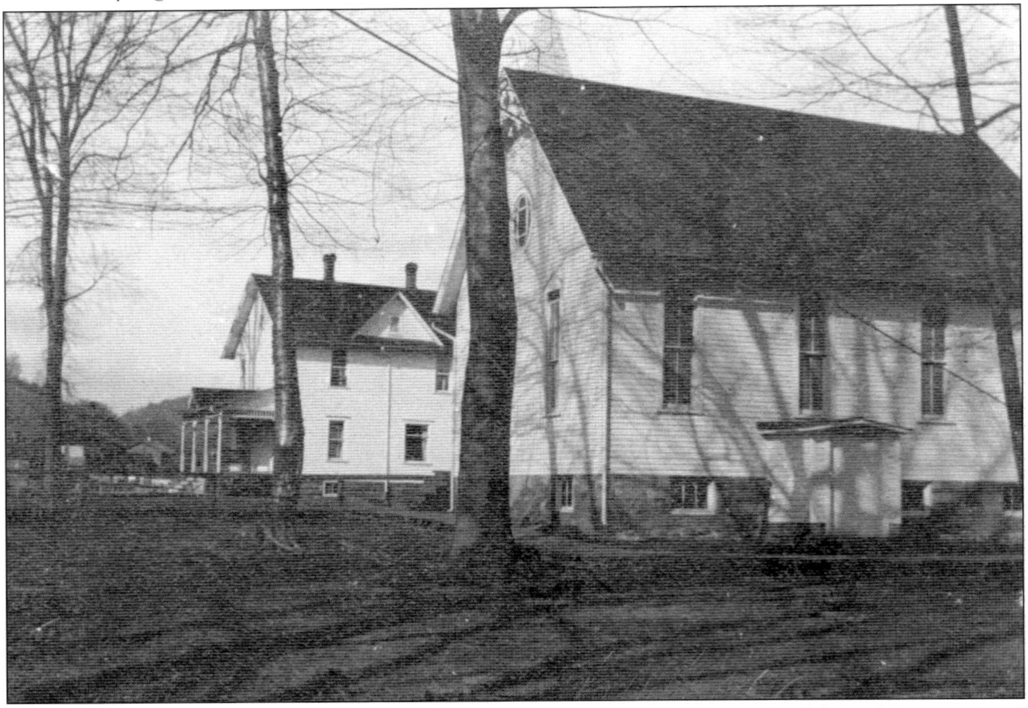

Shown here is a photograph of the Methodist church in Kellettville, established by Reverend Torrey in 1906. The church sat on a plot of land that was often referred to as the Methodist church grove. On certain occasions, the Kellettville Concert Band entertained families while they picnicked and enjoyed a twirl on the permanent merry-go-round. The church also served as the annual meeting place for Kellettville residents who were displaced due to the construction of the Tionesta Dam.

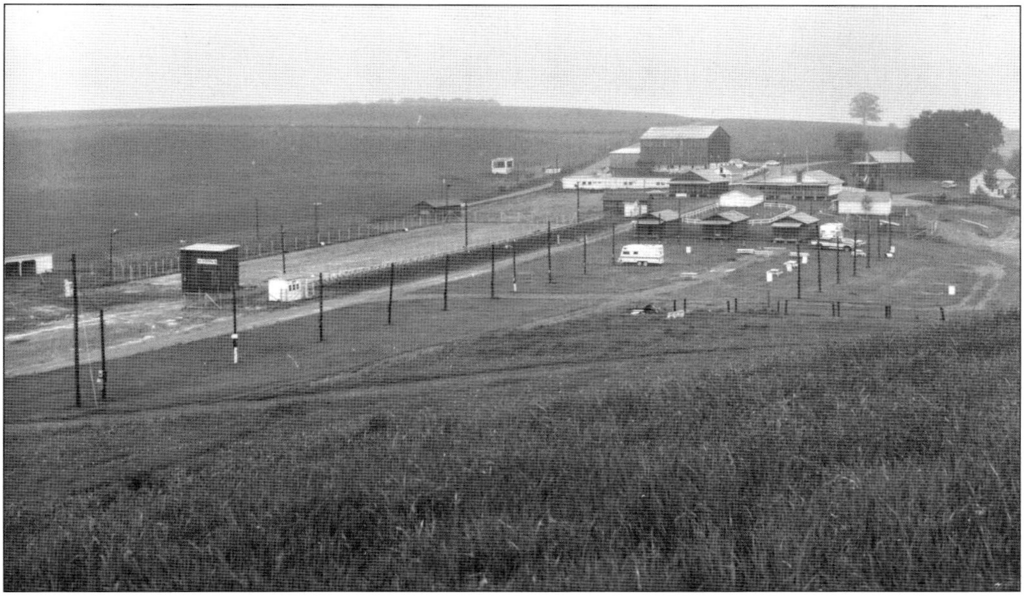

The Flying W Ranch is a working ranch surrounded by the Allegheny National Forest in Kellettville. It was opened in 1974 by part owners and managers Ronnie and Joyce Weller. A popular vacation destination, it consists of a campground, bunkhouses, a tack shop, and the Trails End restaurant. The ranch made many activities, such as trail rides, pony rides, riding instructions, swimming, and youth summer camp available. In 1979, it hosted the first annual Allegheny Mountain Championship Rodeo.

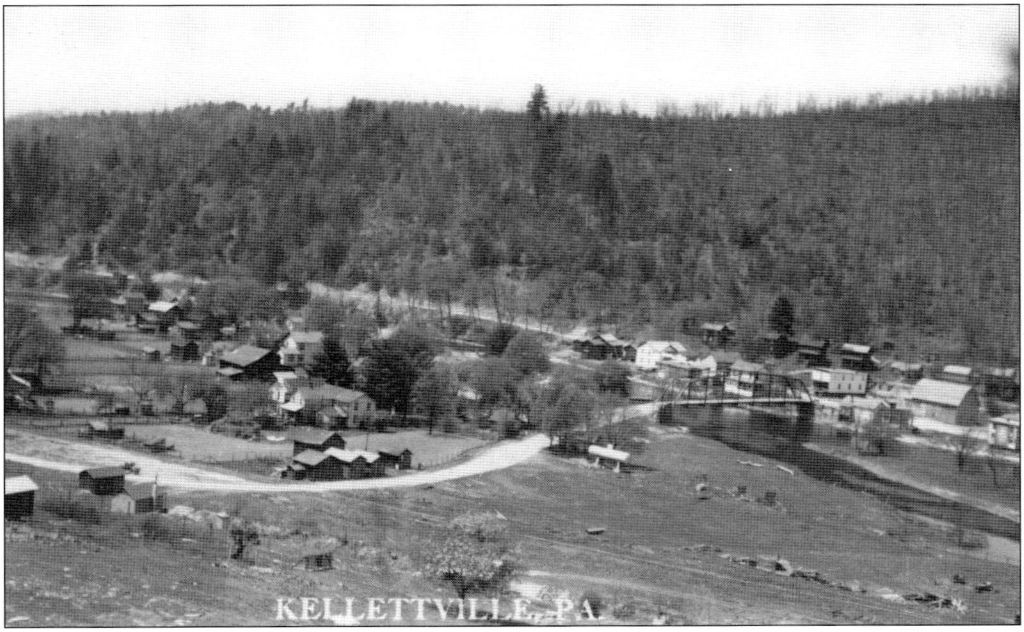

Kellettville is a small community in Kingsley Township located on what was formerly the Daniel Cole farm. The town was named in honor of W.W. Kellet, who came to the area and developed a tannery along Tionesta Creek. The tannins were extracted from hemlock bark, boiled and barreled, and used to cure leather. The Civil War spurred the development of the industry, which gave a boost to the community.

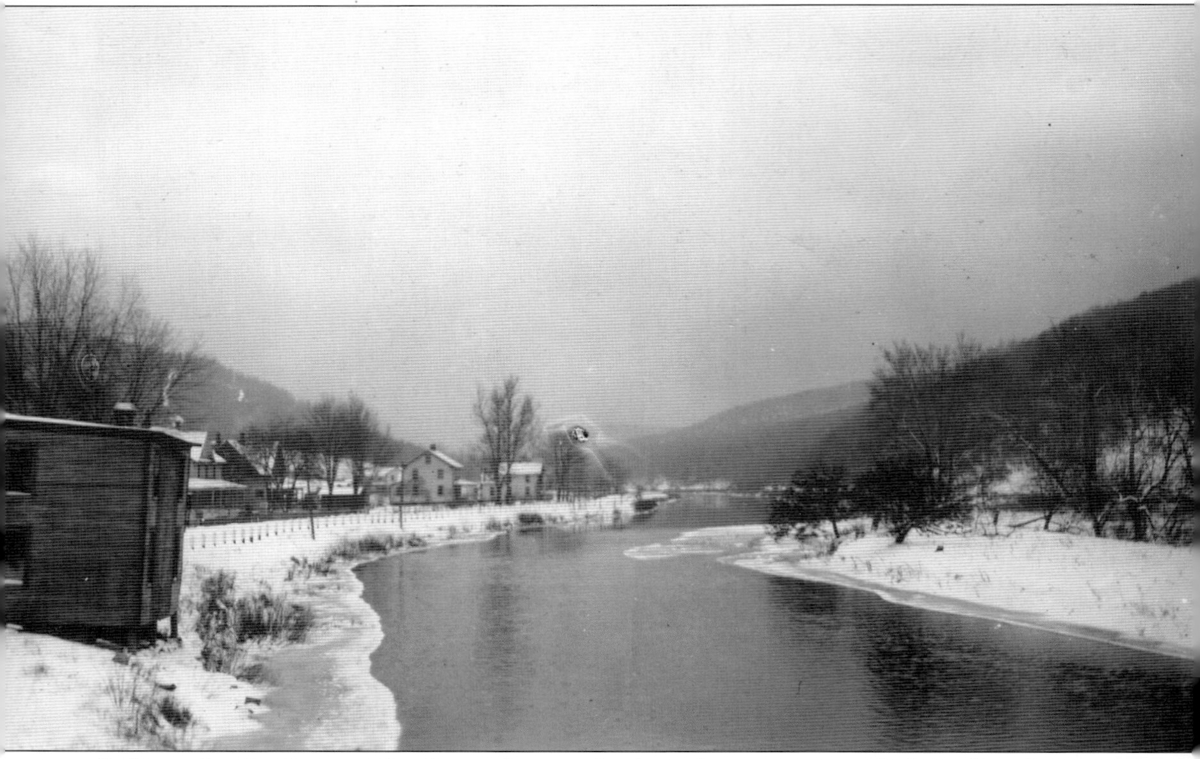

Before railroads, Tionesta Creek was the main highway for transporting the large logs that were felled in the forest and cut into smaller pieces to be transported to the sawmills. The giant cuts of timber were gathered into rafts that were floated down the creek to the Allegheny River. The waterways not only helped, but also hindered residents and businesses. In the winter, ice would form and break into huge blocks that migrated over the banks causing much hardship, damage, and loss of life.

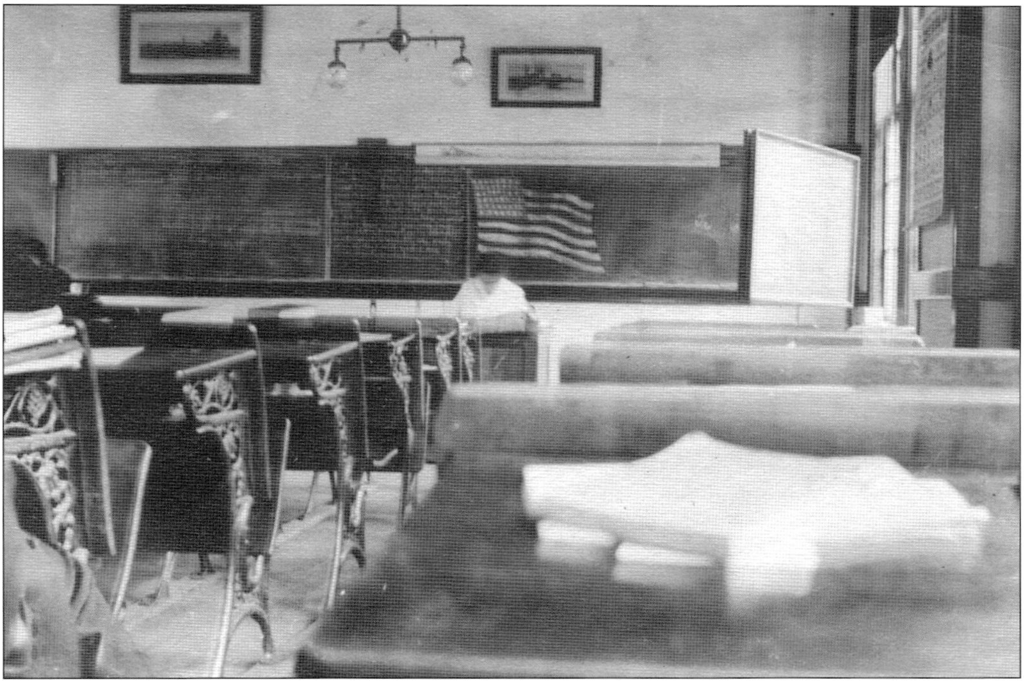

This photograph was taken during the early 1900s inside the Kellettville High School. After the school succumbed to a fire in April 1926, classes resumed in the Collins Hall community center, with seventh and eighth graders also having classes in the building. During the late 1800s and into the mid-1900s, many schools in Forest County fell victim to fire damage.

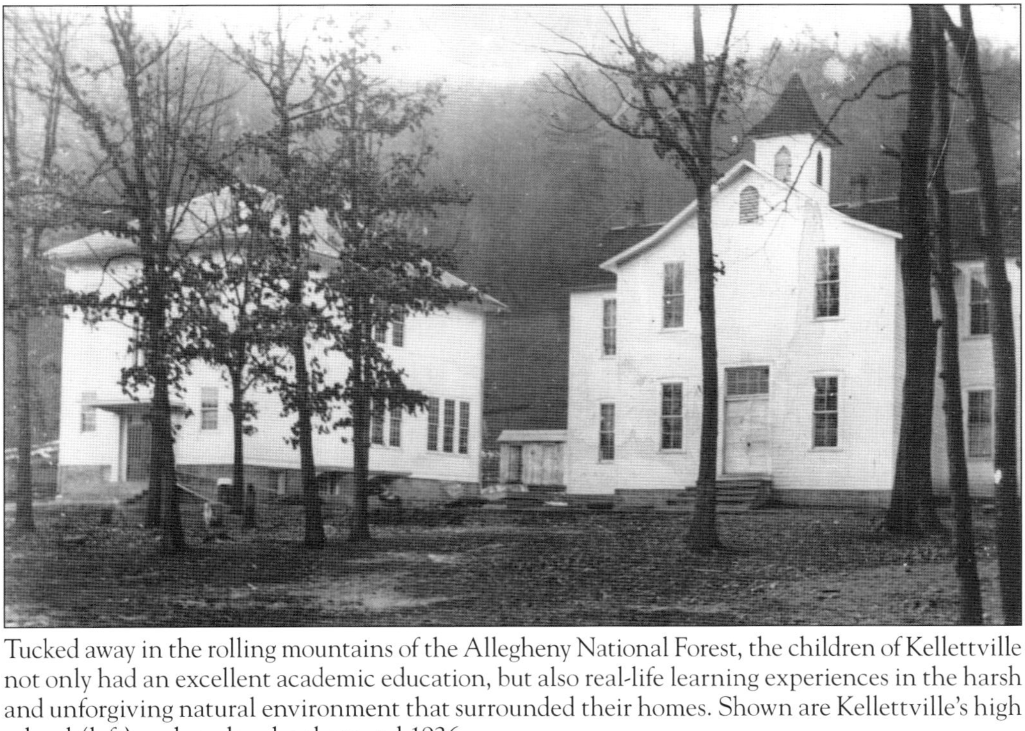

Tucked away in the rolling mountains of the Allegheny National Forest, the children of Kellettville not only had an excellent academic education, but also real-life learning experiences in the harsh and unforgiving natural environment that surrounded their homes. Shown are Kellettville's high school (left) and grade school around 1926.

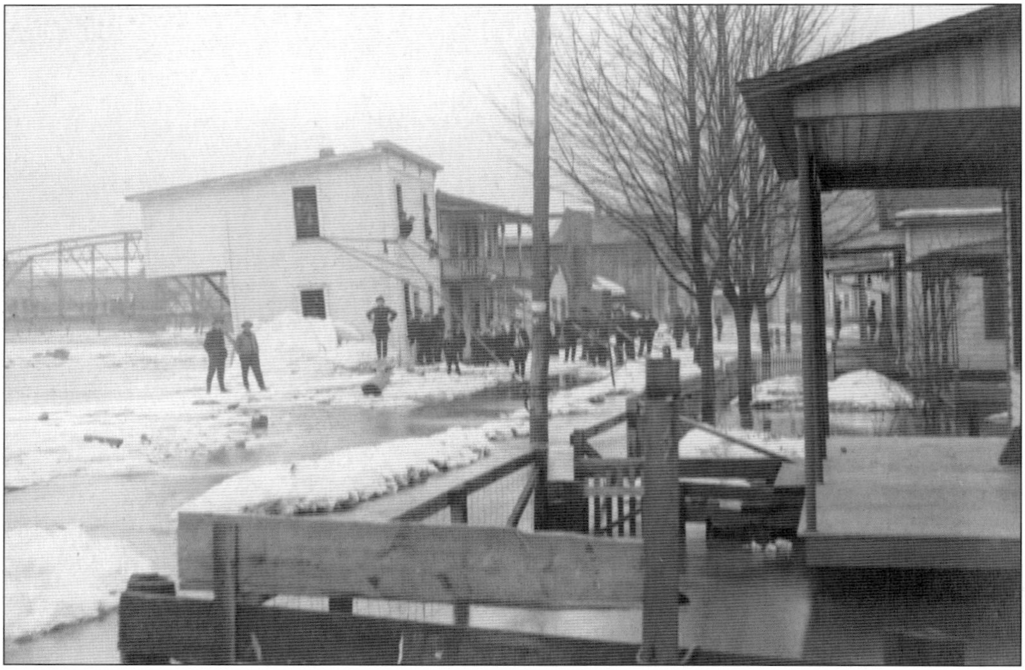

During its peak, Kellettville became a thriving town of laborers and their families with a population of 1,300. They supported several businesses such as the Kingsley House (a four-story hotel), the Watson and Company general store, Harkless Drugstore, Kribbs and Ray Livery, and many others. Employment was commonly found harvesting hemlock or working in the local tannery, the hub factory, the kiln factory, or the sawmills.

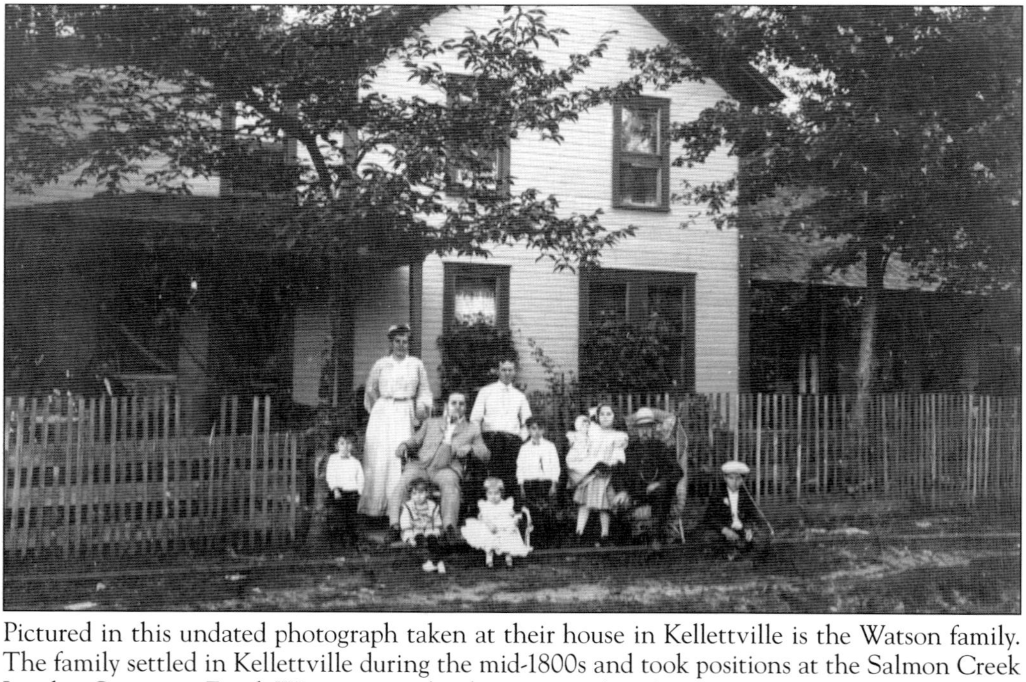

Pictured in this undated photograph taken at their house in Kellettville is the Watson family. The family settled in Kellettville during the mid-1800s and took positions at the Salmon Creek Lumber Company. Frank Watson was school superintendent from 1934 to 1958. John G. Watson held an associate judge position from 1927 to 1928.

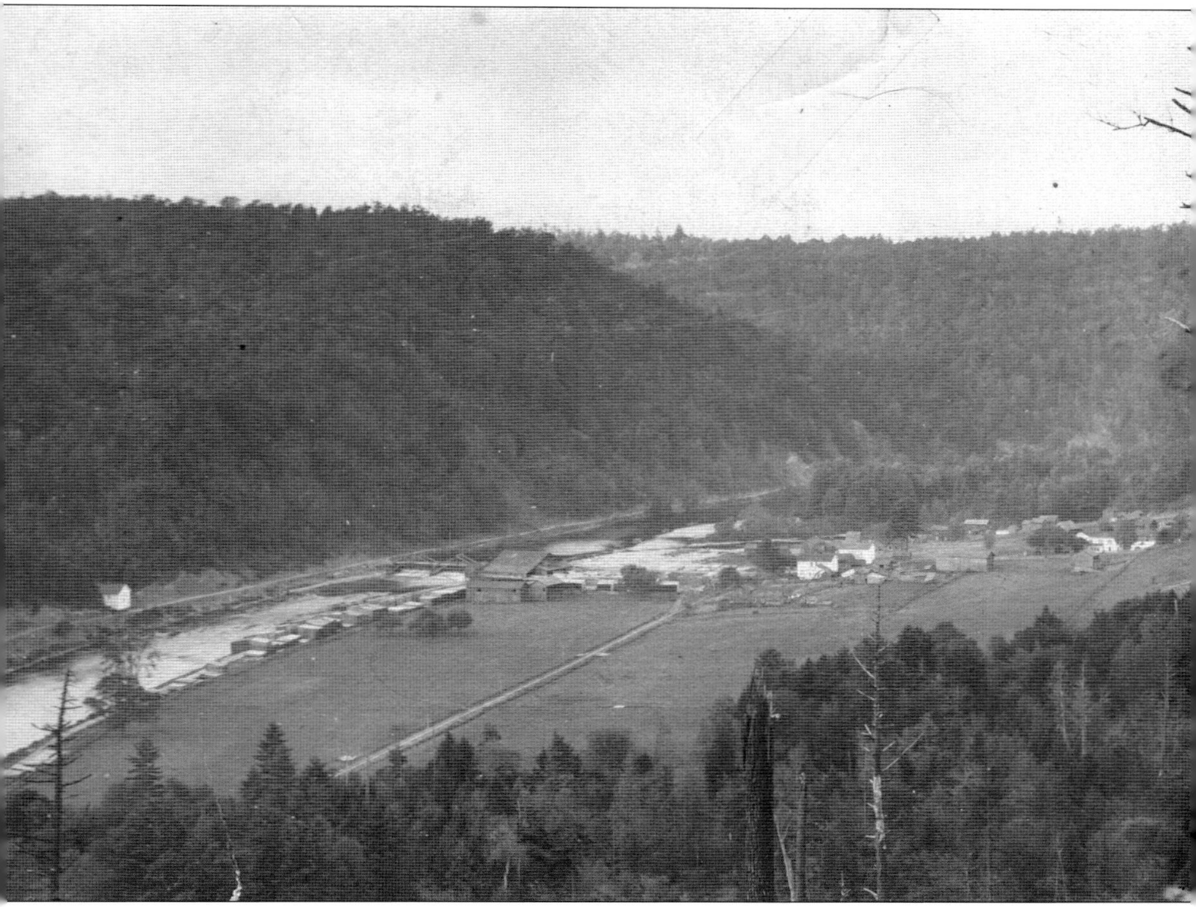

This photograph taken during the late 1800s illustrates how Newtown, or Newtown Mills as it had often been referred to, operated along Tionesta Creek and Allegheny Plateau. During the evacuation of the town around 1940 to make way for the Tionesta Lake, Newtown only had a population of approximately 20 residents.

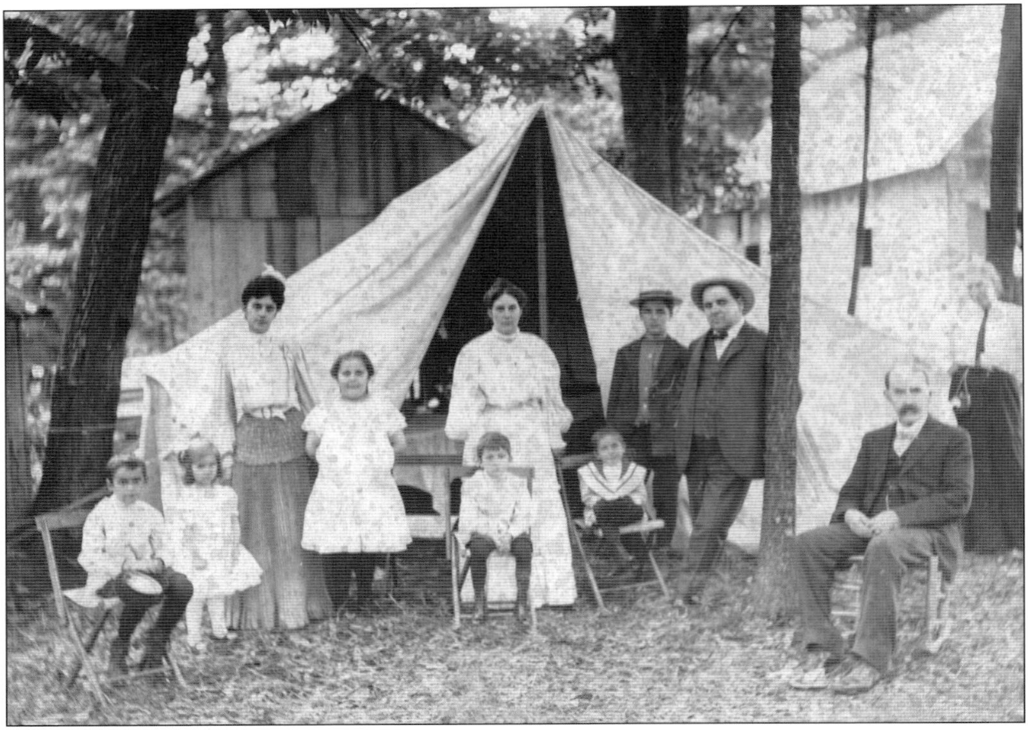

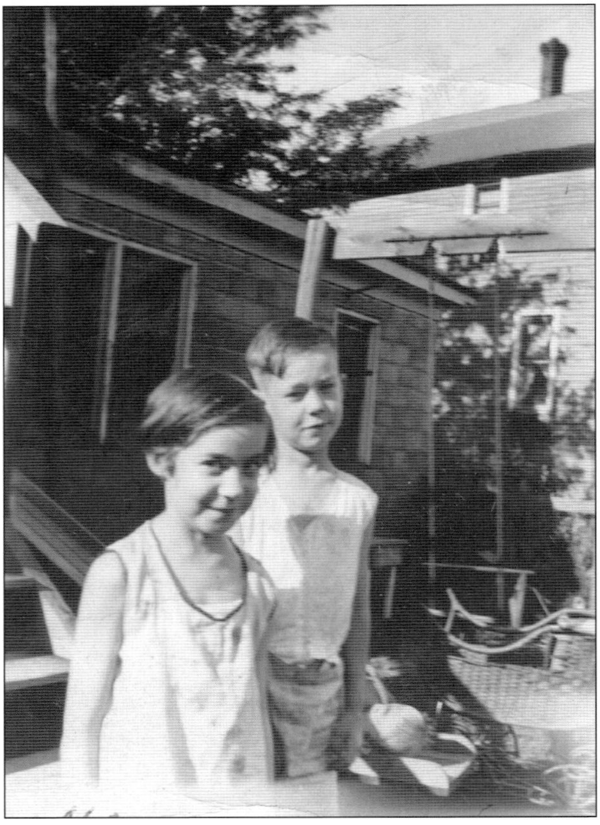

Pictured here is the Leon Watson family partaking in a Methodist church camp meeting in 1912. This particular meeting was the last to be held at Whig Hill, a village in Kingsley Township. During the summer, families pitched tents in preparation for long hours at the event, which consisted of preaching, prayer meetings, singing, and picnics.

Judson "Jud" Wilson is pictured here with his sister Alice M. Wilson. The siblings were lifelong residents of Kellettville as were their parents, Plummer and Julia (Silze) Wilson. As longtime members of the Forest County Historical Society, the Wilson family chronicled much of the recorded history of Kellettville. Both Alice and Jud were instrumental in preserving the Kellettville Old Home Day, an event that reunited residents displaced by the construction of the Tionesta Dam.

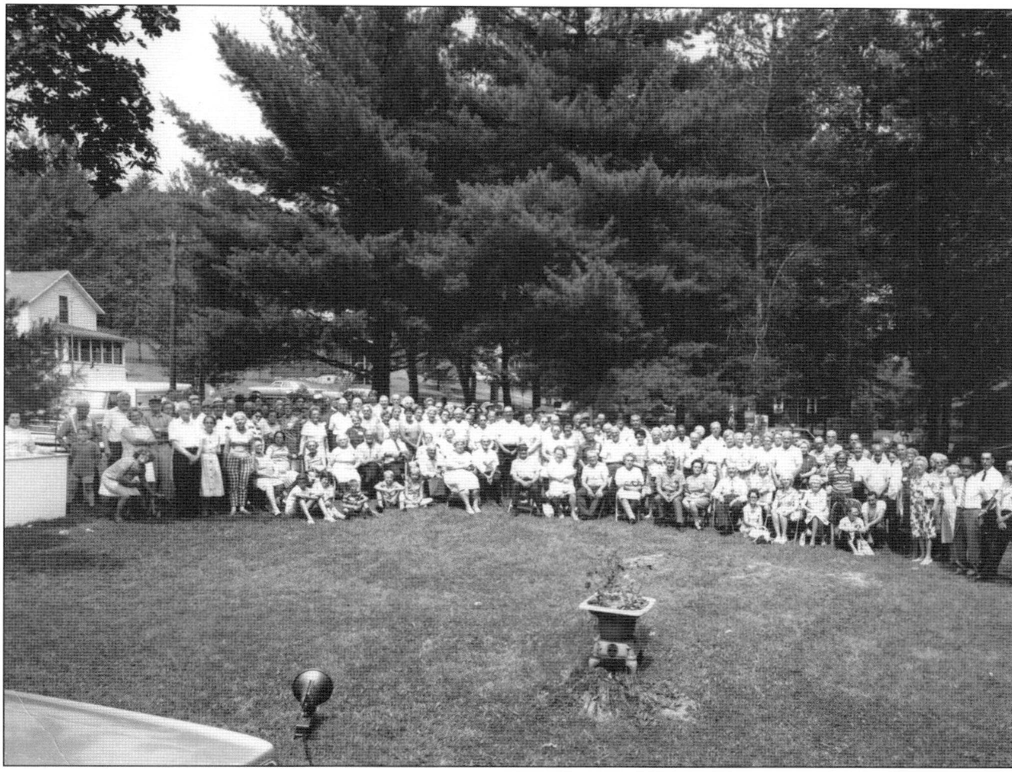

Every summer on the last Saturday in July, residents current and past gathered to celebrate Kellettville Old Home Day. In time, with the closing of the sawmills, the town's economy could not be sustained, and some folks moved elsewhere. In later years, the expected flooding of Tionesta Lake caused others to do the same. The first Kellettville Old Home Day took place in 1926 and the last, shown here, in 1970.

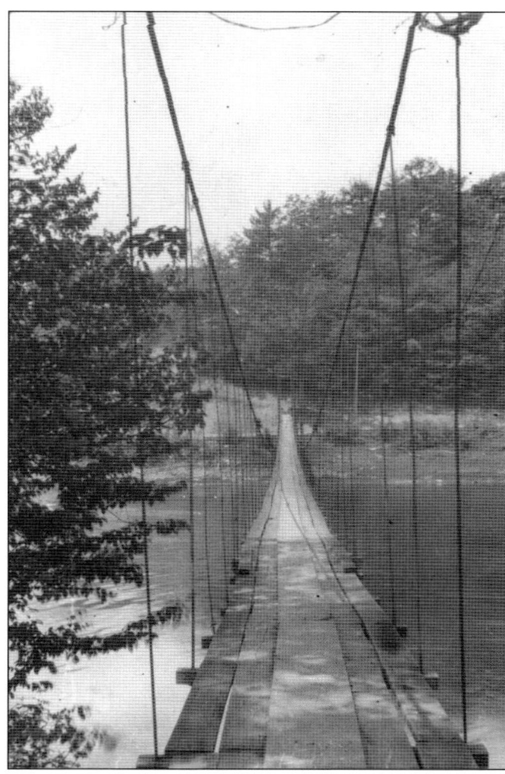

Several creeks, rivers, and other bodies of water that can impede traveling by foot or vehicle break up the vast woodland areas of Forest County. For the more remote and smaller communities, swinging bridges are installed to traverse the creeks. This swinging bridge was brought to Kellettville from Kinzu, Pennsylvania, on a team of horses led by Jay Catlin.

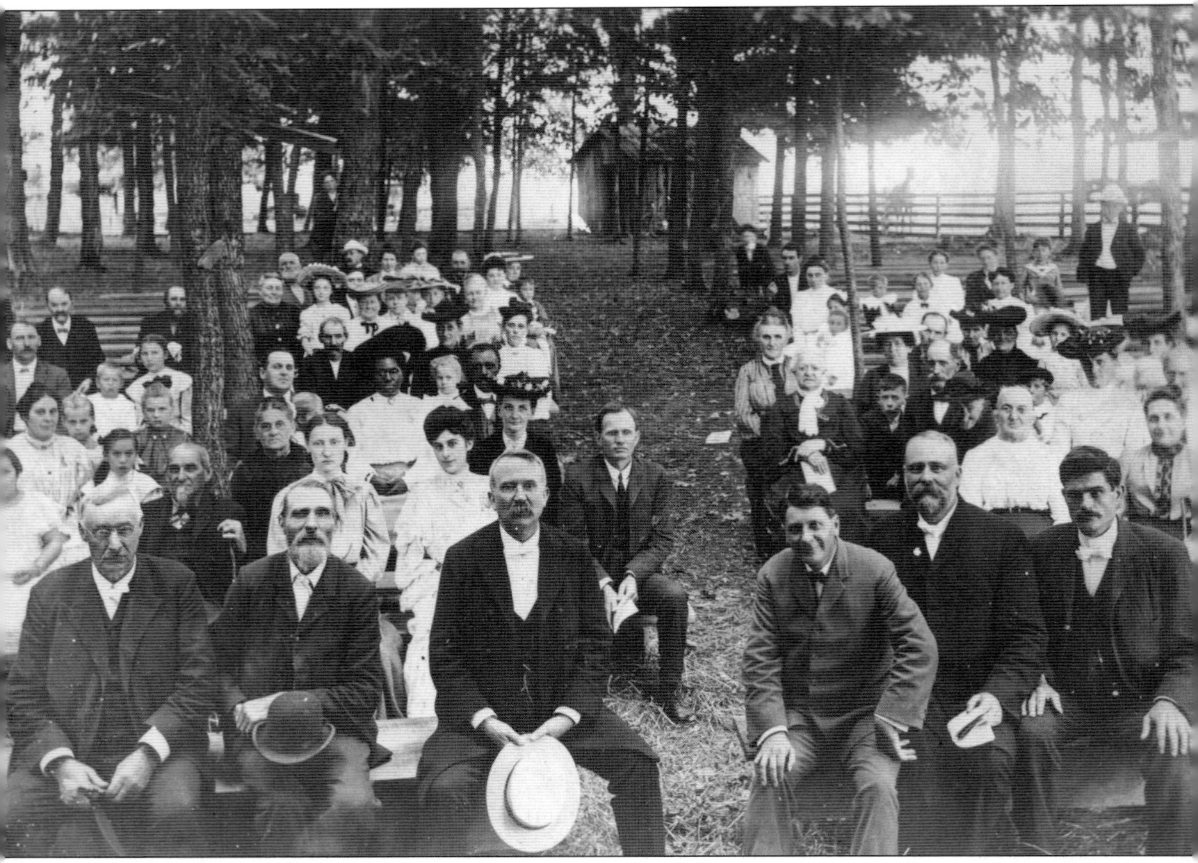

This Methodist church camp meeting was held on the farm of C.W. Zuendel on Whig Hill in Kingsley Township. Three churches, the Methodist (1880), the Free Methodist (1882), and the Townline Evangelical (1887), were established in Whig Hill to serve the increasing population.

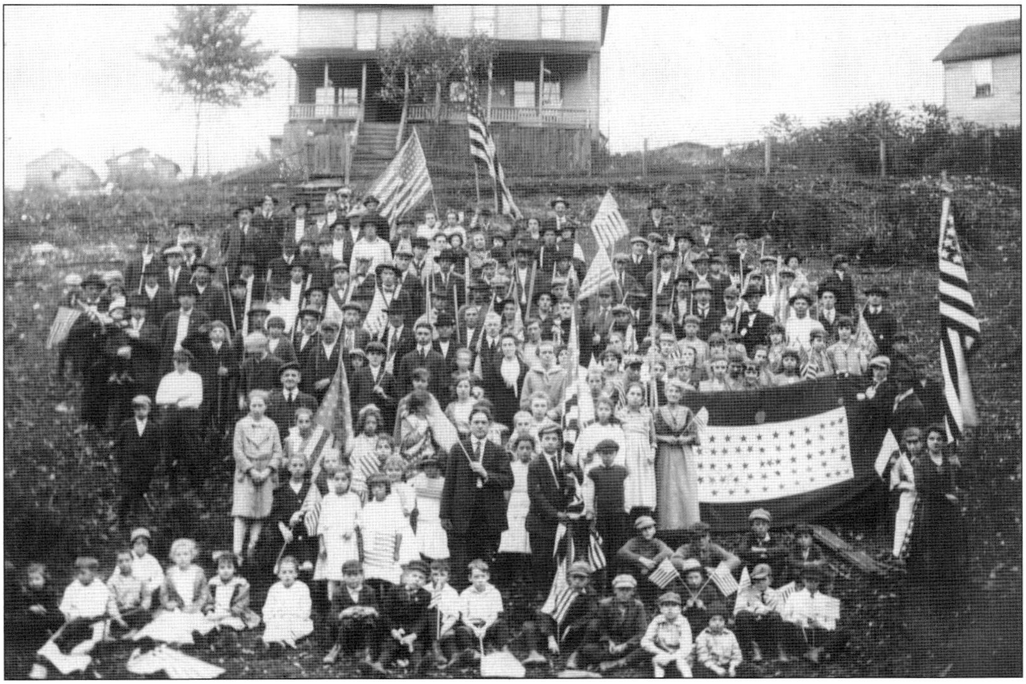

The residents of Forest County have a rich history of military service dating back to the service of John Range in the French and Indian War. Shown in this photograph are the men, women, and children of Kellettville gathering to celebrate Armistice Day on November 11, 1918.

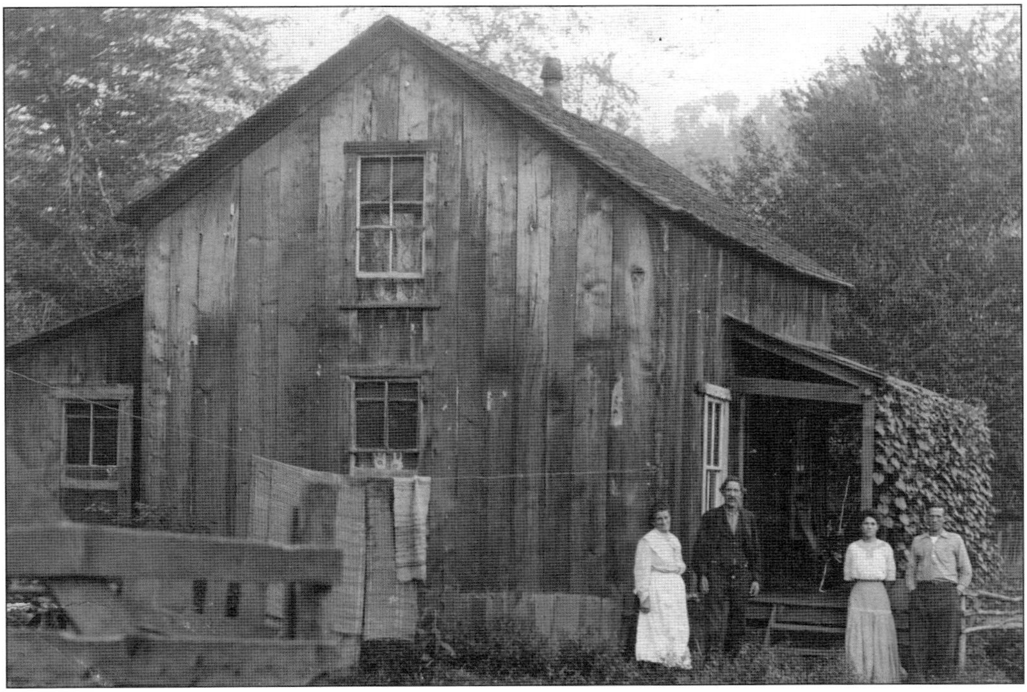

The town of Minister is situated among the rolling mountains in Howe Township and was active in the late 1800s as an oil boomtown. Pictured is a typical house in Minister during the late 1800s. A schoolhouse, which closed in 1934, was also located in the village.

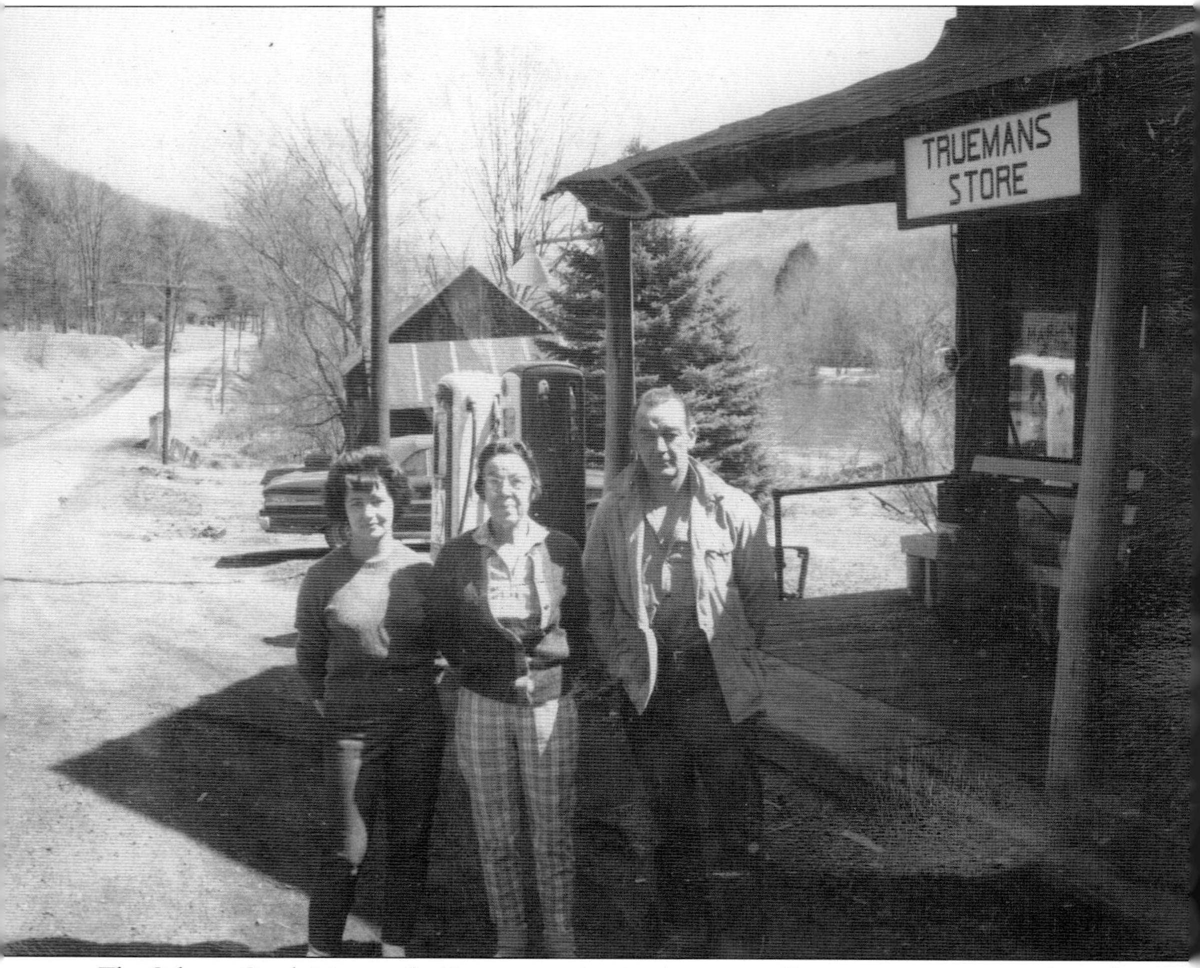

The Salmon Creek Mercantile Company maintained a store at Trueman, a community named after Teddy Collins, while logging operations took place in the Fools Creek and Minister areas for Buck Mill. The store was established in 1900 by Collins to provide goods to the workers in his logging camps. In 1913, it was purchased by Dell Spencer, who ran it for 54 years until selling it to Sue Scalfero, who passed it on to new owners in 1967. It still stands today and is one of the few enduring sites from the lumbering days along Tionesta Creek.

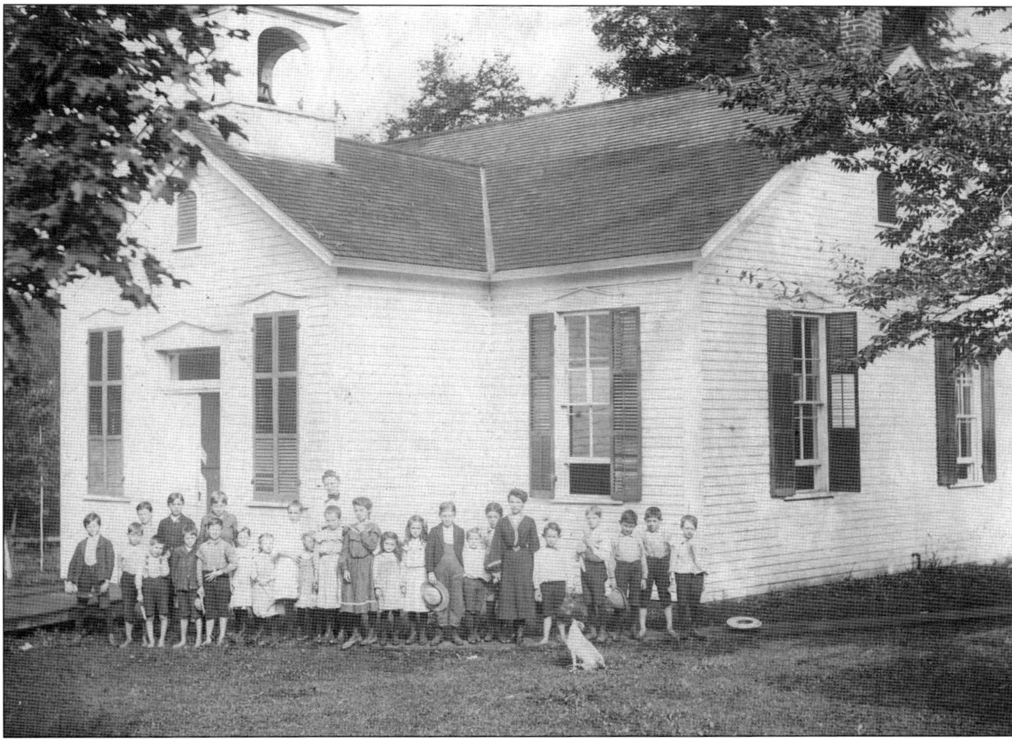

The rural community of Mayburg lies along Tionesta Creek about five miles from Kellettville. The village was named in recognition of the May family who managed oil wells in the surrounding area. A small number of families who were oil lease laborers made their homes among the beautiful landscape. The Mayburg Grade School was in session until its closing in 1941. After that time, the children were schooled in Tionesta by LeWanda Flynn.

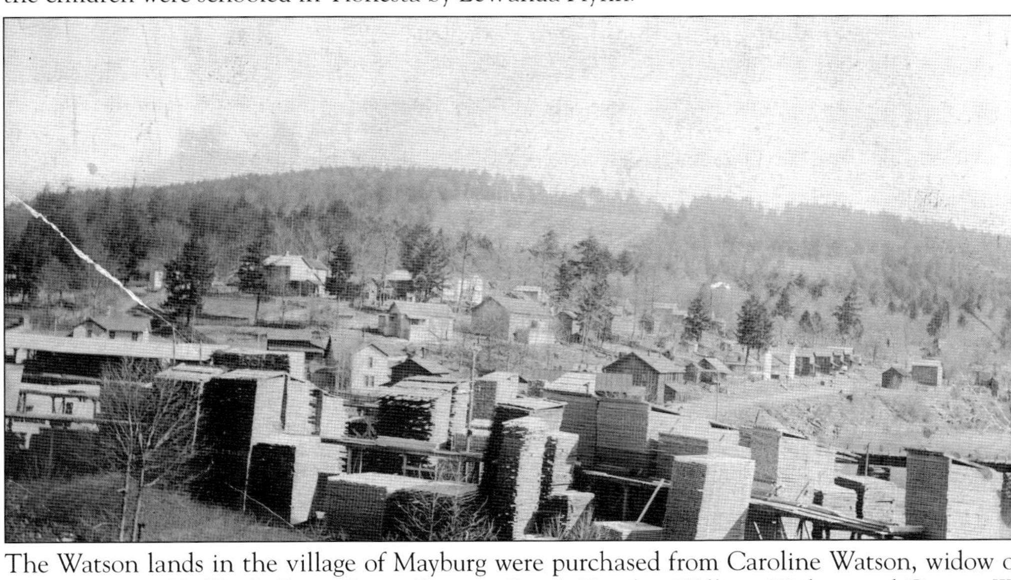

The Watson lands in the village of Mayburg were purchased from Caroline Watson, widow of Lewis Watson. Teddy Collins, Orion Siggins, Frank Kreitler, William Dickey, and George W. Hoover named the firm Watson Lands Lumber Company. Collins was aware of the land's value as it held a tract of high-quality virgin white pine.

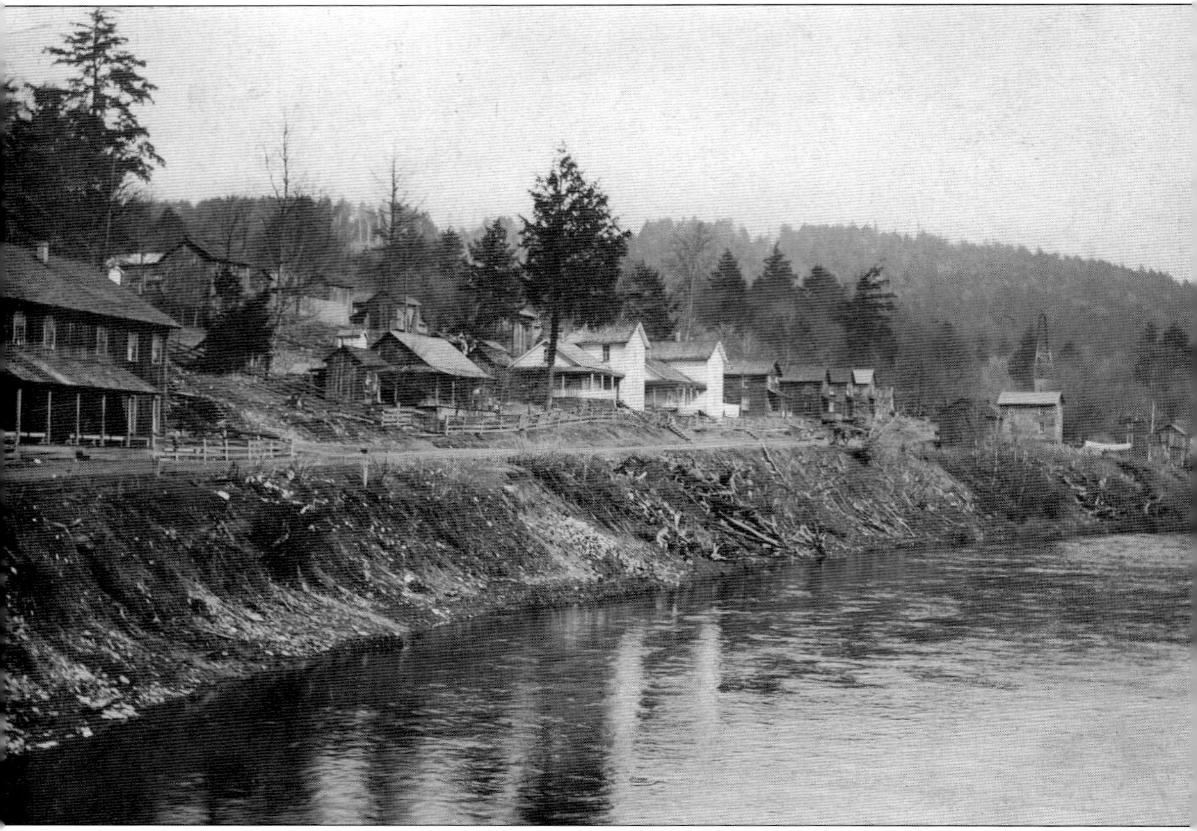

Seen here from a bridge crossing Tionesta Creek, Mayburg was a community that flourished due to the lumber industry, oil boom, and chemical production of charcoal, acetone, and wood alcohol. The village is named after the May family who owned oil wells in the area prior to Teddy Collins establishing his sawmill. The area is still home to some residents, while many others set up hunting camps or cottages to enjoy all the forest has to offer.

Four

Barnett Township and Jenks Township

Barnett Township is in southern Forest County, bordered to the south by the Clarion River. Communities within the township are Clarington, Cooksburg, Hottelville, and Redclyffe. Once called "the Black Forest," Cook Forest State Park was a great expanse of dense virgin evergreens, with a remnant of its former expanse having been preserved for public use. The forest is draped with lacey veils of hemlock, clusters of rhododendron, and carpets of ferns, trillium, and jack-in-the-pulpit. Long ago, the Seneca Nation of the Iroquois Confederacy inhabited this forest. John Cook was the first permanent white American settler, arriving in 1826. He built a cabin and several sawmills at the mouth of Tom's Run and wrote wonderful accounts describing his adventurous log rafting days. Andrew Cook, John's son, built up the logging business and the forest town of Cooksburg. Pittsburgh author Neil Swanson wrote a novel set in 1759 about the Native Americans and the frontiersmen who were pawns of the French and British in their battles over Pennsylvania territory. It was titled *Unconquered*, and in 1946, it was made into a movie that was filmed in Cooksburg. Many locals were extras in the film, and Native Americans from Salamanca and Red House were hired as well. A walk along Longfellow Trail beneath 400-year-old pines is a sacred experience. Cyrus Blood, founder of Forest County, settled in the town he named Marienville in 1833 after clearing a 12-mile road through the dense wilderness from Clarington to Marienville.

Jenks Township was named for the county judge, John W. Jenks. Other villages in Jenks are Byromtown, Duhring, Lamonaville, McCrays, Parrish, and Penoke. Duhring was the site of the Civilian Conservation Corps camp No. 1, which was a work relief program operating from 1933 to 1942. Enrollees planted trees, constructed trails, and built lodging facilities. A few early establishments in Marienville are still operating today, like the Kelly Hotel, Bucktail Hotel, and until recently, Baughman's Market.

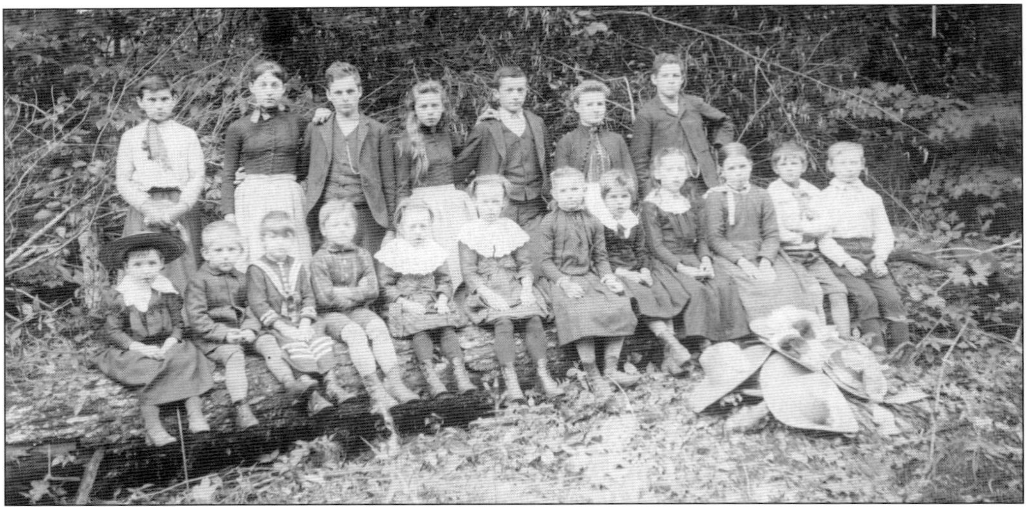

Forest School students in Lamonaville pose for a class photograph in September 1889. Pictured from left to right are (first row) Florence Southworth, Johnnie Marshall, Delia Henry, Glenn Chapman, Esther Anderson, Freda Anderson, Gracie Saint Clair, Lois Henry, Hattie Southworth, Viola Vandenburg, Willie Henry, and Lambert Ohlsson; (second row) Grace Marshall, Minnie Southworth, Wilmur McArthur, Lillie Henry, Gussie Herman, Lillian Loveland, and Elmer McArthur. Not pictured is the teacher, Lillian Loveland.

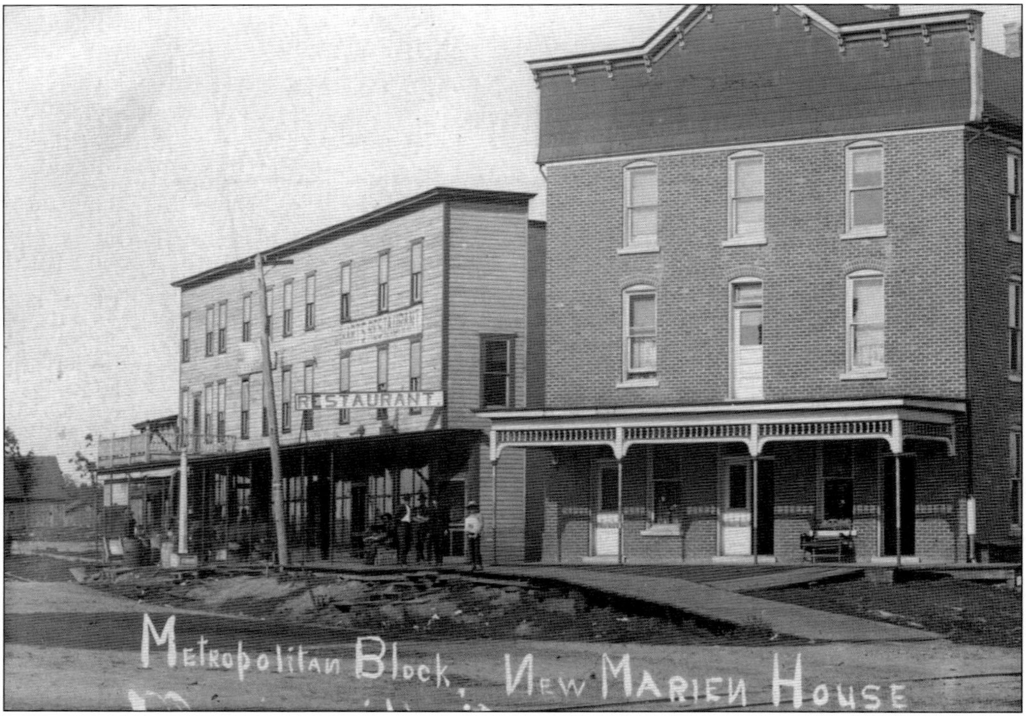

In October 1833, Cyrus Blood, the founder of Forest County, had settled in an unclaimed portion of land in Northwestern Pennsylvania with his family. He named the settlement of Marienville after his daughter Marien. The two would become examples on how the rich should treat the poor. Shown in this 1914 postcard are Harts Restaurant and the New Marien House Hotel, both located in the metropolitan block of Marienville.

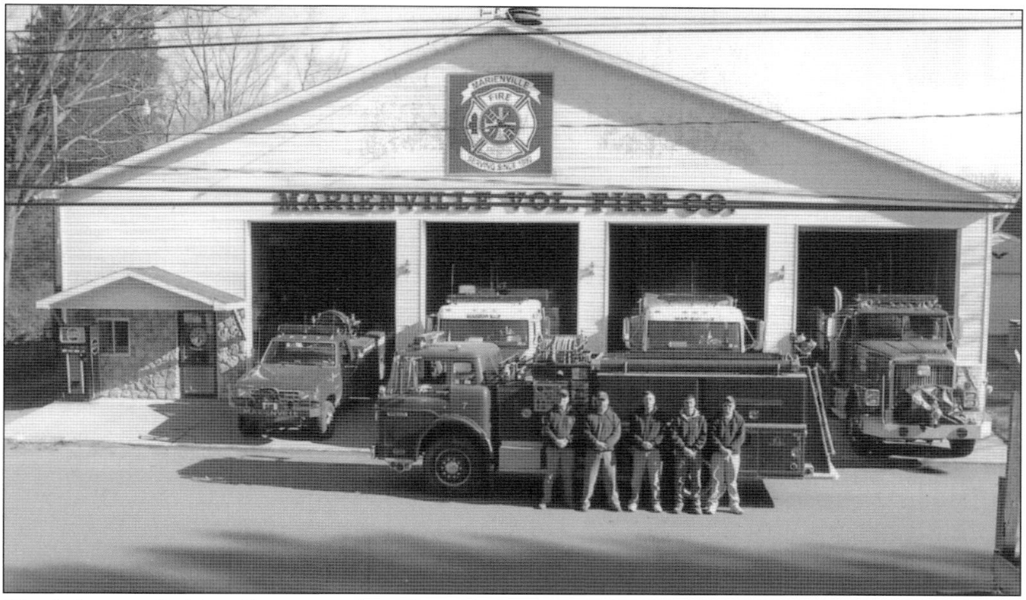

The Marienville Fire Company first formed in 1892 with only a handful of men, a pump and wagon, and many buckets for water. After a large fire in 1902, the group reorganized to form a more cohesive and better-equipped unit. Not only do these brave firefighters battle flames, they also search for lost hunters and hikers and host a variety of community events.

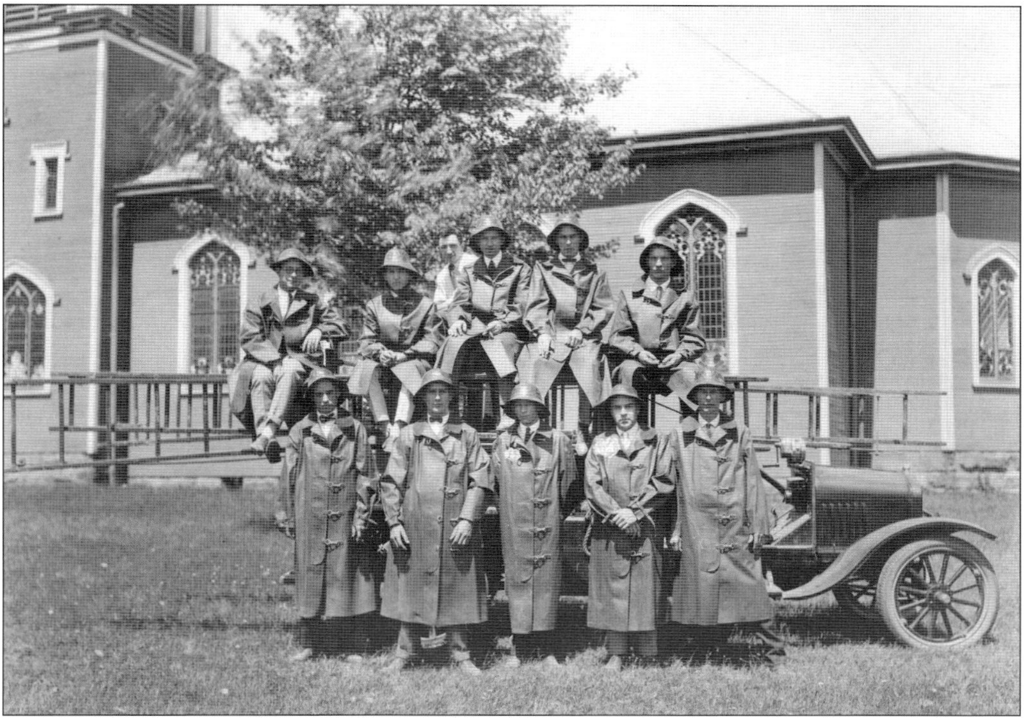

Pictured are members of the Marienville Volunteer Fire Company on July 26, 1923. From left to right are (first row) unidentified, Fred Grulman, Shed Blymiller, Bill Altman, and Fred Mortimer; (second row) Lawrence Songer, Ray Songer, Cecil Baughman, Earl Cunningham, Babe Mortimer, and Andy Lubold.

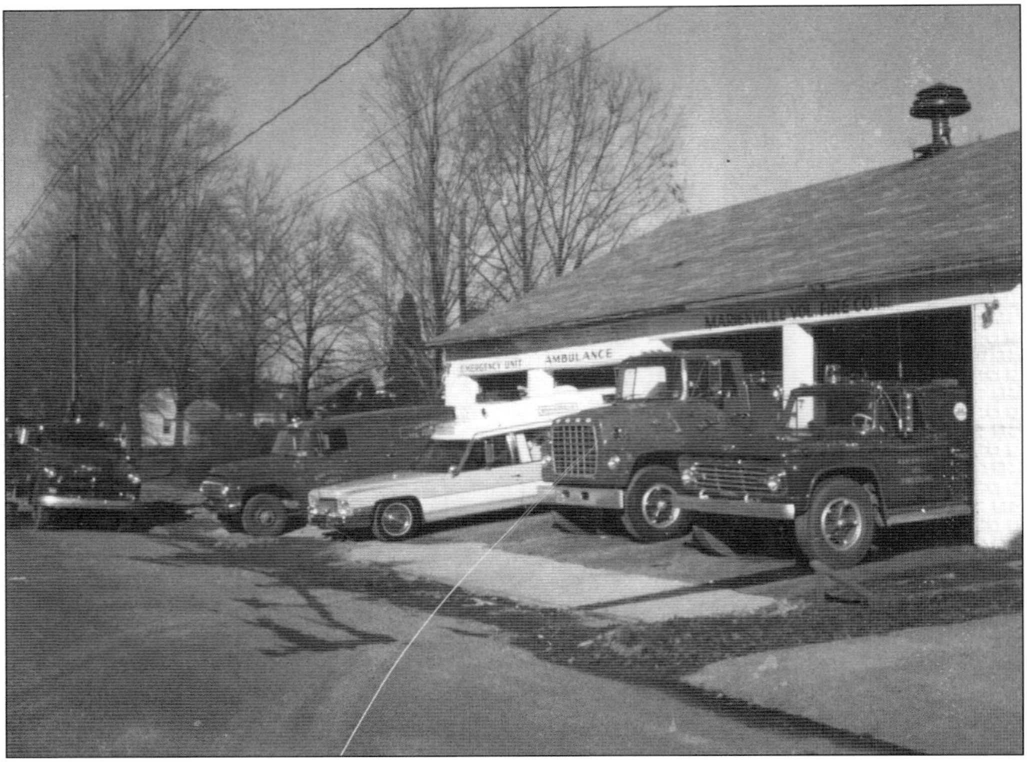

As the Marienville Volunteer Fire Company began to grow during the mid-1900s, a new building was built across the street from their old one. The new firehouse held three trucks. Later, two more bays were added, which eventually housed ambulances. The fire company and ambulance service became incorporated but remained separate entities for funding purposes.

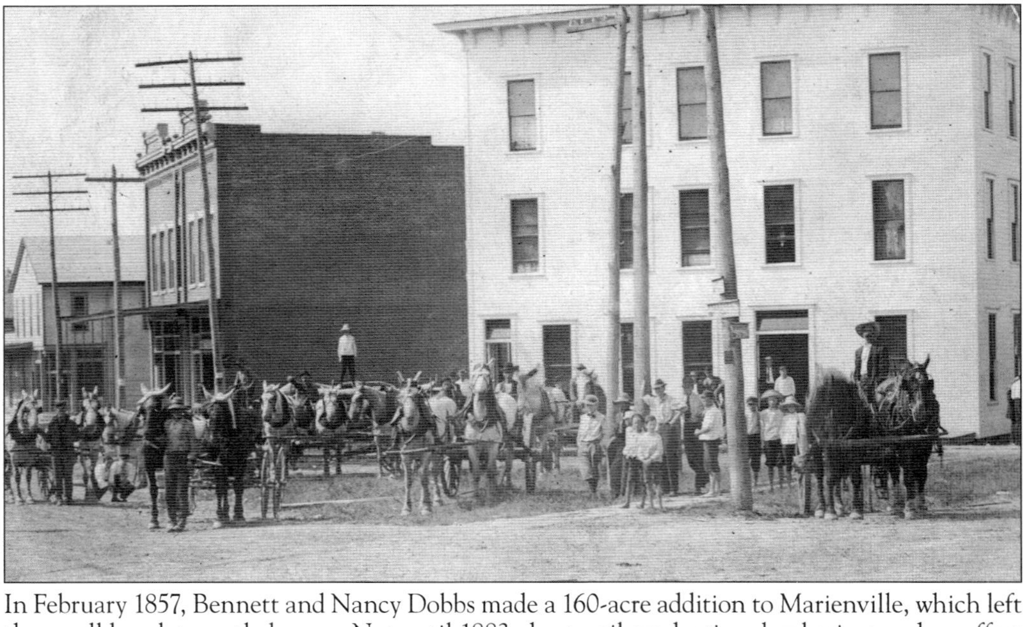

In February 1857, Bennett and Nancy Dobbs made a 160-acre addition to Marienville, which left the small hamlet mostly barren. Not until 1883, due to oil production, lumbering, and an effort put forth by the residents, did Marienville become a thriving village.

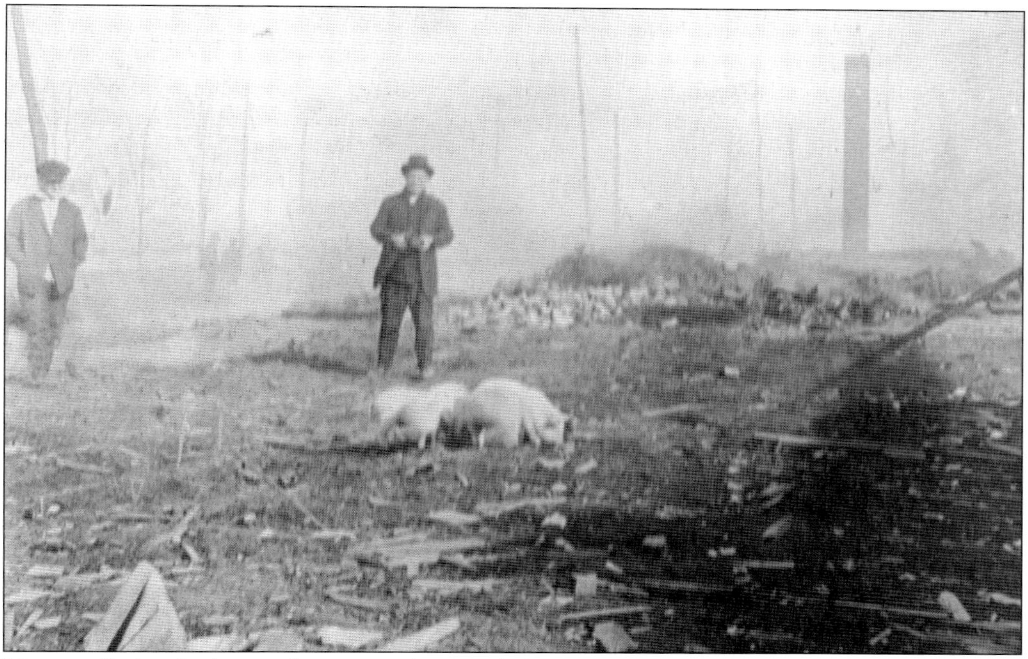

Marienville has had several structure fires, including multiple business fires on January 1, 1890; house fires on April 23, 1902; the Mintz Department Store fire in June 1913, and the Keystone Hotel fire in September 1924. Shown in 1914 are Fish Matthews (left) and Denis Carmen as they inspect the site of a recent fire, along with several pigs that wandered onto the scene.

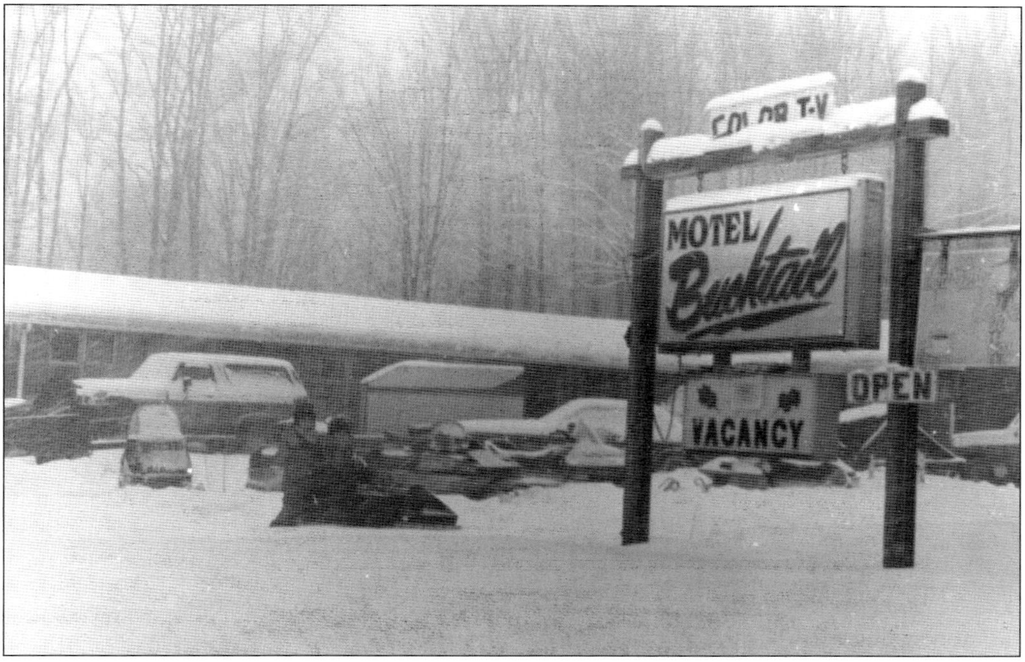

In 1936, the Bucktail Inn opened for business in Marienville under the ownership of Frank Regina and his wife. After an expansion during the 1940s and the addition of bedrooms, the business became known as the Bucktail Hotel. It was later sold in 1951 to Andrew Pastilock and his wife.

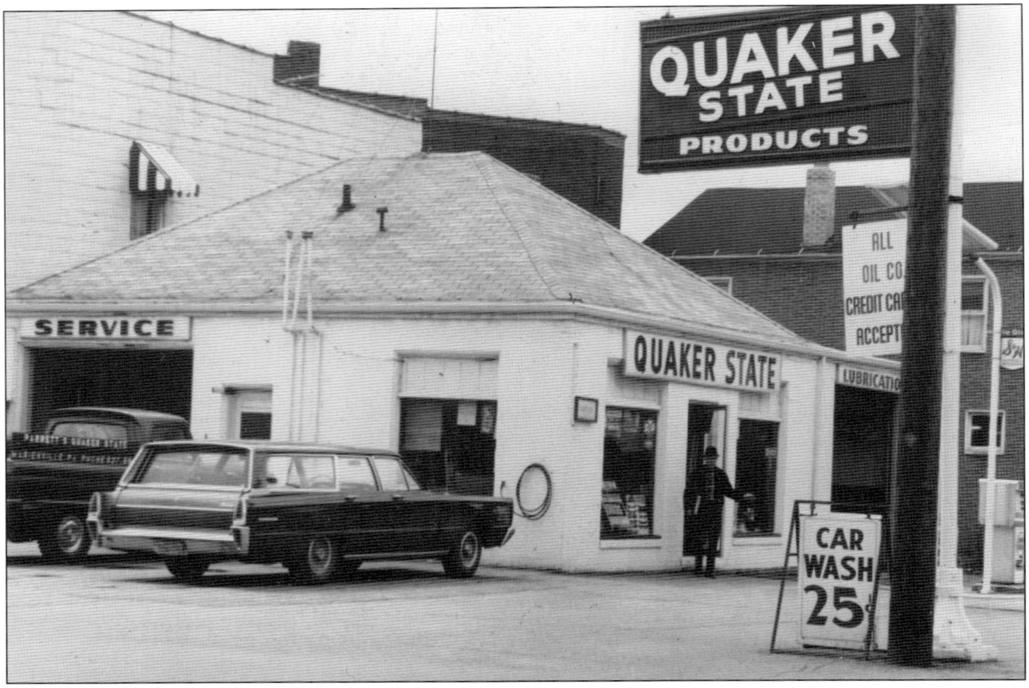

Throughout the 20th century, Marienville was home to many locally owned businesses, including the Clown Restaurant (closed in April 1975), Marienville Airport (closed in 1948), and Harp's Garage (closed in 1975). Many other businesses have changed hands over the years and subsequently changed names.

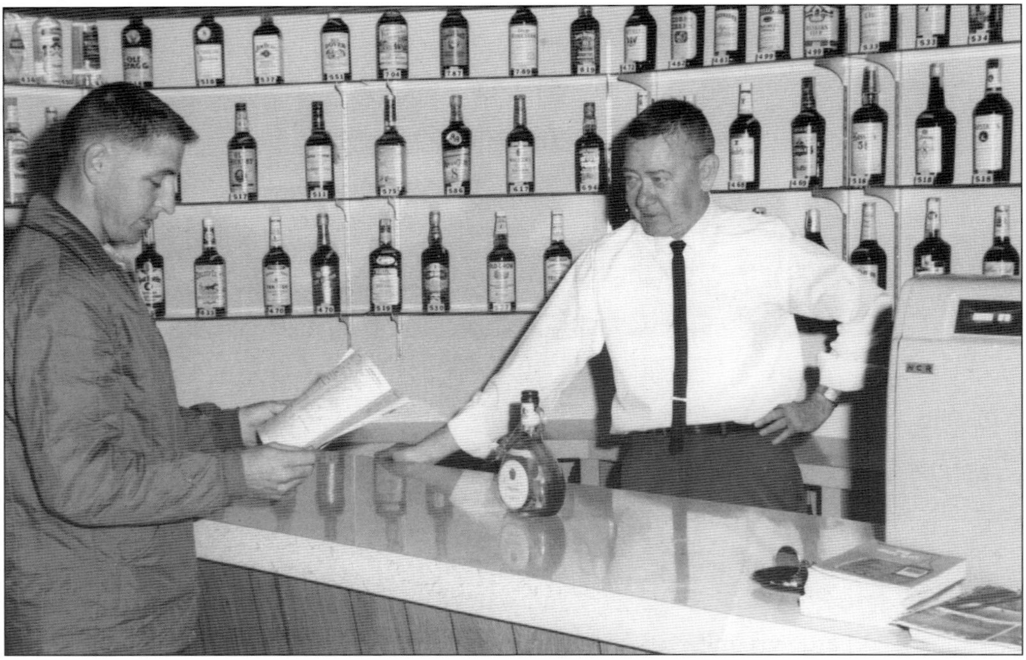

Marienville has been home to several alcoholic beverage companies. In 1959, Marble Reaghart opened one of the largest beverage companies in Marienville, the Marienville Beverage Company. Posing for a photograph in the Marienville State Liquor Store are Bob Snyder (left) and Russ Johnson.

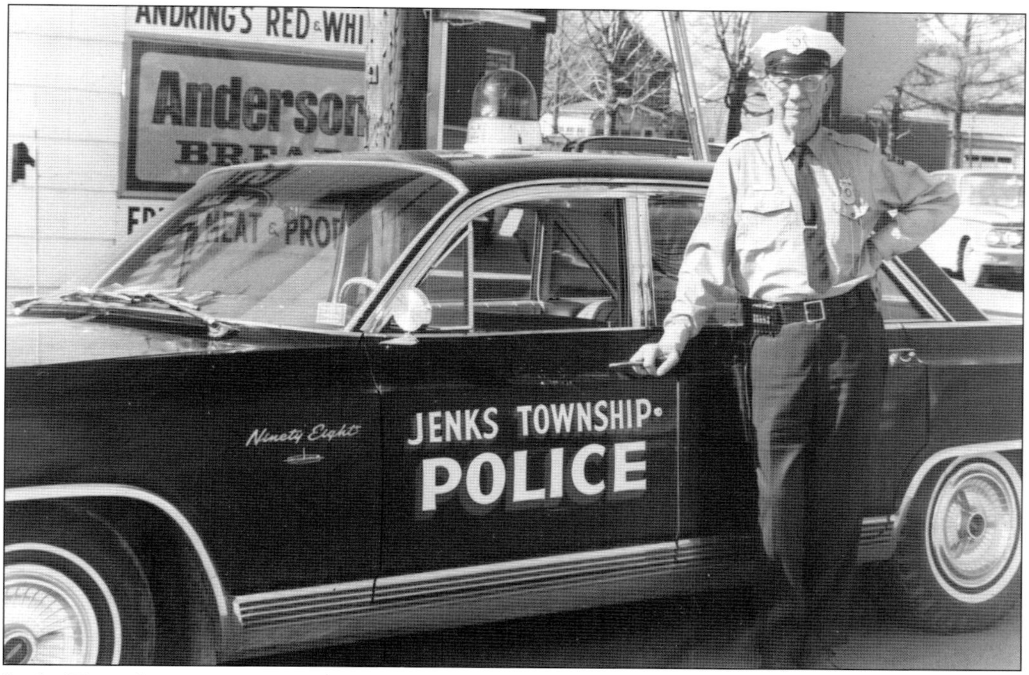

Jenks Township was organized in 1838 and named in honor of Hon. John W. Jenks, one of the associate judges of Jefferson County. The first courthouse in Forest County was built in Marienville, in Jenks Township. Marienville is located near the center of Jenks Township with Pennsylvania Route 66 acting as the main thoroughfare.

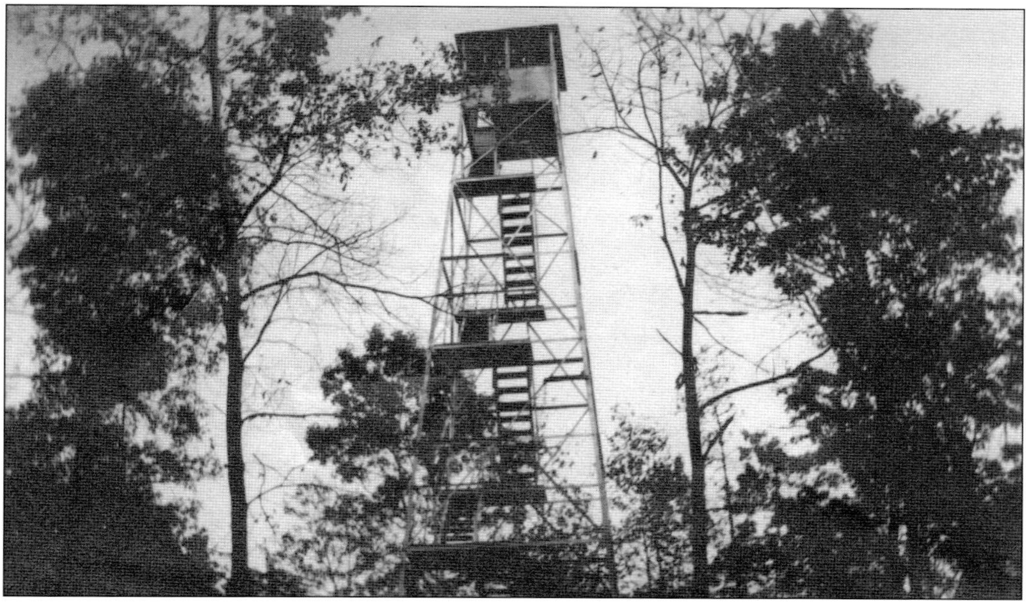

In 1921, the Department of Forests and Waters built the Marienville Fire Tower on Eldridge Summit, which is named after the first settlers in this region. The tower, which is open to the public, was originally 60 feet high with a ground elevation of 1,860 feet, but was enlarged to 86 feet in 1933.

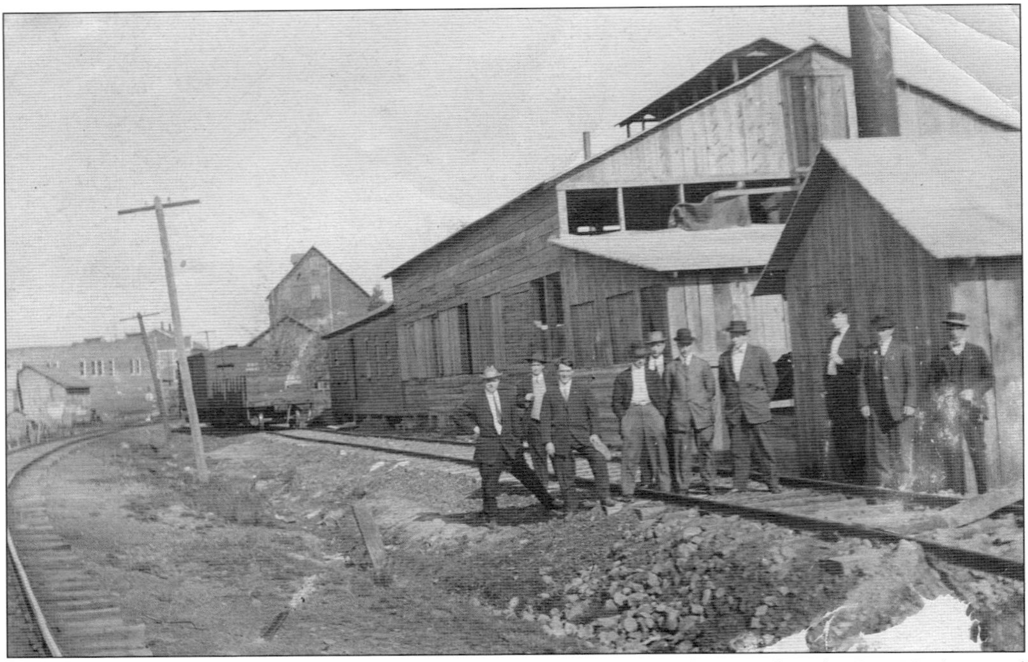

On April 15, 1914, the residents of Marienville came together to discuss plans by Roy Underwood to build a plant to produce glass bottles. By late August, the necessary building and equipment were in place for the South-West End Marienville Glass Bottling Plant to begin production. Company employees are shown outside the plant in 1914.

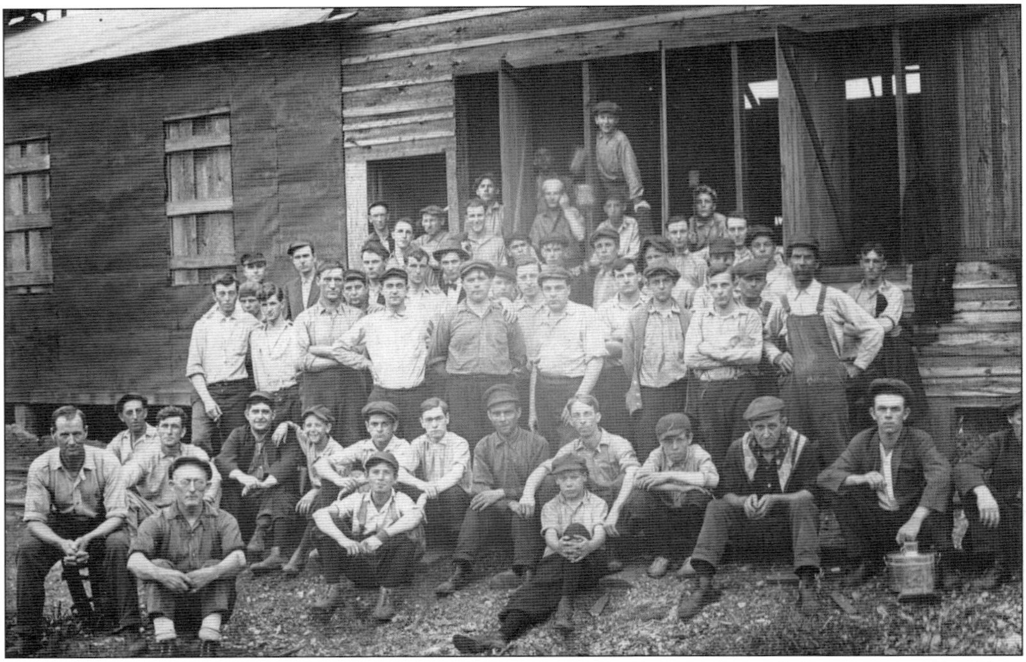

The South-West End Marienville Glass Bottling Plant was later renamed the Marienville Glass Plant when it merged with several other plants throughout the United States. In 1982, after 68 years of nonstop operations and being the largest Forest County employer, the plant closed its doors for the last time. Plant workers are seen here around 1914.

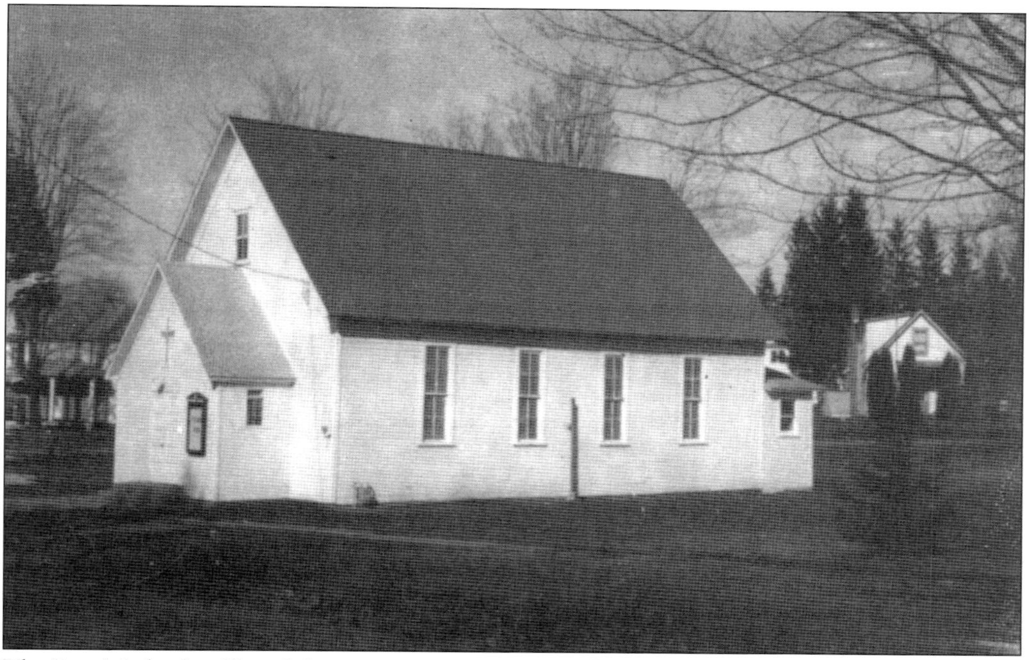

The Free Methodist Church began services in Marienville around 1892 when Reverend Witcomb was appointed pastor until his replacement took over in 1894. As the annual conference of the Free Methodist Church met, a pastor would be selected to replace the old one or to cover various Free Methodist churches in the area.

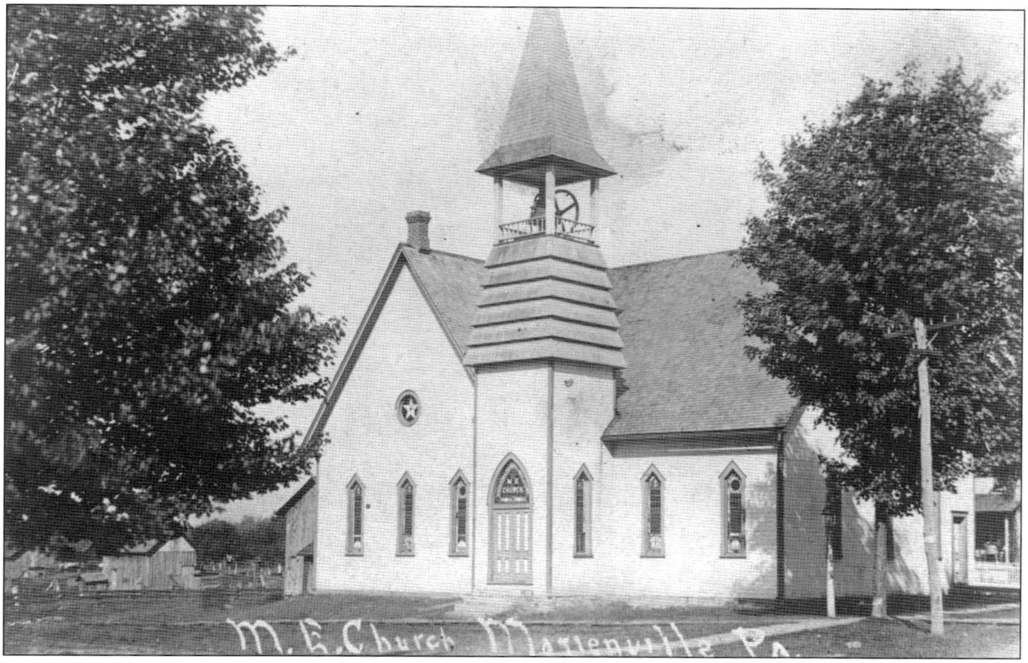

In 1883, Edwin Hull introduced Marienville to Methodism by gathering with six other people to worship. With the population growing and interest in Methodism also increasing, a new church was built for $900 in 1894. The building was later remodeled in 1951, and again in 1965 with the addition of a fellowship hall and kitchen. The church is pictured on October 25, 1907.

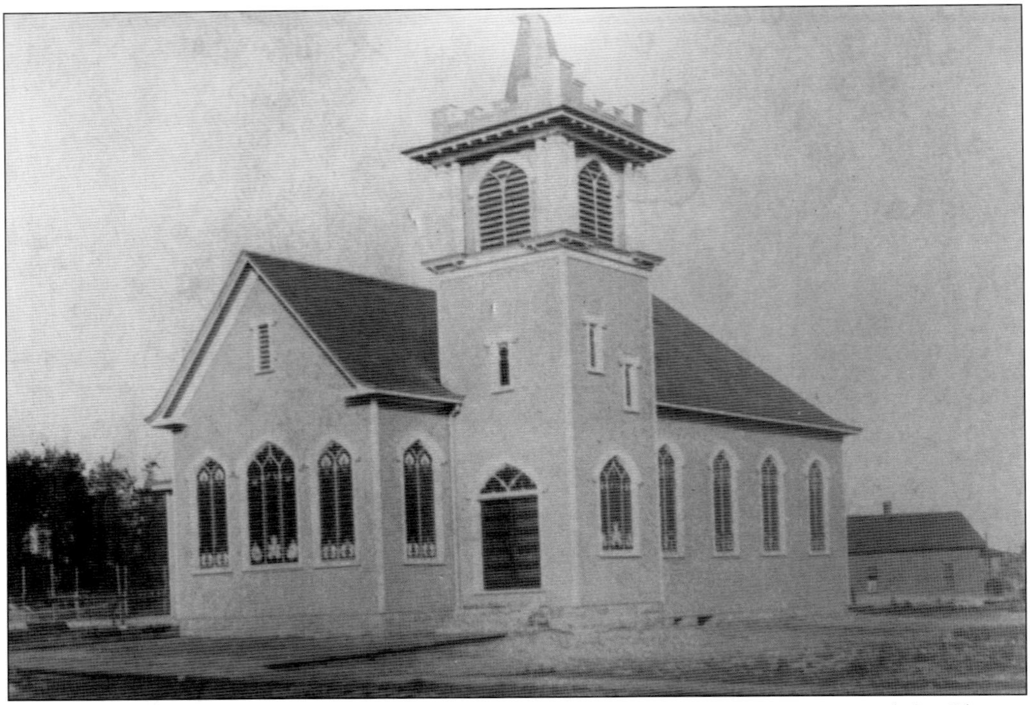

The First Presbyterian Church was constructed in 1887 after a committee petitioned the Clarion Presbytery to establish a church in Marienville. The original building succumbed to flames on April 23, 1902, but through the sheer tenacity of the members, a new church was erected in 1903.

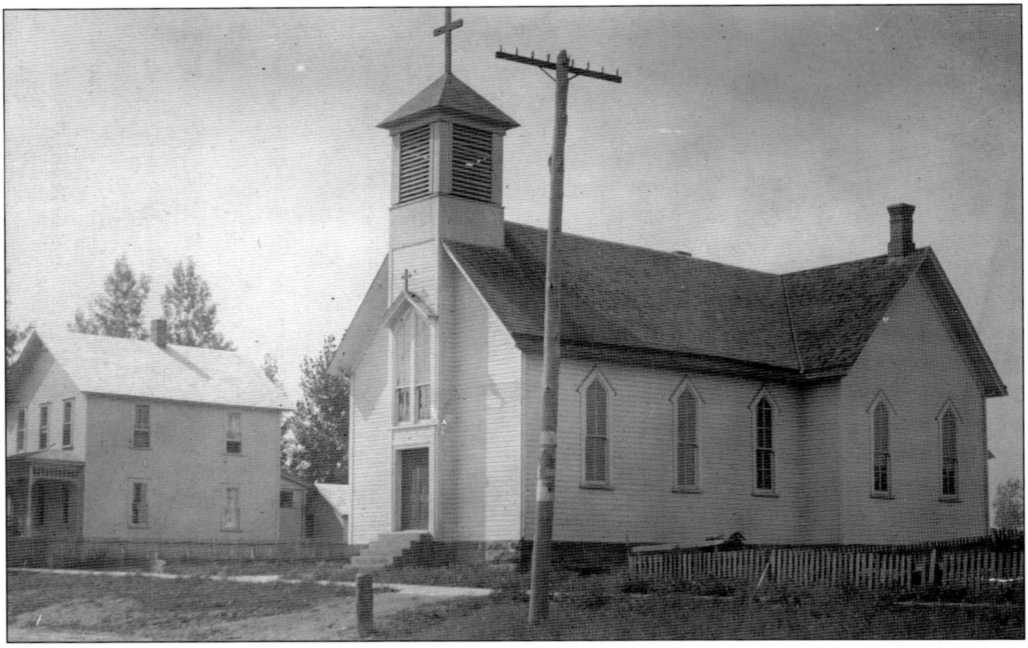

In 1892, through the fundraising efforts of eight families in Marienville, construction of the St. Anne's Roman Catholic Church was complete. Due to a growing congregation, a new church was erected in 1967, with a consecration on October 20, 1968. Pictured is the original building around 1910.

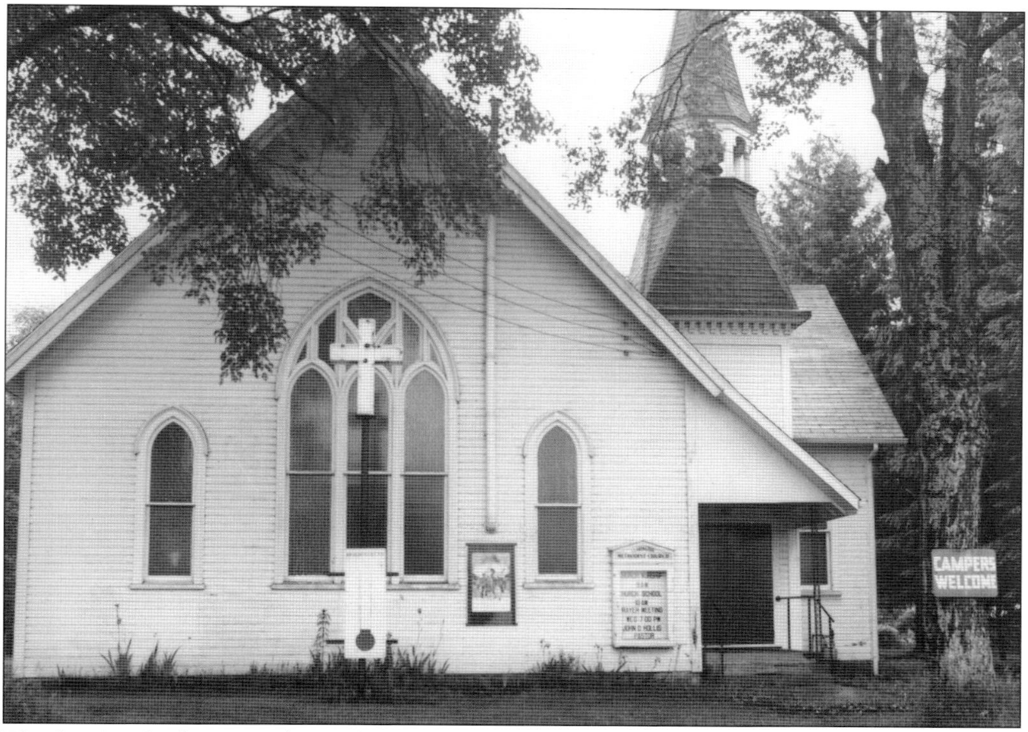

The first Methodist to settle in Clarington was William Coon, who, along with Edwin Hall and several others in 1845, formed a Methodist gathering in the area. The first Methodist church in Clarington was built around 1850, and a newer building was later erected around 1900 in a different location. Pictured is the Clarington Methodist Church with a sign welcoming campers.

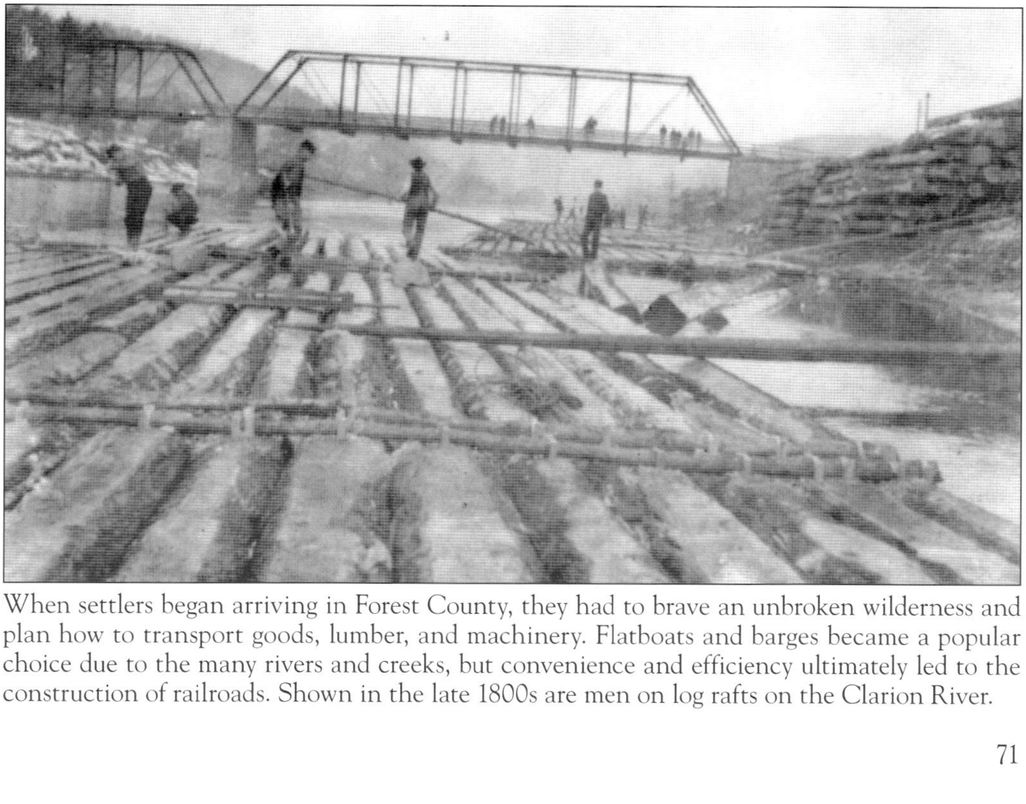

When settlers began arriving in Forest County, they had to brave an unbroken wilderness and plan how to transport goods, lumber, and machinery. Flatboats and barges became a popular choice due to the many rivers and creeks, but convenience and efficiency ultimately led to the construction of railroads. Shown in the late 1800s are men on log rafts on the Clarion River.

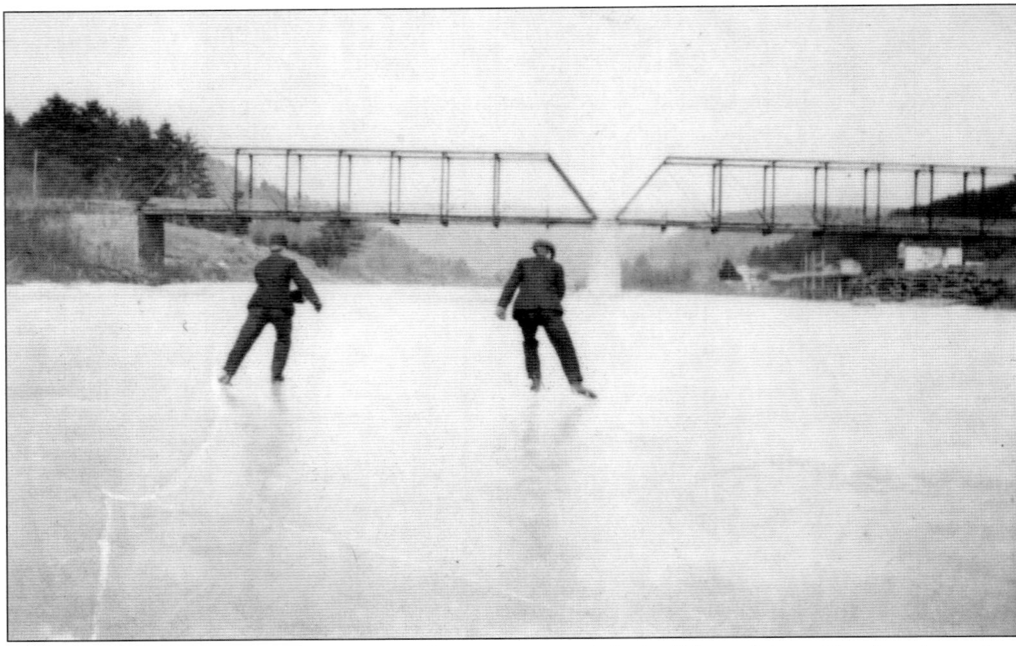

The cold winters in Forest County may have temporarily halted the rafting of lumber, but a deep freeze allowed these two men to enjoy a skate on the Clarion River. Ahead of them, the old Route 899 bridge crosses the river into the village of Clarington.

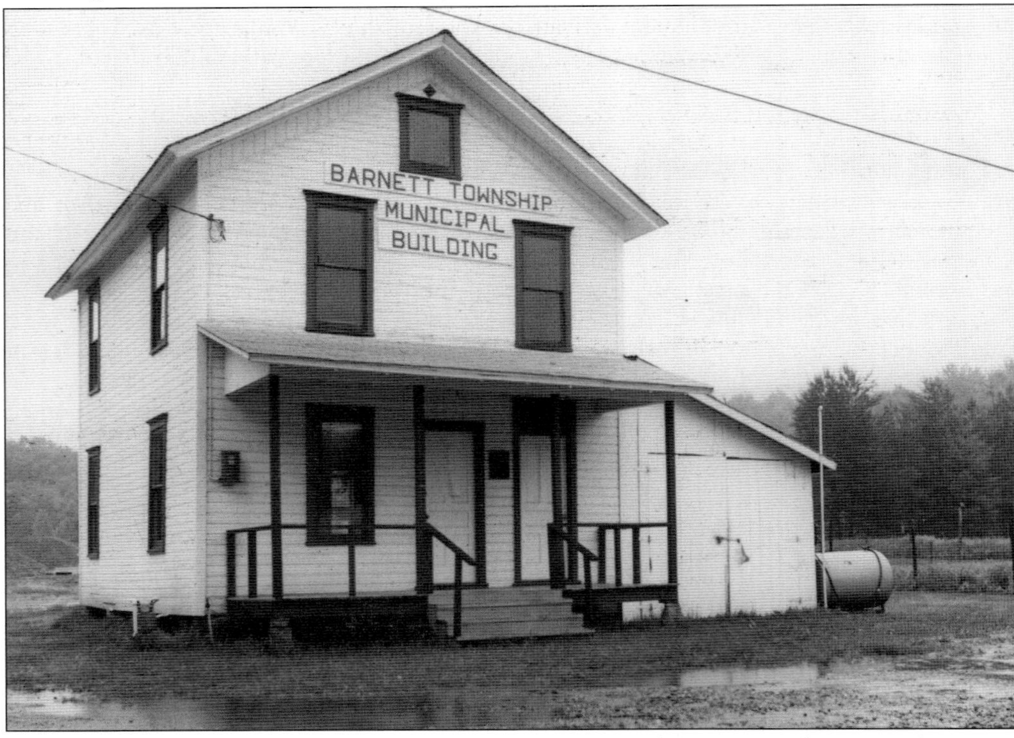

Organized in 1833, Barnett Township was named after Joseph Barnett and contained Tionesta Township and Jenks Township until their departure in 1838. Barnett Township was the filming location of forest scenes in the 1946 movie *Unconquered*, starring Gary Cooper and Paulette Goddard.

Five

Industry

Early industry was quiet in Forest County despite the discovery of coal and oil in the mid-1800s. Most of the trade excitement was centered on the timber business. Quality lumber was coming out of Forest County beginning in the 1850s, which spawned many other industries. Hemlock bark was shredded and boiled to produce tannins for curing leather. Tool handles, wagon wheel hubs, and shingles were other lumber derivatives. The growth of sawmills and their byproducts contributed to the county's economic expansion and population growth, which soared in the late 1890s.

Devastating floods and fires slowed down progress, causing property damage and deaths, but enthusiastic business owners rebuilt, at times more than once. The 1900s were quite prosperous for Forest County communities. Evidence of this is apparent in the building of churches, schools, and a variety of businesses. The railroads gave the lumber industry increased speed and reach, and the railroad owners profited from freight and passenger fares. The end of World War II brought an economic slump to the area. But as in the rest of the country, it also encouraged transformation and diversification. Some local businesses established after World War II include Tionesta Mantle Company, Marienville Foundry Company, Tionesta Sand and Gravel, Knox Glass Company, Crator Manufacturing (plastics), Purinton Pottery Company, Evenflo (baby bottles), and Endeavor Lumber Company. Also, the tourism industry increased during this time.

Forest County possesses a spirit of optimism historically demonstrated with every new venture. The residents and businesses have incredible tenacity and a great respect for their industrial heritage. Above all, Forest County is most proud of the timeless beauty of its natural surroundings.

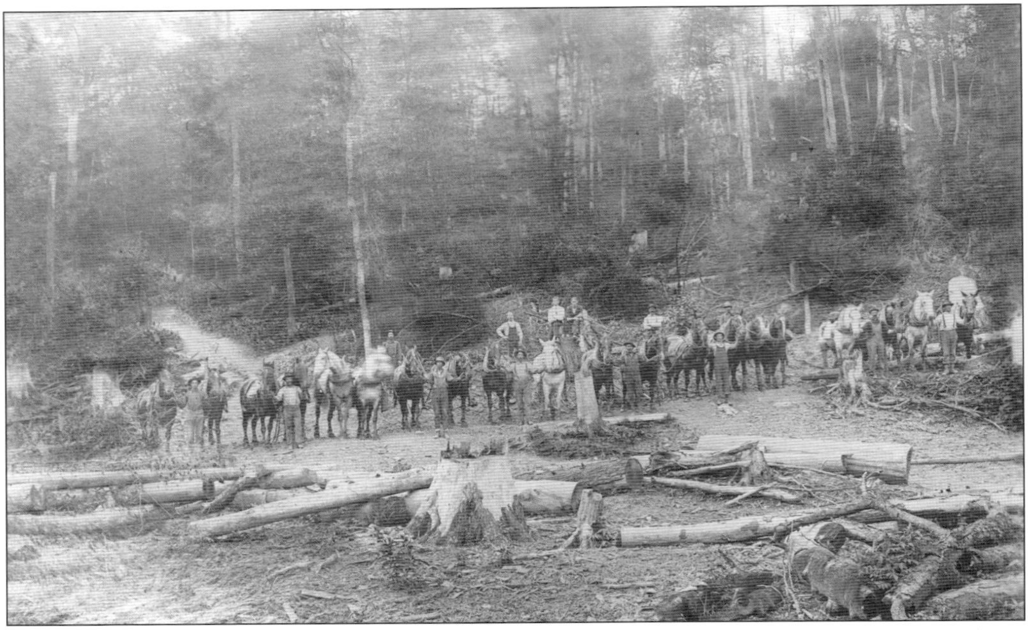

Pictured are two teams of 10 horses with workers from the Collins, Watson, & Company Golinza Mill. George Lacey and F.C. Lacey owned the mill at Golinza until an employee murdered George Lacey. Around 1890–1892, Teddy Collins and George Watson purchased the mill and ran it until its closure sometime between 1905 and 1906. Shortly after the closure, the mill was relocated to a new facility in Kellettville.

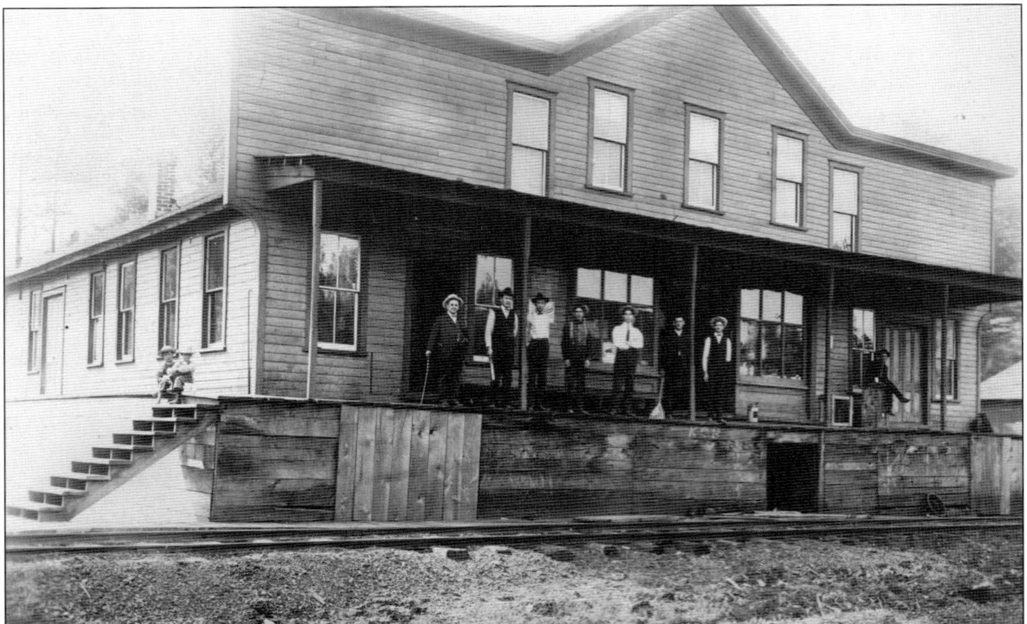

Pictured in this undated photograph are men standing in front of the Salmon Creek Mercantile company store. From left to right are store manager Leon Watson, George Klinestiver, Mark Wilson, unidentified, Clarence Cloke, Hump Brisel, Kooman Mealy, and Vinton Mealy. The two boys sitting on the steps to the left are unidentified.

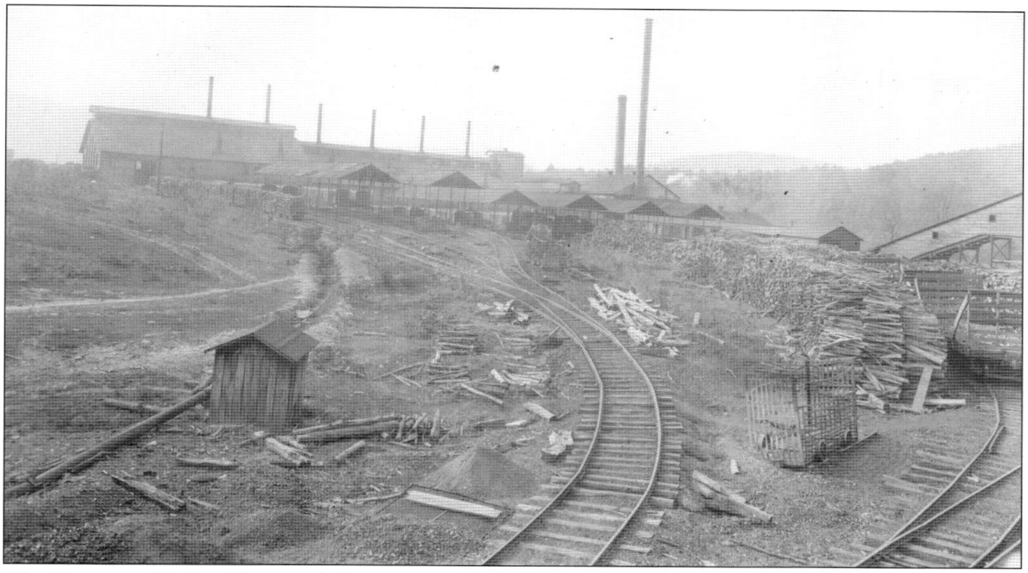

The Tionesta Valley Chemical Company was Teddy Collins's final venture. With partners Frank K. Brown and Frank X. Kreitler, plans were made to build a plant in Mayburg that produced wood chemicals from culled hardwood left on logged lands. Teddy Collins died in 1914, one year after operations began. His ownership passed to his son E.S. Collins. Brothers Martin F. Quinn and Thomas H. Quinn gained control of the company around 1916, with their heirs managing the plant until 1930. At that time, Wheeler & Dusenbury took over and changed the name to the Mayburg Chemical Company. It closed its doors in 1942, the last large wood chemical plant in Pennsylvania.

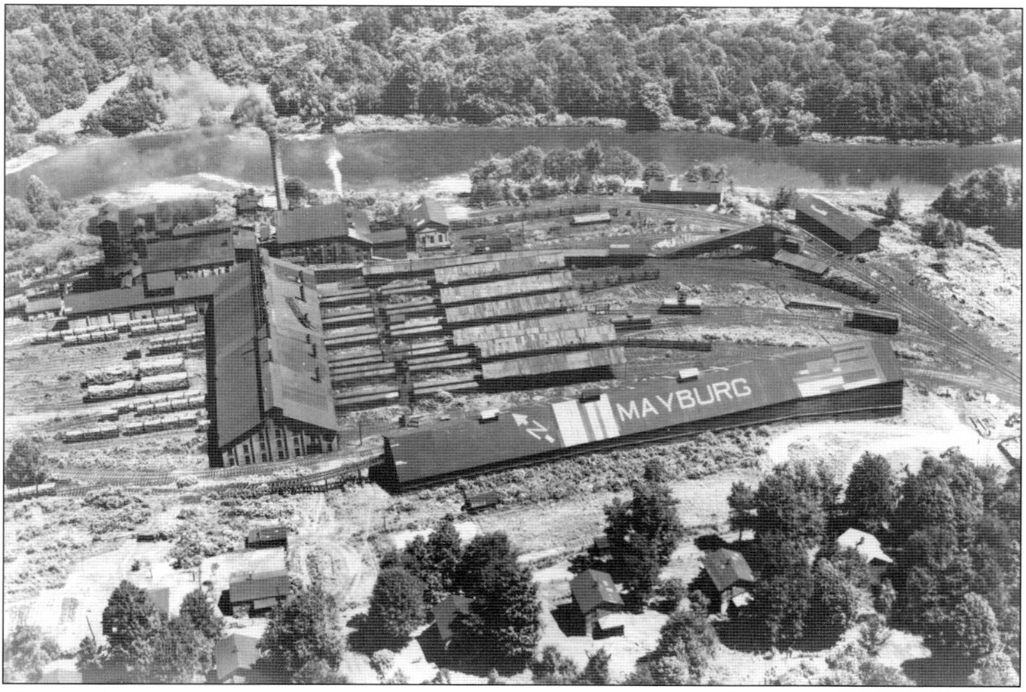

The Mayburg Chemical Company plant, as seen in 1941, was the largest remaining chemical company in Pennsylvania at the time. The plant, which began operation in February 1913, was located on the east side of Tionesta Creek near Kingsley Creek.

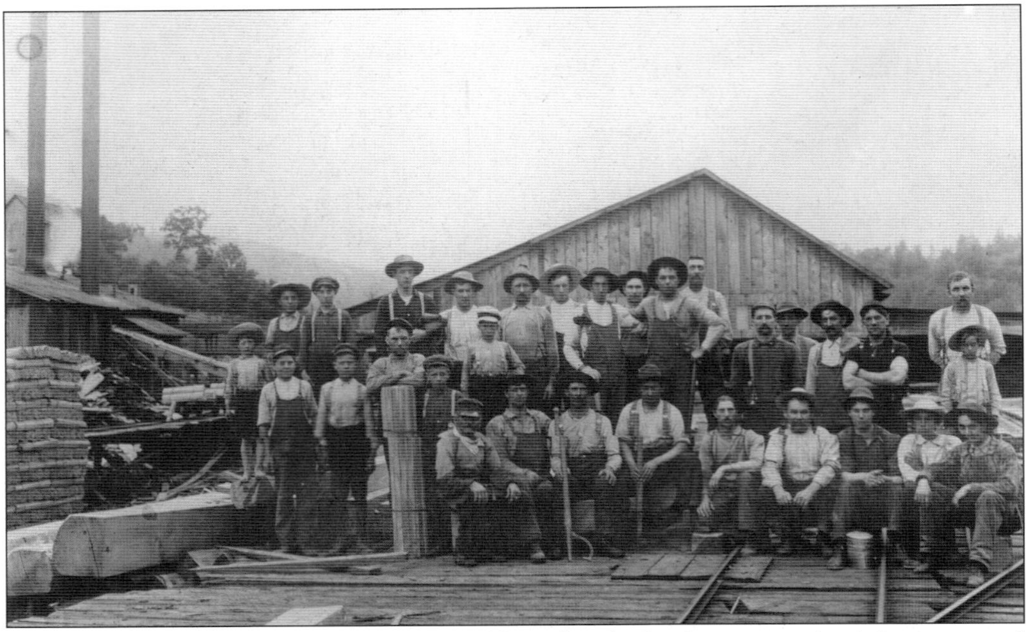

During the early 1900s, L.S. Clough and Teddy Collins had a dispute over land that pertained to the lumber industry. Clough owned the Clough Mill, which sat on approximately 5,000 acres, some of which overlapped with land owned by Collins. After a lengthy court battle in 1911, Collins and his associates Frank K. Brown and Frank X. Kreitler purchased the Clough lands to expand their enterprise.

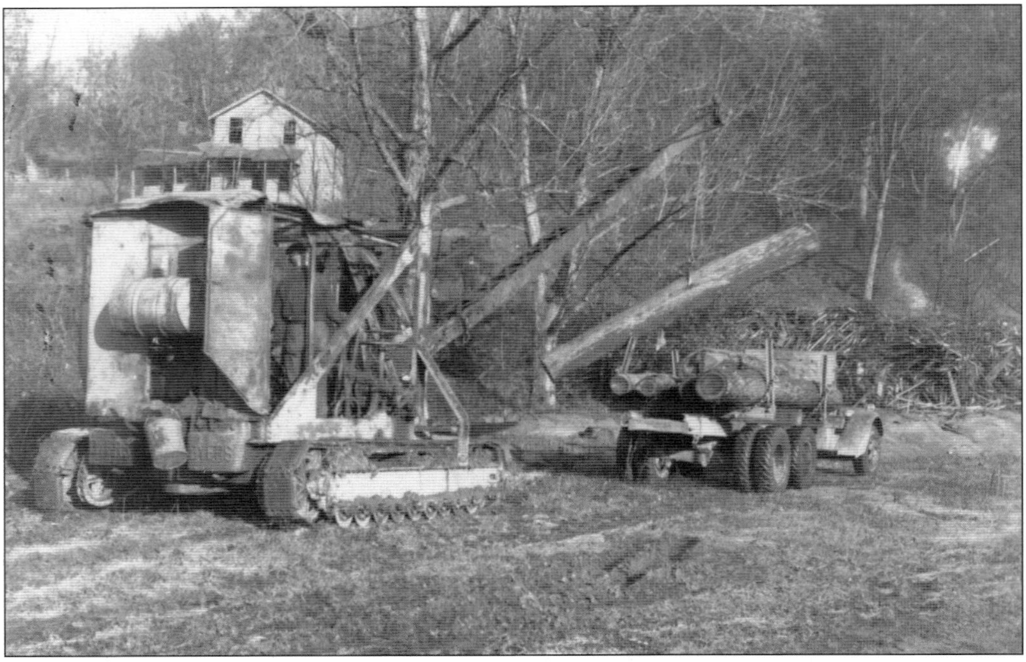

Trees below what would soon be the high-water mark of Tionesta Lake are being moved with a log loader in Nebraska in 1940. The government suggested that the residents of Nebraska vacate their homes by Wednesday, November 13, 1940, to avoid the possibility of being flooded. Twelve families chose to remain.

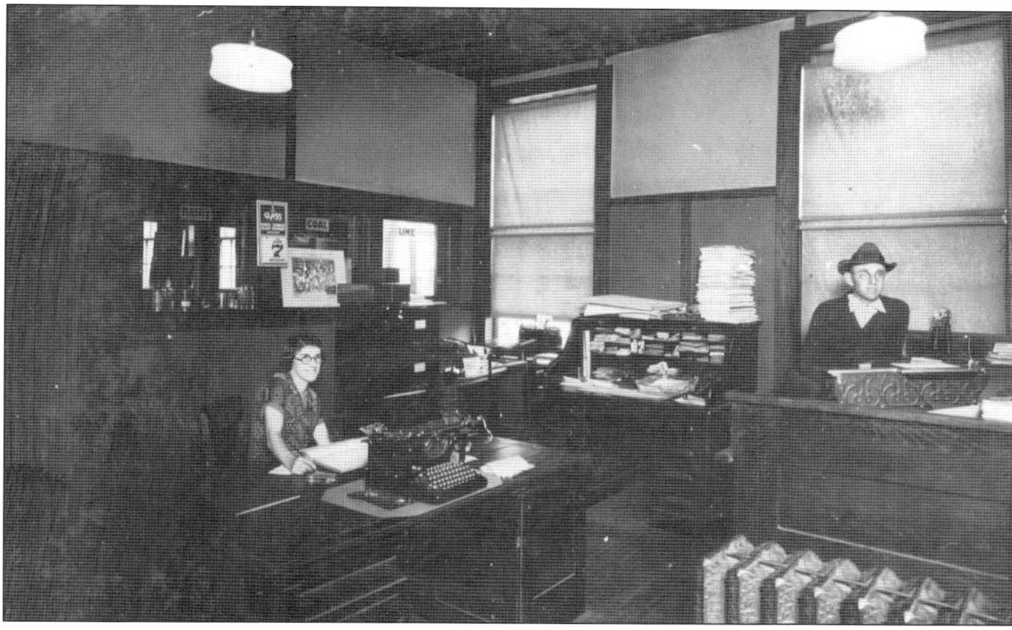

During the late 1800s, several planing mills and sawmills began operating in Tionesta, with many sprouting up near Tionesta Creek. In 1916, the Jamieson Lumber Company purchased a mill that had previously changed owners and names several times due to economic decline. The mill was subsequently altered to meet the needs of the company and became a thriving business. Siblings Janet and Harry Jamieson pose in the Jamieson Lumber Company office.

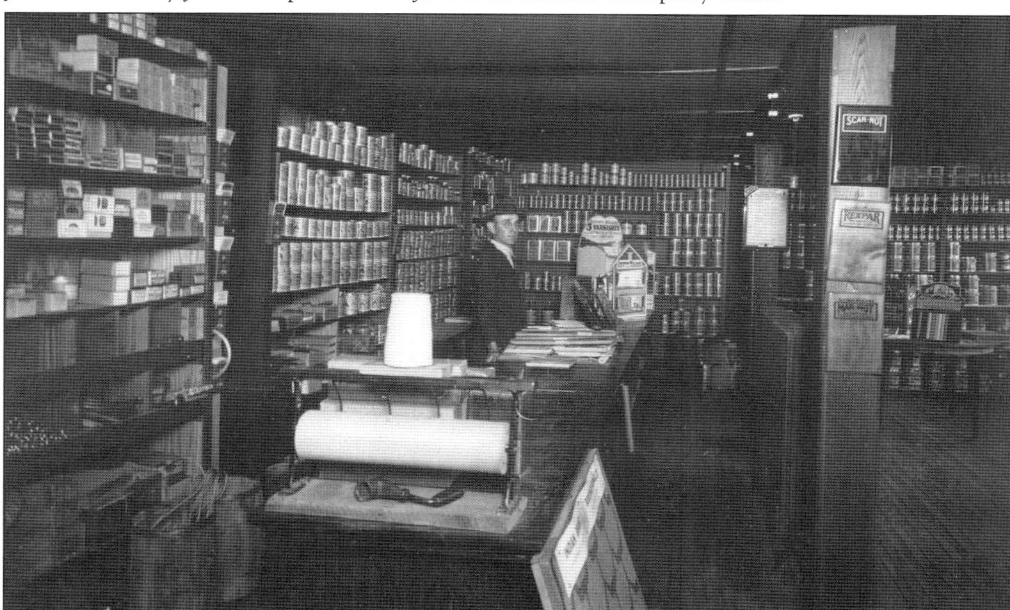

The Jamieson Lumber Company was incorporated in 1921 and changed its name to the Jamieson Lumber and Supply Company that same year. On April 15, 1948, the factory suffered a catastrophic loss by fire. Eventually, it was rebuilt as a smaller and more contemporary building that operated until the 1950s, when it was sold to the Cropp Lumber Company. Shown here is Harry Jamieson in the Jamieson Lumber Company paint supply room.

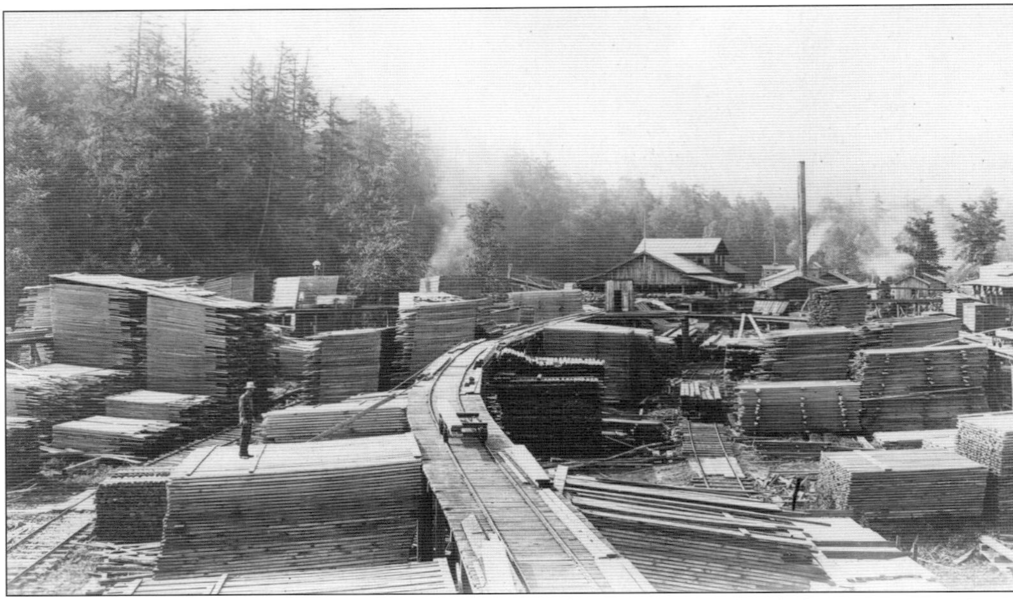

In 1870, Teddy Collins purchased the Lacy Mill and 7,000 acres of land along Tionesta Creek in Nebraska. Collins's partnership with Frank X. Kreitler, Frank K. Brown, and William Dickey was known as the Watson Lands Lumber Company. Pictured is the finished lumber area of the company.

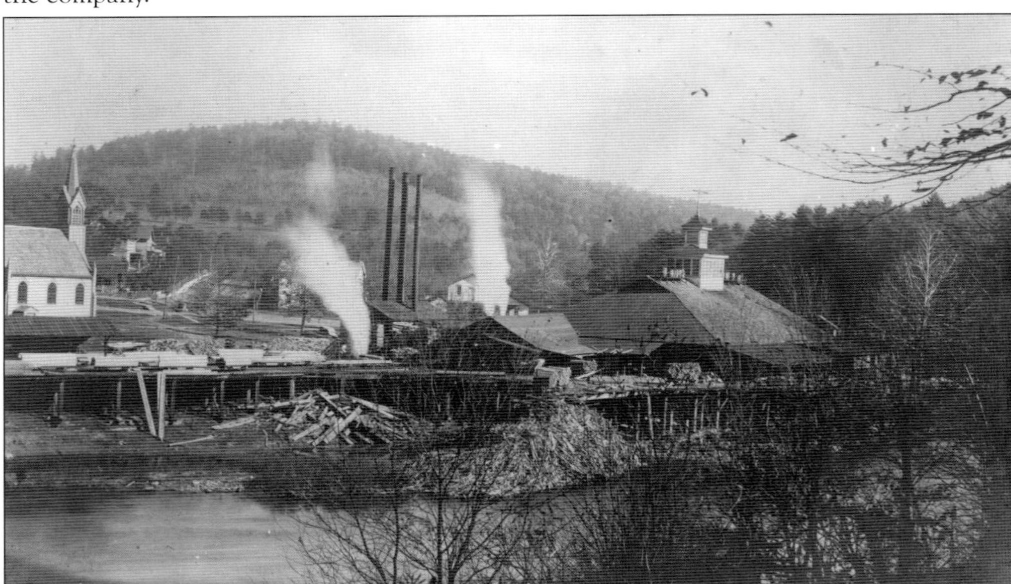

The lumber operation of Collins and Holbrook, established in 1867, purchased 7,000 acres in 1870 along Tionesta Creek and its tributaries, Big Coon and Little Coon Creeks. Virgin white pine was the dominant species along the creek valley, some measuring four feet thick and 150 feet tall. A 1,100-acre warrant contained approximately 25 to 35 million feet of pine. The Nebraska Mill took three years to build, and despite continuous use, it lasted 45 years. A large cupola, unique to this mill, adorned its roof, perhaps for ventilation. The mill housed a circular saw with a tandem carriage capable of sawing long pine logs that were used to construct 150-by-30-foot barges. Some were delivered to Pittsburgh, bringing over $1,000 each.

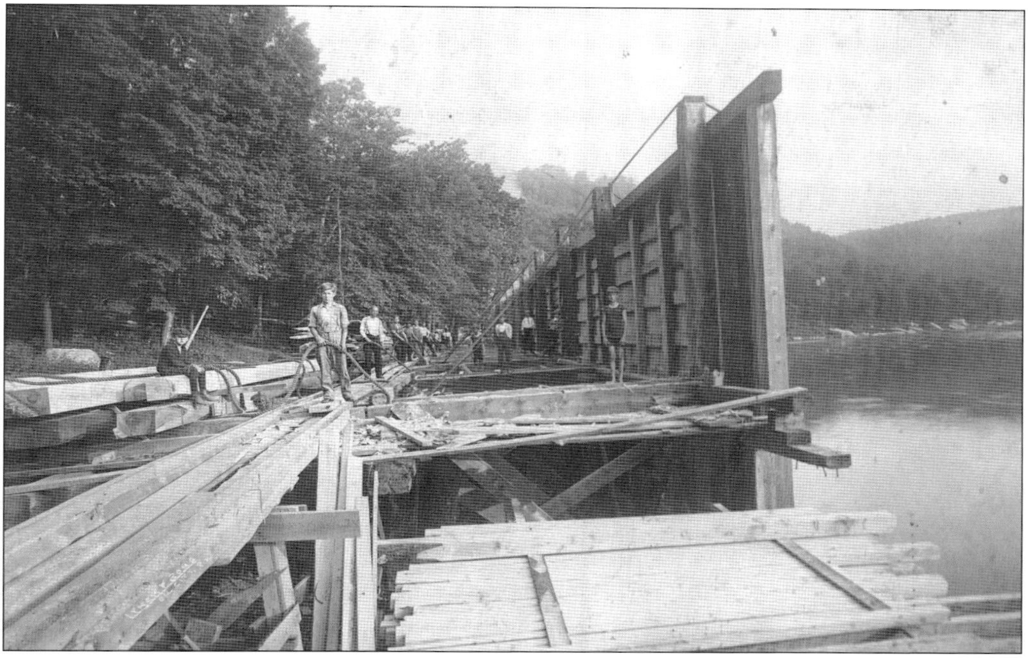

Workers at the Wheeler & Dusenbury yard in West Hickory ready a coal boat bottom to be flipped into the river. The workers used a method called tilting to flip the boat bottom into the water. When a tilting platform was unavailable, the boat bottom was flipped in upside down and, using a large amount of heavy stones on one side, flipped right side up.

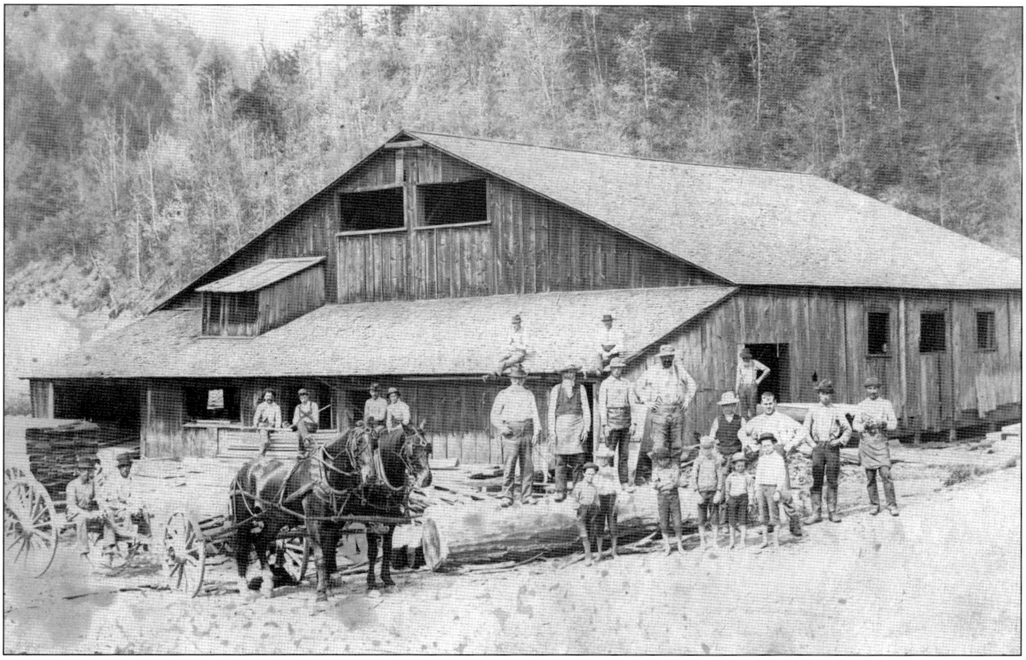

Newtown, or Newton Mills as it was often referred to, was a small town just east of Tionesta Creek near Nebraska, which lasted until the mass evacuations caused by the building of the Tionesta Dam. Pictured are workers and locals outside the Wheeler & Dusenbury Mill. During the height of its operation in the late 1860s, Wheeler & Dusenbury had three mills in Newtown.

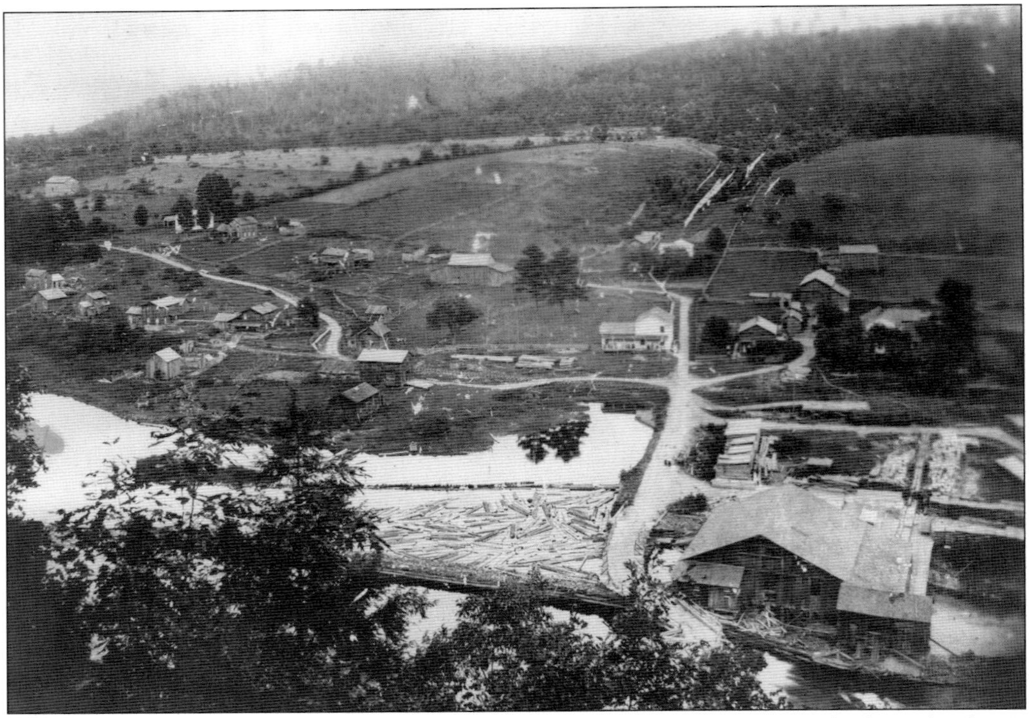

Pictured is the town of Newtown, named by founder Hamilton Stow, with the Wheeler & Dusenbury Mill operating along Tionesta Creek, around 1897. The Wheeler & Dusenbury Mill began operations in 1839, with Hamilton Stow managing the company until 1865. The mill operated until 1911.

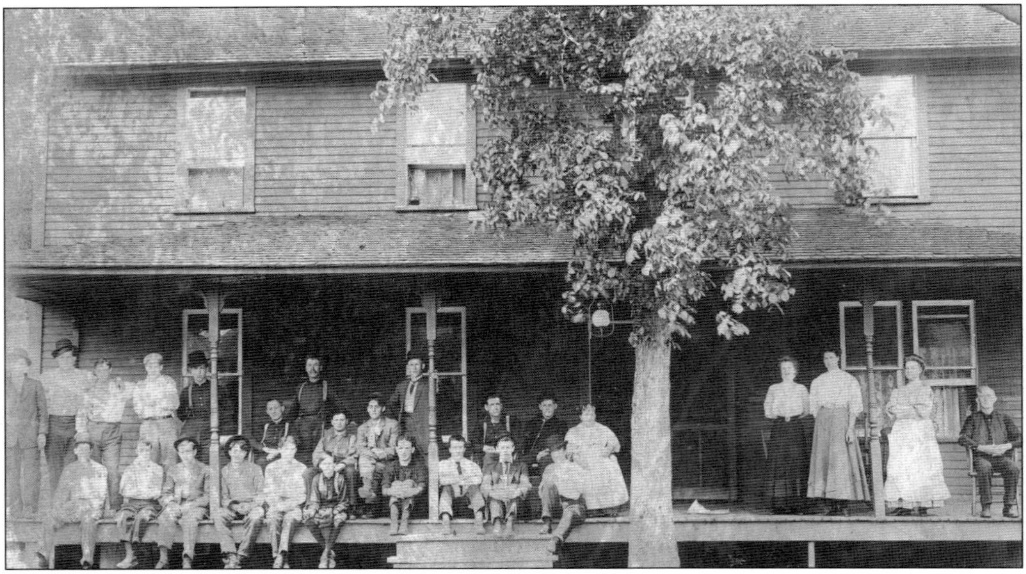

With the logging industry continuously growing throughout Forest County, the area witnessed an increase in population during the late 1800s and early 1900s. People and families came from all over looking for work in the mills and a chance to start a new life. Throughout the county, several boardinghouses were established to fit the needs of loggers and their families. Shown here is the Watson Boardinghouse around 1905.

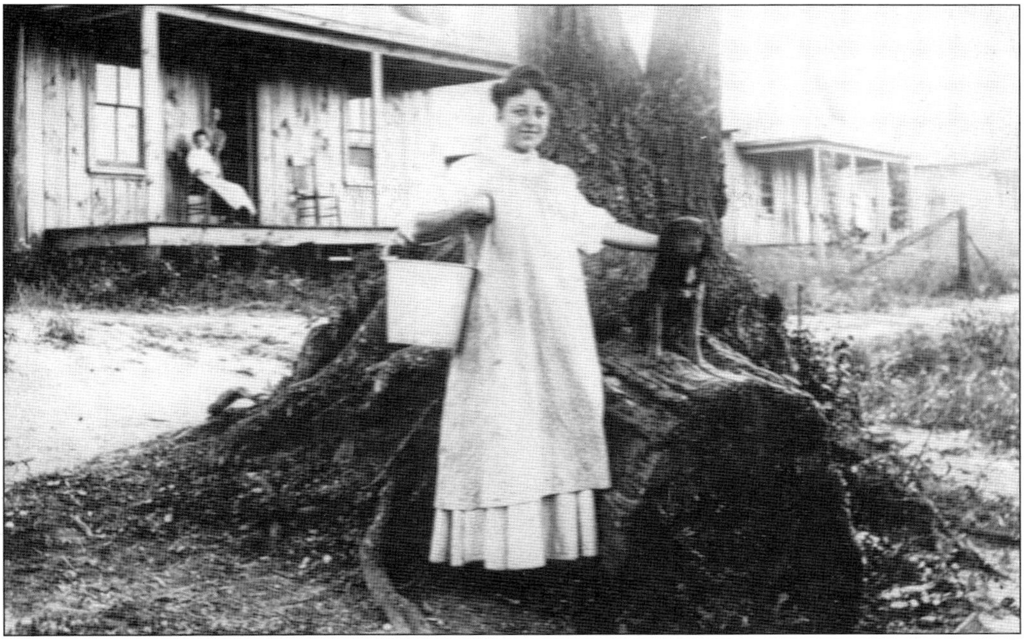

In 1833, a young William F. Wheeler from New York partnered with Henry Dusenbury to establish the firm of Wheeler & Dusenbury Lumber Company. In 1837, they purchased land and mills on Tionesta Creek near what is now known as Endeavor. The company flourished in 1867 when Nelson Platt Wheeler (son of William Wheeler) and William Dusenbury (son of Henry Dusenbury) joined in managing the Endeavor operation, which consisted of two large mills known as the upper and lower mills. There were over 300 employees running the successful band-saw mills. This undated photograph illustrates how early mill workers lived.

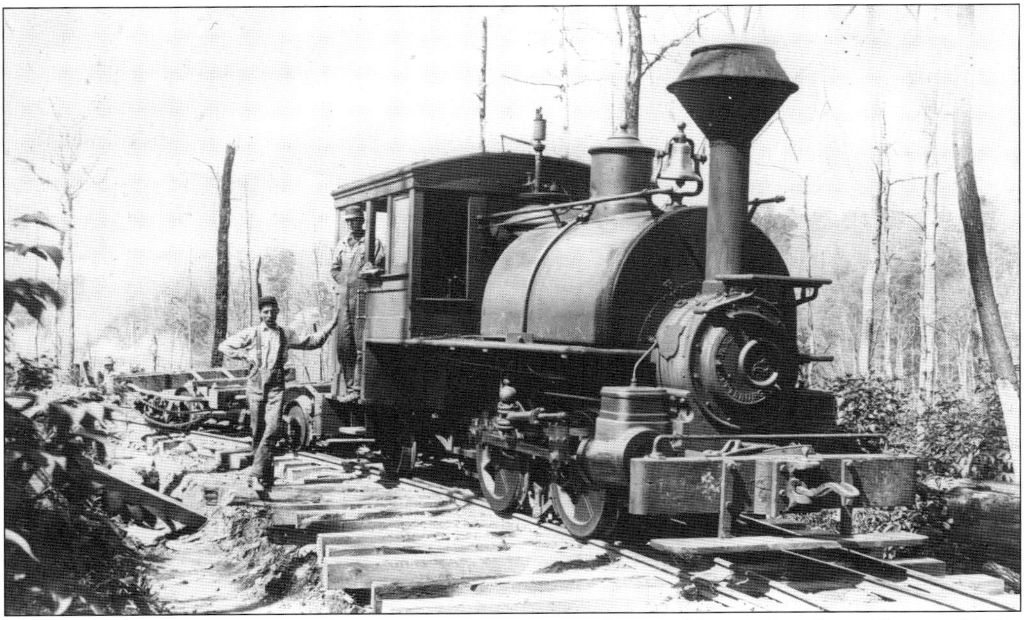

In 1890, Haskel & Company began lumber operations along Millstone Creek and later sold the operation in 1892 to the Wagner & Wilson Company. Wagner and Wilson kept the lumber mill functioning until July 15, 1905. The company was later relocated to Monroe, Washington.

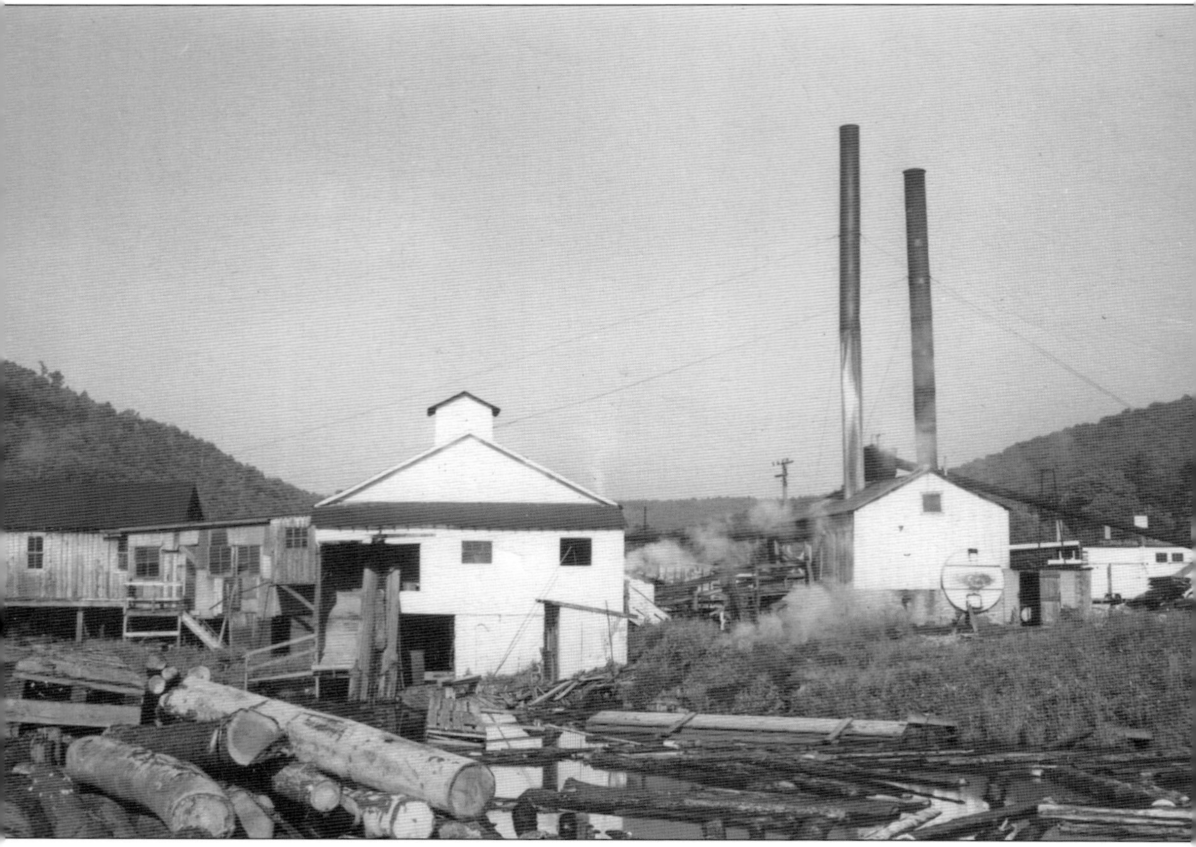

After the Wheeler & Dusenbury Company closed in October 1939, the plant remained vacant until former employees purchased the building in March 1941. That year, Walter Swanson, Lloyd Cleveland, and Russell Gustafson organized to form the Endeavor Lumber Company, which mainly produced hardwood items such as furniture. The mill is pictured here in 1948.

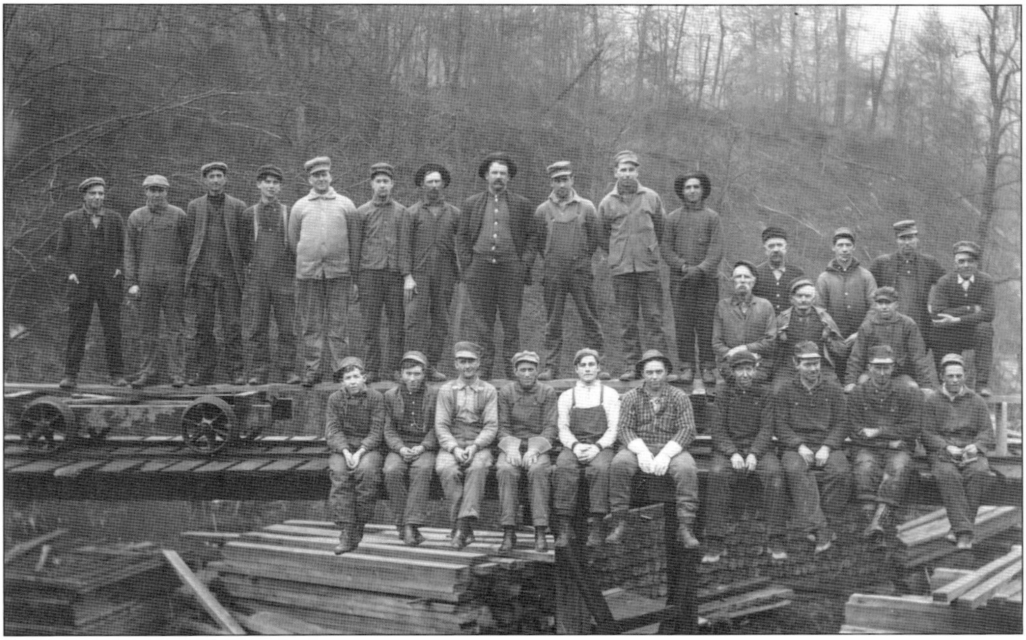

Workers from the Mayburg Sawmill take a break from their duties for a photograph in the lumberyard during the early 1900s. The lumberyard extended from the mill, up Bobb's Creek, to the banks of Tionesta Creek.

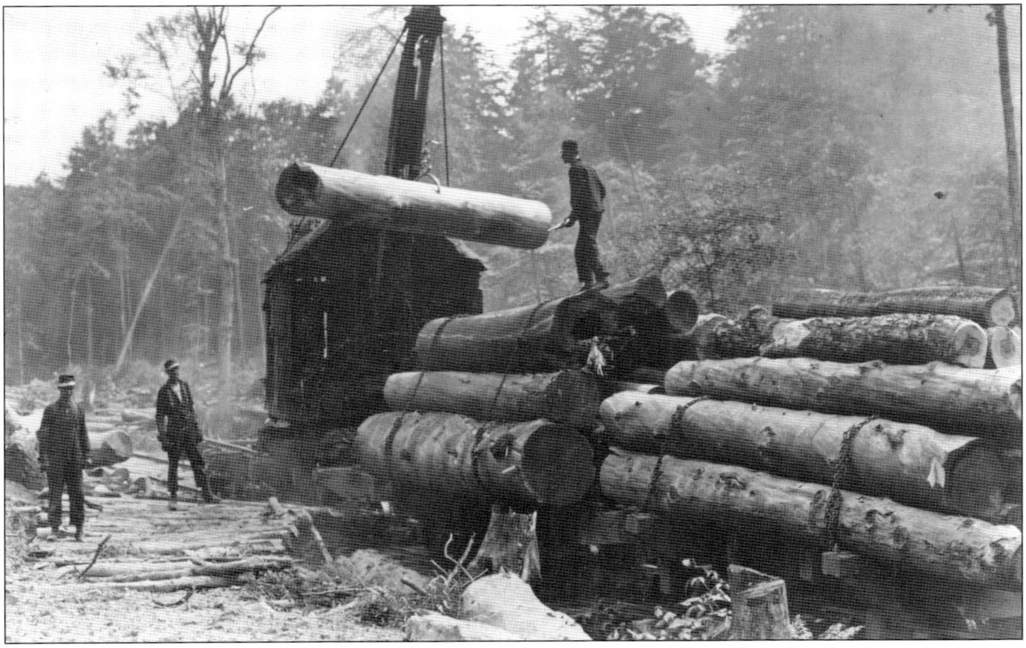

Workers of the Watson Lands Lumber Company load logs with a Barnhart loader for transport to the sawmill in Mayburg. The Watson Lands Lumber Company originated in 1894. The sawmill in Mayburg was completed in 1895, and in that same year, its first locomotive, Shay No. 1, was purchased. The mill was a profitable operation for 22 years. In 1917, it was permanently closed and torn down.

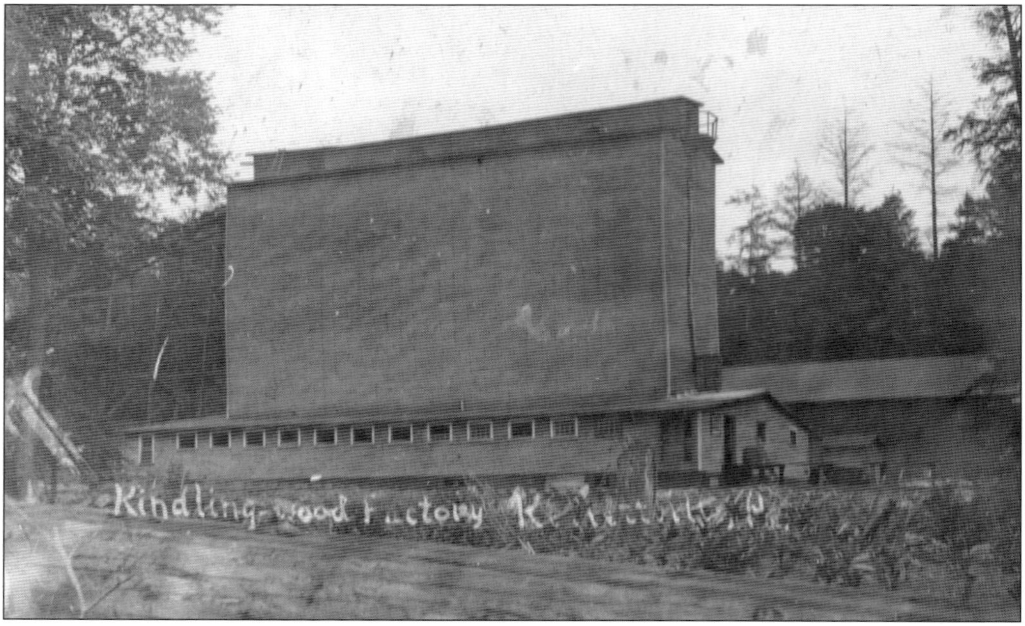

This c. 1905 photograph shows the Standard Wood Company's kindling factory in Kellettville. The factory was on Salmon Creek and across from the Salmon Creek Lumber Company. The kindling factory used an endless belt that transferred hemlock slabs across the creek from one building to the other.

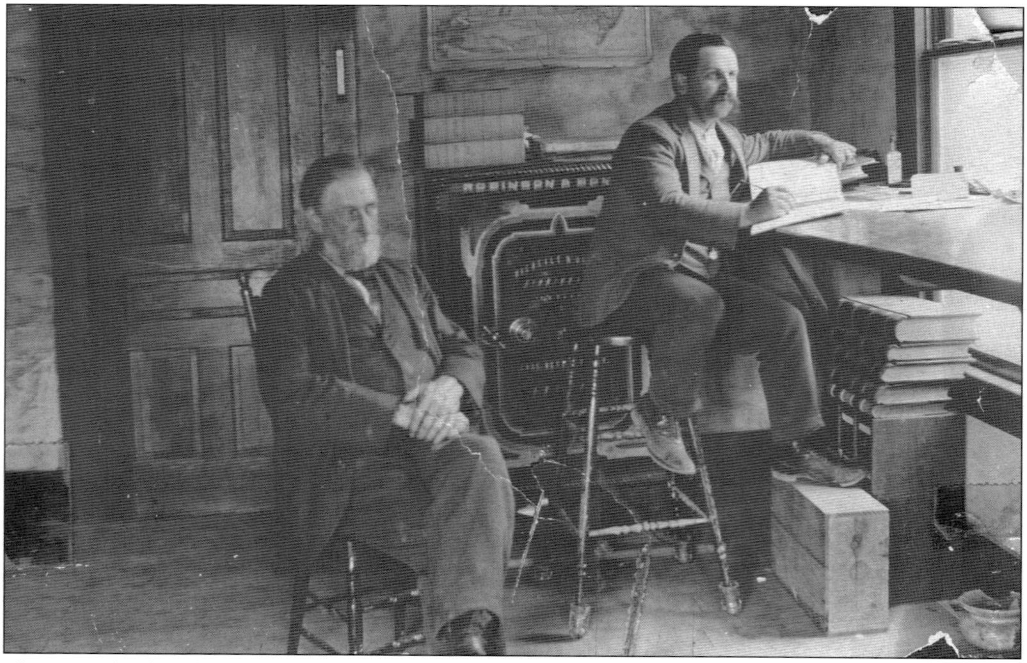

Photographed at the Salmon Creek Lumber Company Office in the late 1800s or early 1900s are Teddy Collins (left) and Walter Leon Watson. Collins, widely known for his lumber business, also enjoyed building churches as a hobby, with several built by him in West Hickory, Tionesta, Nebraska, and Kellettville. Watson was an employee in the lumber business until Collins appointed him general railroad superintendent.

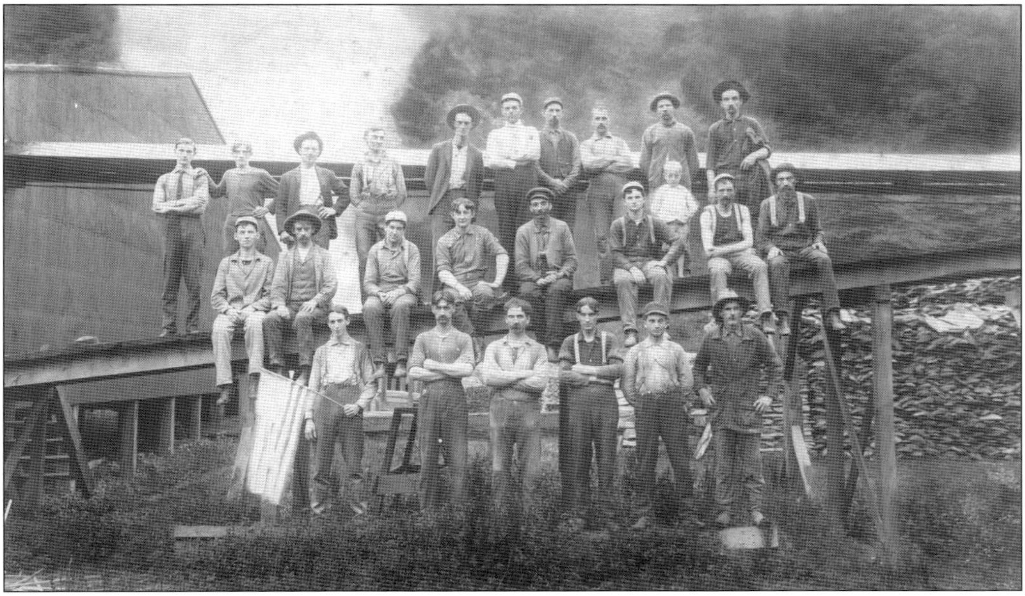

The upper mill in Endeavor was one of two large mills owned and operated by the Wheeler & Dusenbury Lumber Company in the Hickory Valley. The shingle mill sliced sections of pine into tapered wedges, which produced wooden shingles. As towns and cities grew across the east and midwest of Forest County, so did the demand for lumber. The bulk of the timber milled in Endeavor for construction during the 19th century was eastern white pine, which was favored as a roofing material.

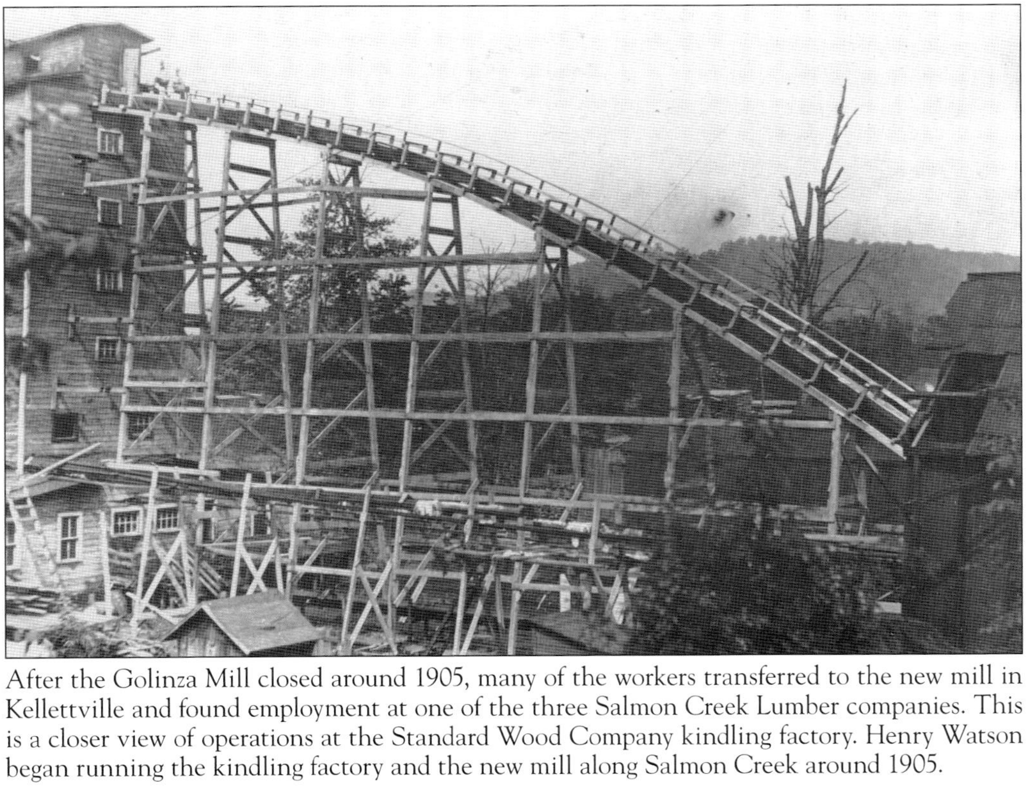

After the Golinza Mill closed around 1905, many of the workers transferred to the new mill in Kellettville and found employment at one of the three Salmon Creek Lumber companies. This is a closer view of operations at the Standard Wood Company kindling factory. Henry Watson began running the kindling factory and the new mill along Salmon Creek around 1905.

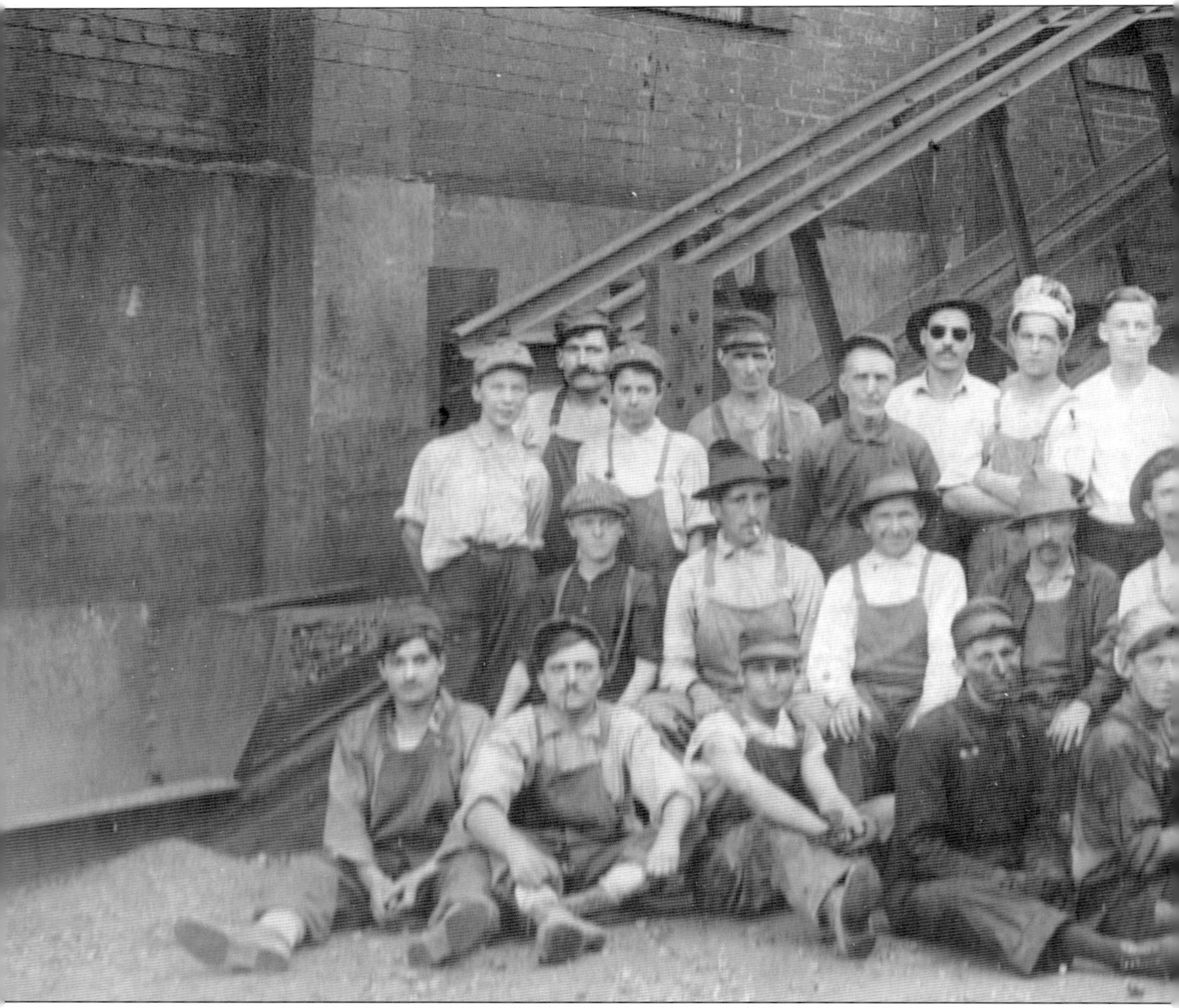

Since the Mayburg Plant had been in operation since the late 1800s, much of the wood in the area became sparse. By 1911, fears of a mill closure were looming amongst the administration and employees. Being the exuberant businessman that he was, Teddy Collins saw the potential in the

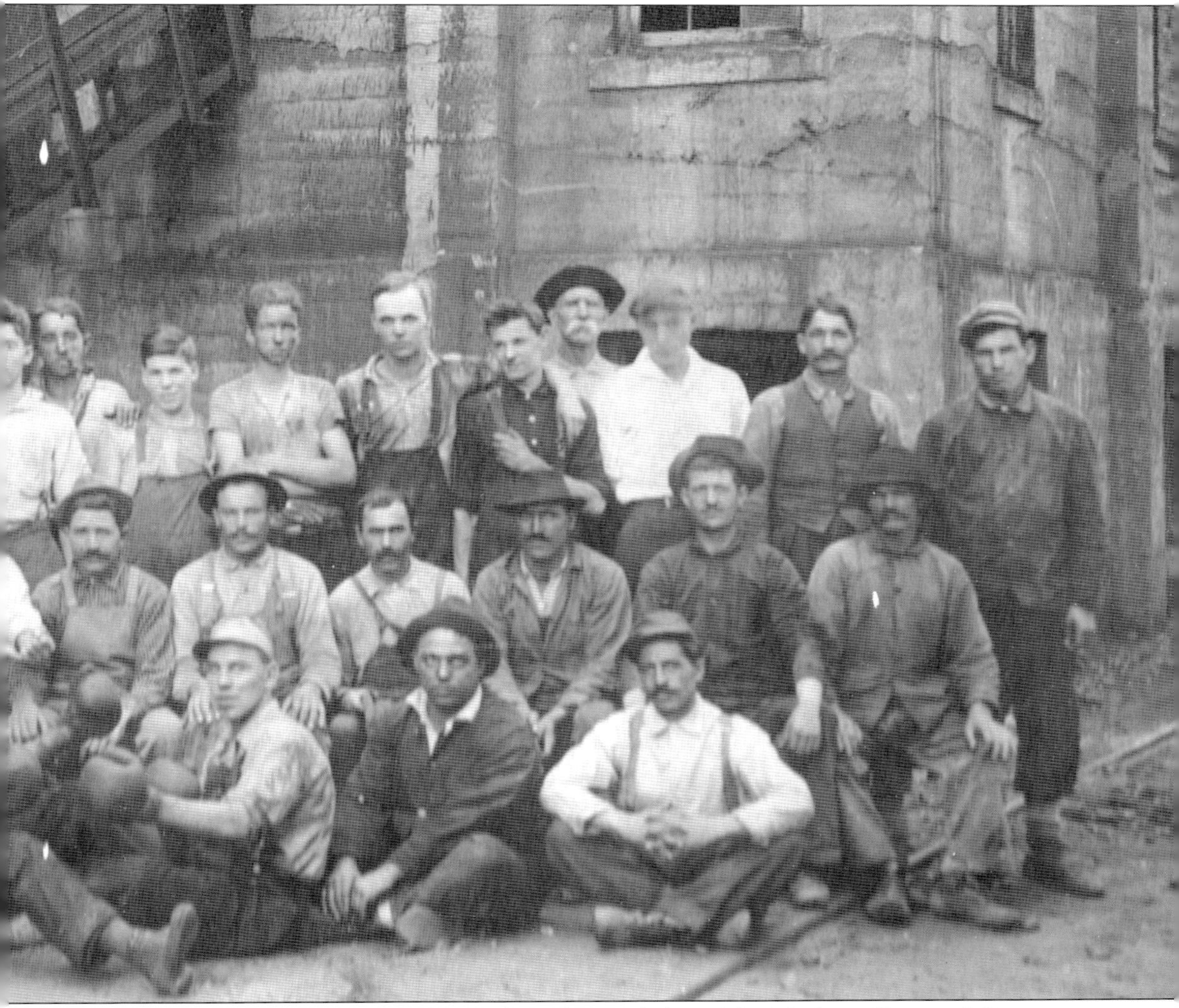

nearby Clough lands along with the use for a chemical plant. The Mayburg Chemical Company operated from February 1913 to July 5, 1943. Soon after its closing, all materials and buildings were sold off or junked. Pictured around 1918 are workers of the Mayburg Chemical Plant.

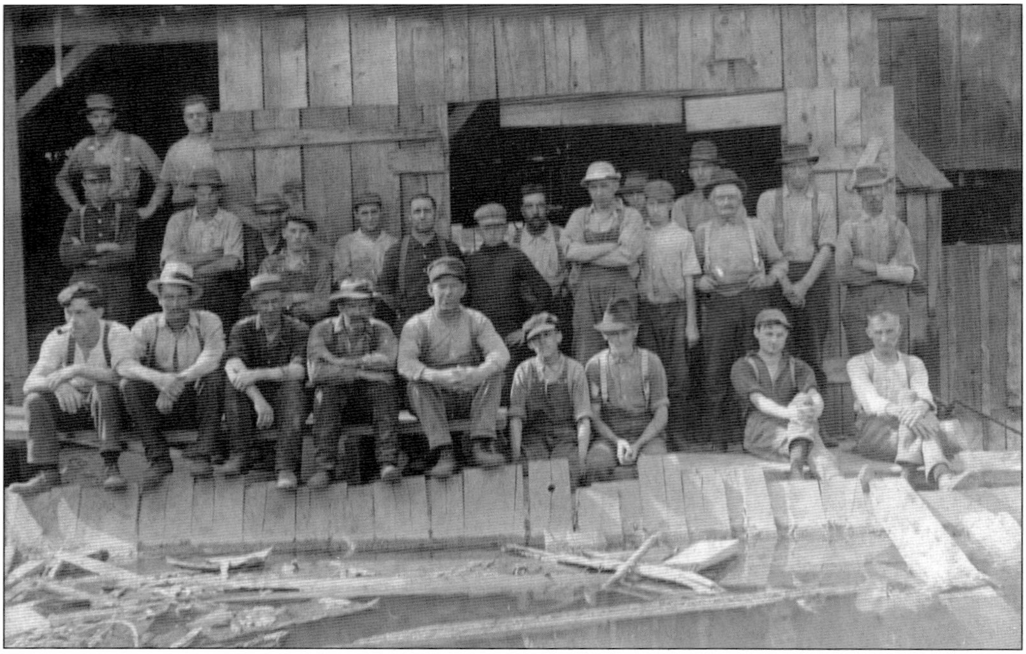

The Salmon Creek Lumber Company, owned by Joseph Adamson, began in 1878 as the Salmon Creek Lumber and Mining Company. Over the course of its operation, which lasted until 1923, the Salmon Creek Lumber Company owned several sawmills and tanneries along Branch Creek and Salmon Creek.

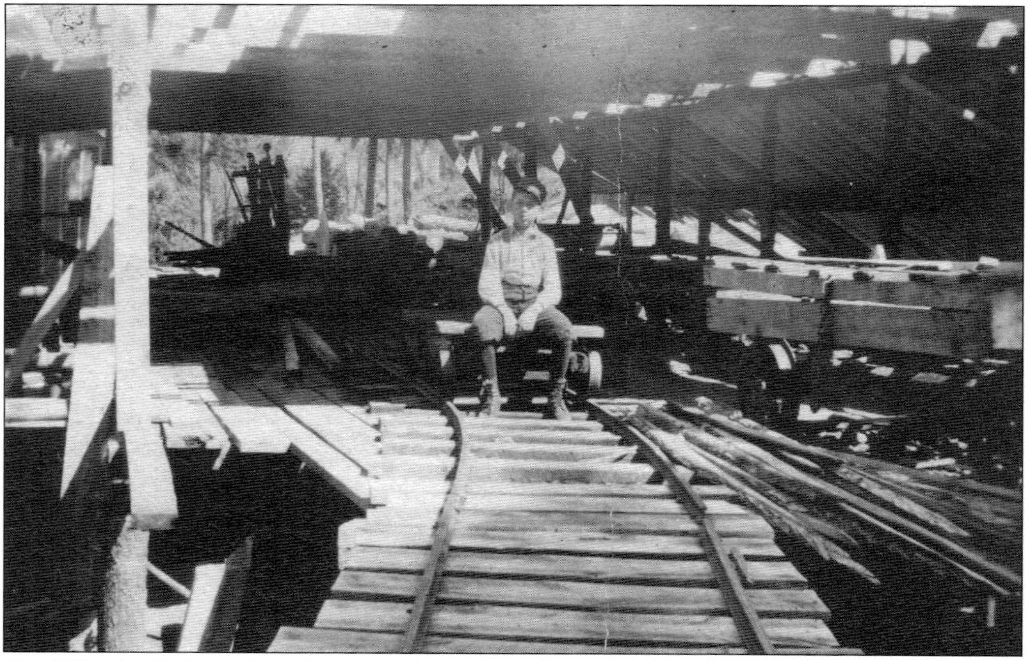

The Wheeler & Dusenbury Lumber Company had purchased land in Hickory Township several years before opening a mill there in 1853. The plant operated as a water mill from 1853 until 1887, when it changed to a steam circular mill. This photograph shows a mill worker at the plant during the early 1900s.

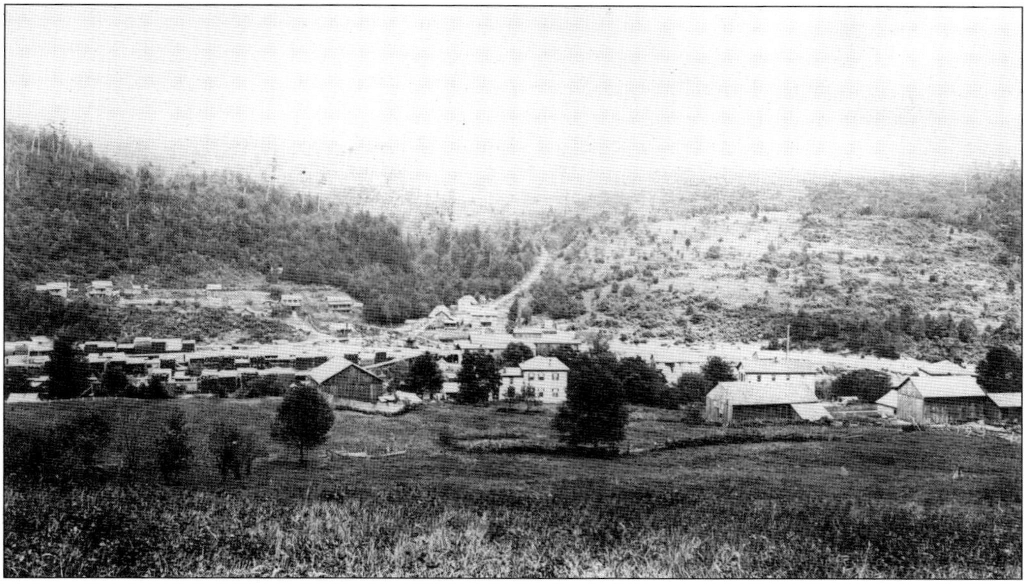

Pictured in the early 1900s, the town of Golinza, originally named Cobbs Mills, is located on Big Coon Creek approximately five miles from Nebraska. The first mill in Golinza was built around 1868 by founder John Cobb and sold to Fredrick and George Lacy several years later. In 1890, Teddy Collins bought over 7,000 acres of land in Golinza from the Lacy brothers in order to build the Collins mill.

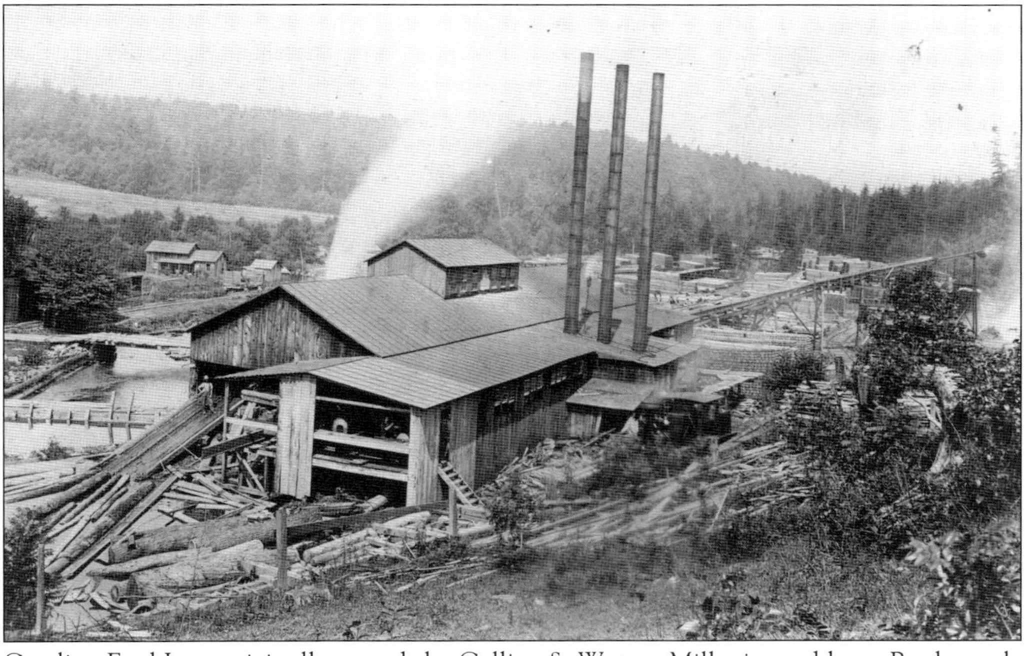

Caroline Ford Lacy originally owned the Collins & Watson Mill, pictured here. By the early 1900s, Teddy Collins and George Watson acquired the Lacy family's Golinza sawmill and built the Sheffield & Tionesta Railroad to handle the large amount of lumber produced by their growing businesses. While imagining more efficient ways to transport logs to the mill in winter (other than on sleds), he was inspired to design a locomotive that could travel rapidly through the forest on maple strips over pine rails.

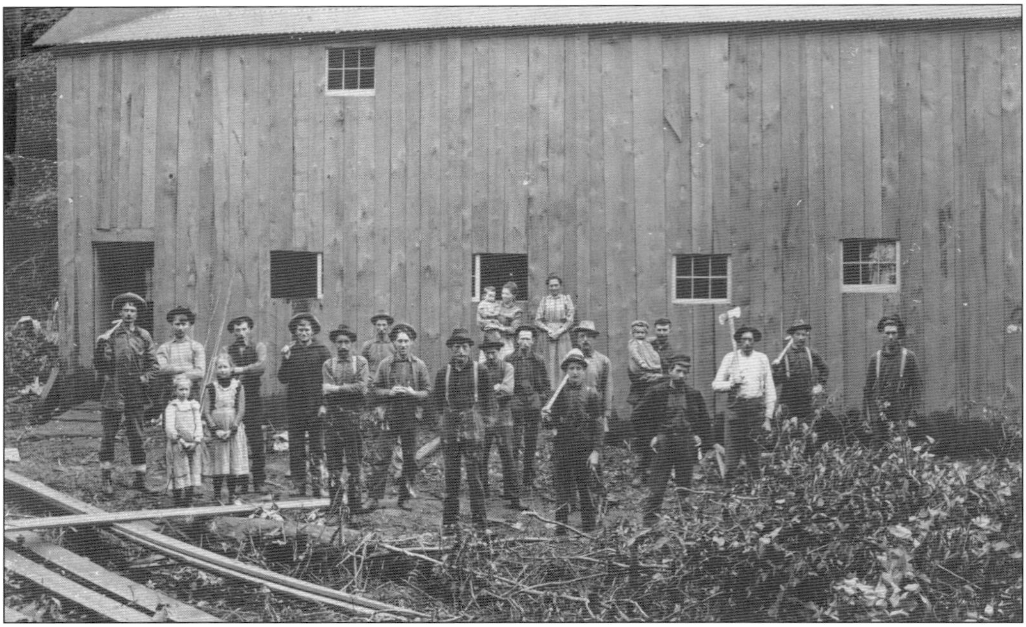

Lumber mills and labor camps were commonly located along creeks and streams, as was Minister Camp, pictured here. Waterways were dammed and released, causing strong currents to push against a large wheel, which in turn powered the saws within the mill. The Wheeler & Dusenbury firm took great care of their laborers. Their camps were lighted electrically, their sleeping quarters had bunks made of steel, and they had kitchens and dining rooms, a store, stables, and a blacksmith shop.

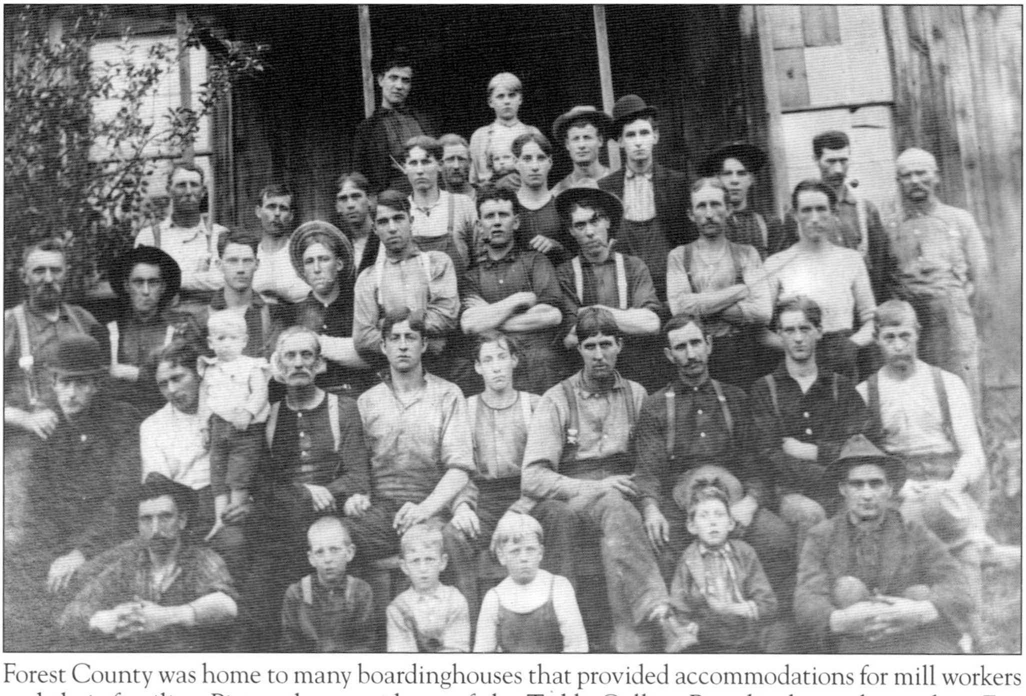

Forest County was home to many boardinghouses that provided accommodations for mill workers and their families. Pictured are residents of the Teddy Collins Boardinghouse located on Fox Creek. Throughout his career, the lumber tycoon owned many of these facilities in order to keep his employees happy and operations running smoothly.

Six

Locomotives and Railroads

Forest County was once one of the most bountiful lumber-producing sections of Pennsylvania. An immense amount of lumber was rafted out on Tionesta Creek, but as time went on, a better means of transporting logs was needed in order to tap the forest pockets of plenty. The Tionesta Valley Railroad was founded in about 1879, and in 1882, Engine No. 1, also known as "Wild Pigeon," took its first ride on the rails. It connected with the Baltimore & Ohio Railroad at Sheffield Junction. The 1880s railroad fever was hitting its peak, and soon, rails from Tionesta to Sheffield (Warren County) were laid down. The Wheeler & Dusenbury Lumber Company had one of the first logging railroads in Forest County. By 1883, the Hickory Valley Railroad (originally known as the Reno Railroad) connected East and West Hickory as it crossed a bridge over the Allegheny River. Teddy Collins created a railroad that ran from Tionesta to Sheffield where it could connect to the Tionesta Valley Railroad and the Pennsylvania Railroad. This line also carried passengers.

The hazardous job of "wildcatting" involved a practice comparable to that of a modern-day extreme athlete. Fully loaded cars were heavy for the small trains, which were guided by one man, called a "wildcatter." He used gravity to send the cars flying down the tracks. Switchbacks were used to help manage the speed. The brakeman would sometimes lose control and have to leap off seconds before the wreck in hopes of saving himself.

Lumber, leather, and chemical wood processing all relied on the forest to supply them. Without a forest, these operations ceased, as did the need for railroads. Shay, Climax, and Heisler were the main builders of logging locomotives used in Forest County. Sometimes, the engines were given nicknames, such as "Old Nellie," the "Big Four," the "Fred Klinestiver," and the "Gold Bug." One of the oldest lines in Pennsylvania, the Pittsburgh & Western Railroad, stretched from Butler County to Mount Jewett. One of its stops was Marienville in Jenks Township. The train station still exists in Marienville and is currently being renovated.

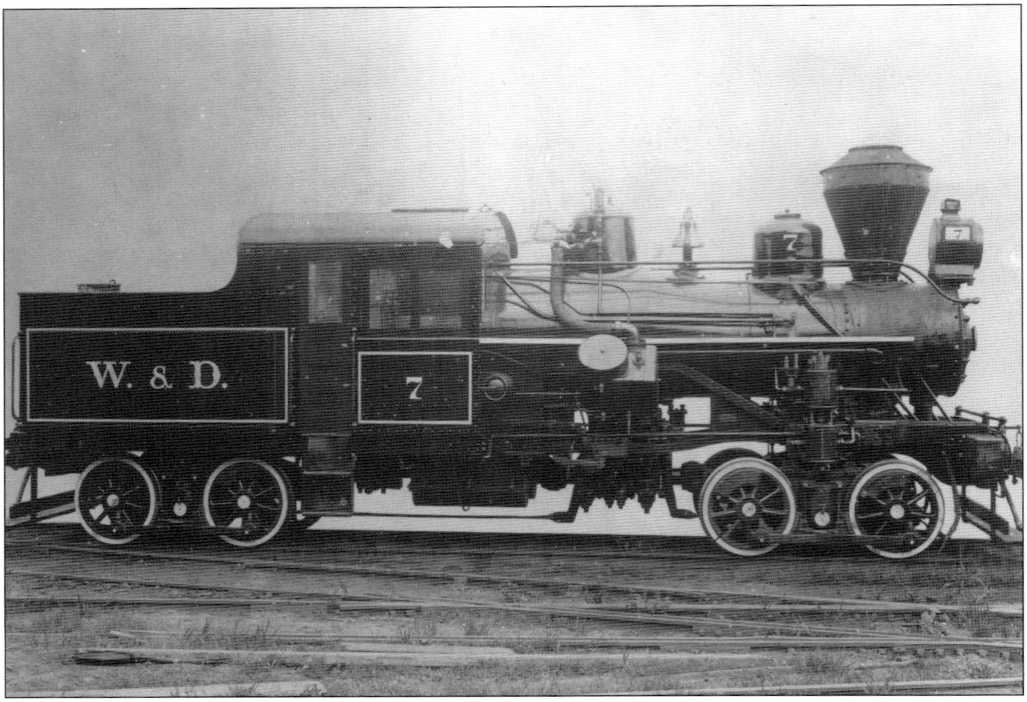

Pictured is a brand new Heisler locomotive destined for the Wheeler & Dusenbury Lumber Company of Endeavor, Pennsylvania. The Wheeler & Dusenbury Railroad operated for over 55 years with only seven engines. Relatively few Heislers were used in Pennsylvania, as Climaxes and Shays were preferred. This No. 7 locomotive was built in 1918 and weighed 47 tons.

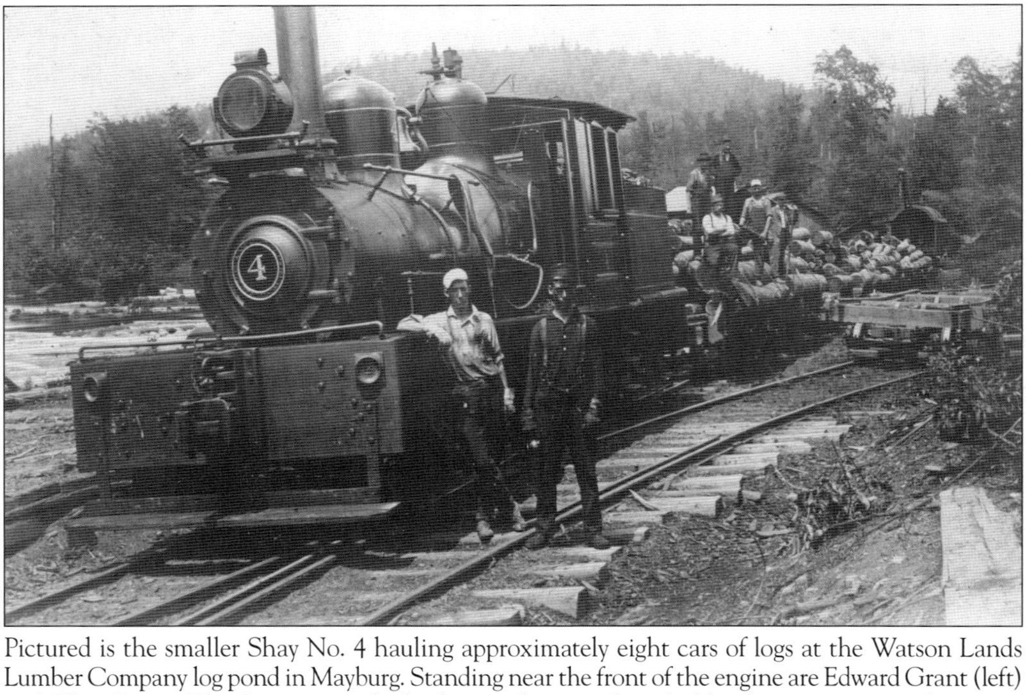

Pictured is the smaller Shay No. 4 hauling approximately eight cars of logs at the Watson Lands Lumber Company log pond in Mayburg. Standing near the front of the engine are Edward Grant (left) and Chas Grant. The five men in the background are unidentified lumber company workers.

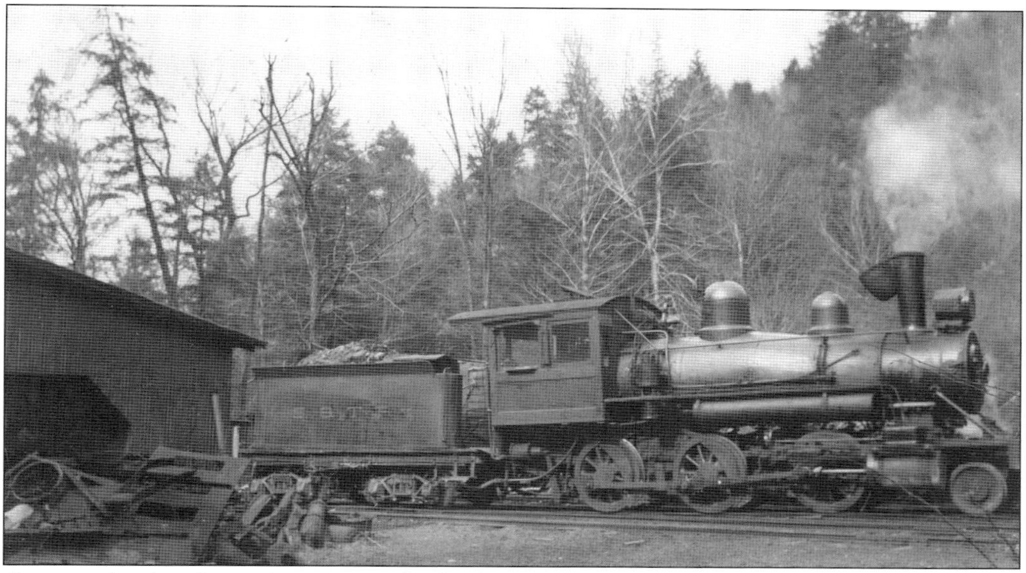

Carrying lumber from Tionesta to Sheffield, locomotives traveled along Tionesta Creek and various streams on the Sheffield & Tionesta Railroad line. Log trains and bark cars were used for hauling logs to the sawmills and bark to tanneries. This engine is passing through an area known as Blackhole in Nebraska. It was given its name by Teddy Collins, the owner of Nebraska and most of the surrounding area, who, upon observing the large amounts of coal smoke produced by the many engines rolling through the roadhouse, quipped, "this part of Nebraska is a black hole."

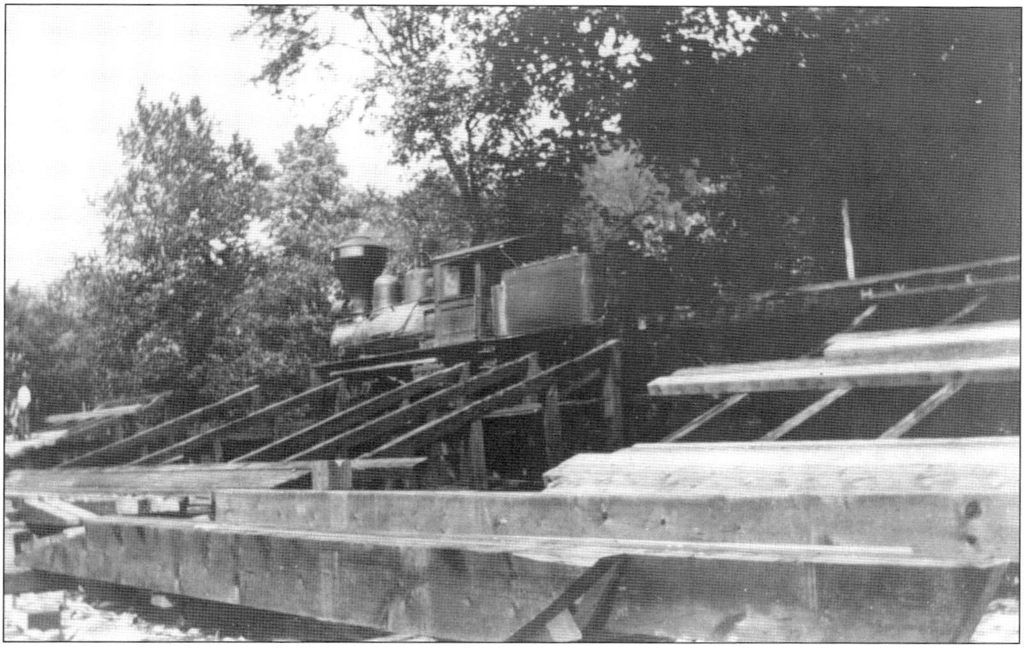

During the early years of the lumber industry in Forest County, railroads were scarce if present at all in some locations. Barges and flatboats were used extensively to transport locomotives and railroad materials into the county in order to construct transportation lines. Once the railroad lines were set, large building yards such as the one pictured in West Hickory could be constructed and used to haul coal and farm products.

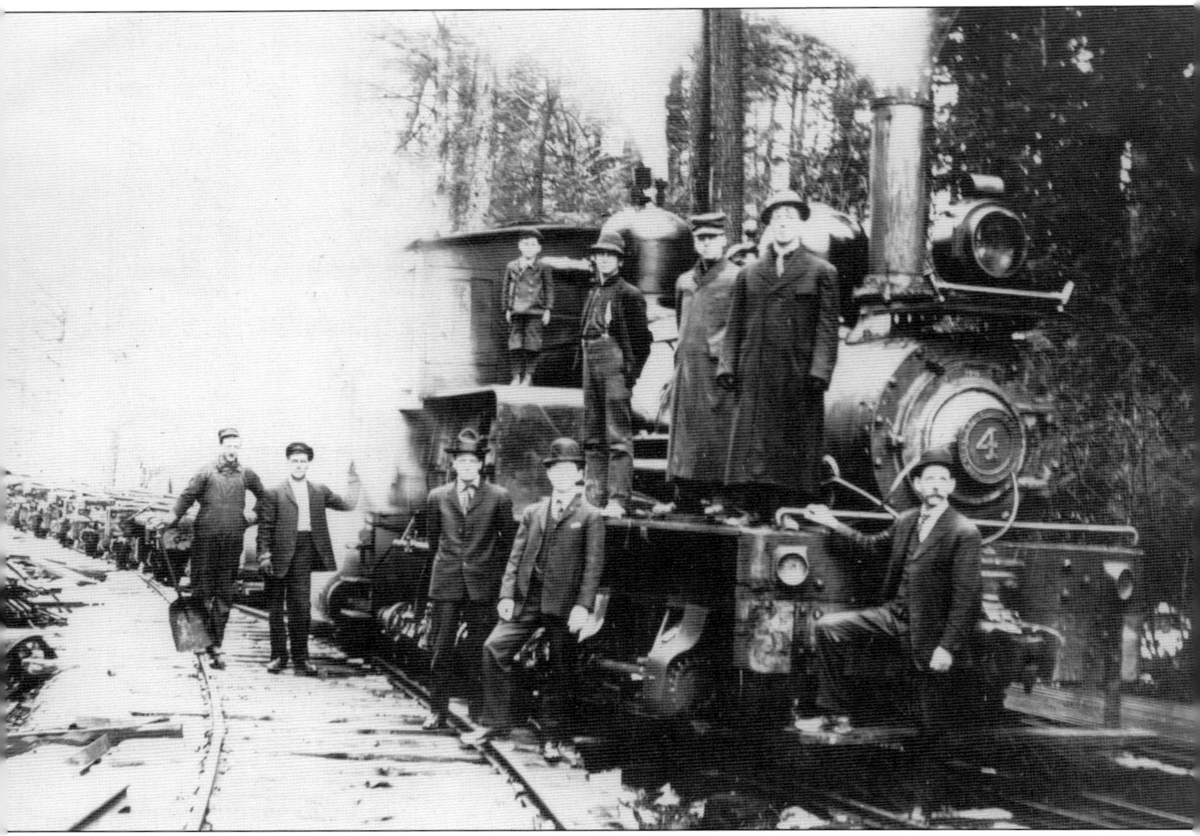

This 42-ton Shay No. 4 engine was purchased around 1906 for use on the new standard-gauge railroad built on Lamentation and Bear Creeks by the Watson Lands Lumber Company. The Shay engine was designed to navigate steep hills and sharp curves as it burrowed into the previously inaccessible forest. Log trains made several trips per day, hauling wood back from the harvest to the mill in Mayburg. By 1917, the 2,300 acres of virgin white pine that dominated the Watson Lands had been completely slashed, and the Mayburg mill was closed. Shay No. 4 was subsequently given a new job hauling lumber from Salmon Creek. When the Salmon Creek Lumber Mill shut down around 1923, several engines, including Shay No. 4, were stored in the planing mill at Kellettville.

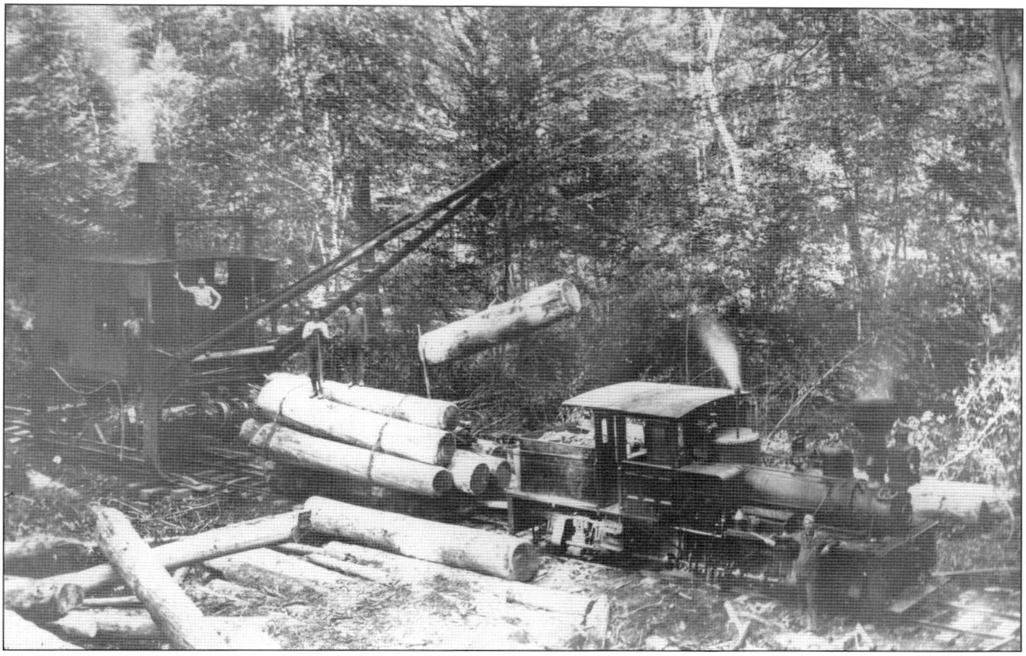

The McGiffert log loader shown on the left was possibly the only such machine in Pennsylvania during the early 1900s. Operated at the Watson Lands Lumber Company in Mayburg, the loader straddled the tracks while empty train cars were maneuvered under it. The engine hauling the logs is Shay No. 1, which was purchased in 1895.

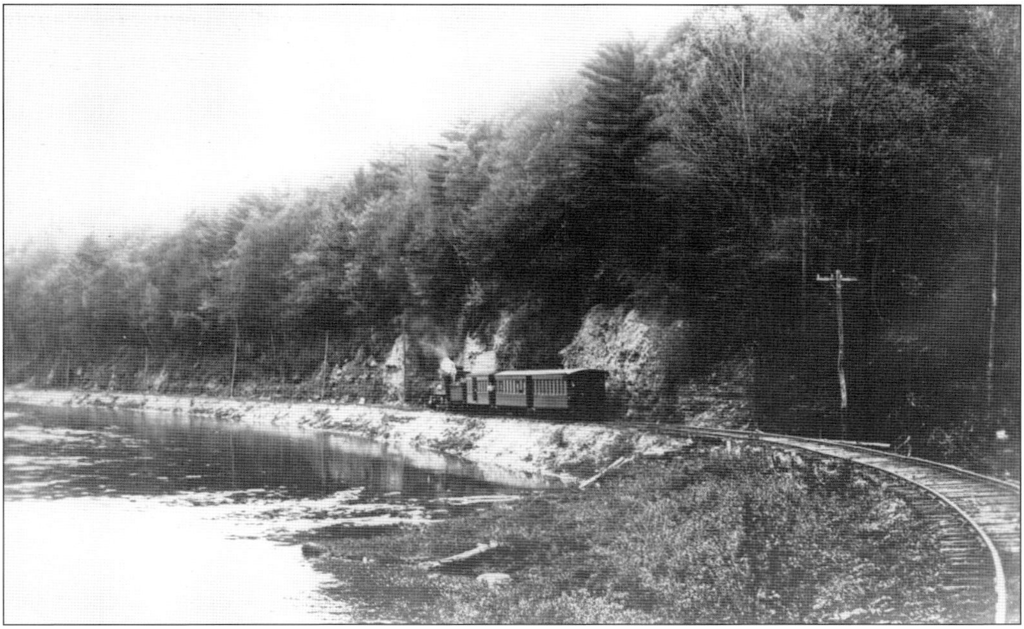

Pictured on the Sheffield & Tionesta Railroad is a passenger train pulled by engine No. 4 along Tionesta Creek near Balltown. On August 10, 1911, the Sheffield & Tionesta Railroad purchased the Tionesta Valley & Hickory Railway Company. By 1911, Teddy Collins had control over the Sheffield & Tionesta Railroad, Tionesta Valley & Salmon Creek Railway Company, and the Tionesta Valley & Hickory Railway Company.

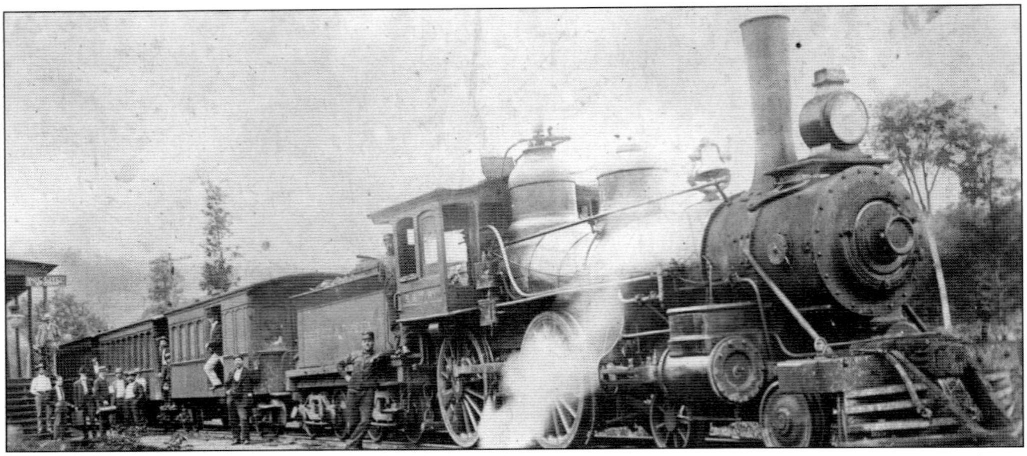

The Tionesta Valley & Salmon Creek Railway Company incorporated on May 12, 1893, and ran tracks from Ross Run to Kellettville. On May 16, 1901, the Sheffield & Tionesta Railroad merged with the Tionesta Valley & Salmon Creek Railway Company. Shown in this photograph is the Sheffield & Tionesta Railway engine No. 4 in front of a passenger train in Kellettville.

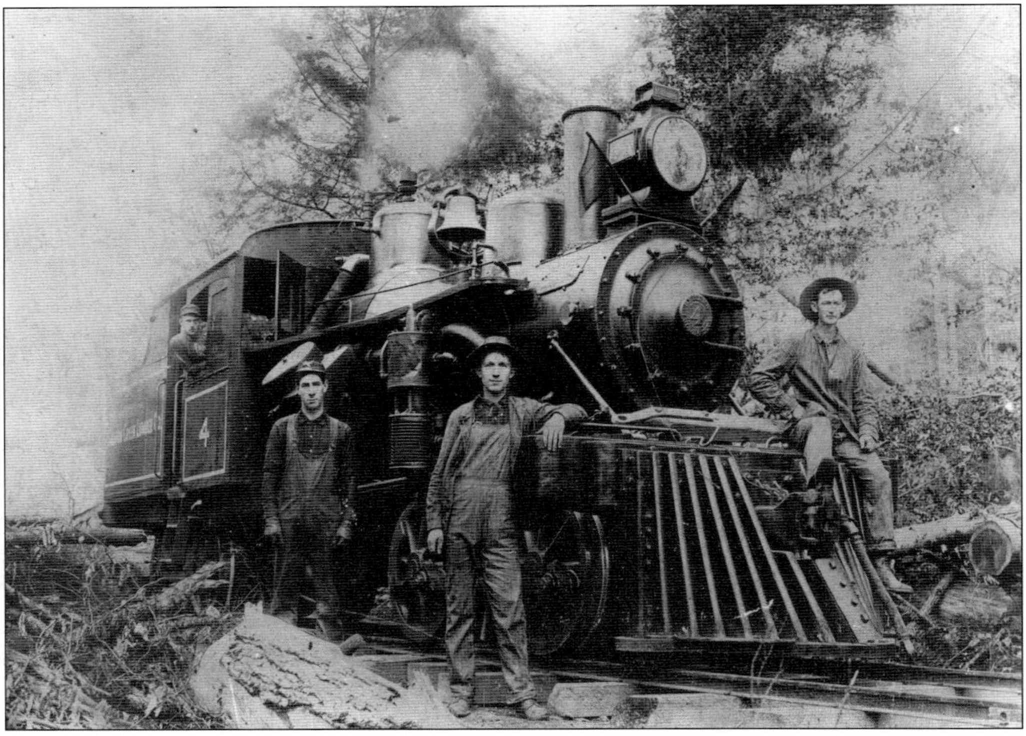

Taking a break for a quick photograph on the Sheffield & Tionesta Railroad engine No. 4 in Kellettville are, from left to right, engineer Wynn Zerbe, fireman Steve West, brakeman John Olson, and pilot James Gult.

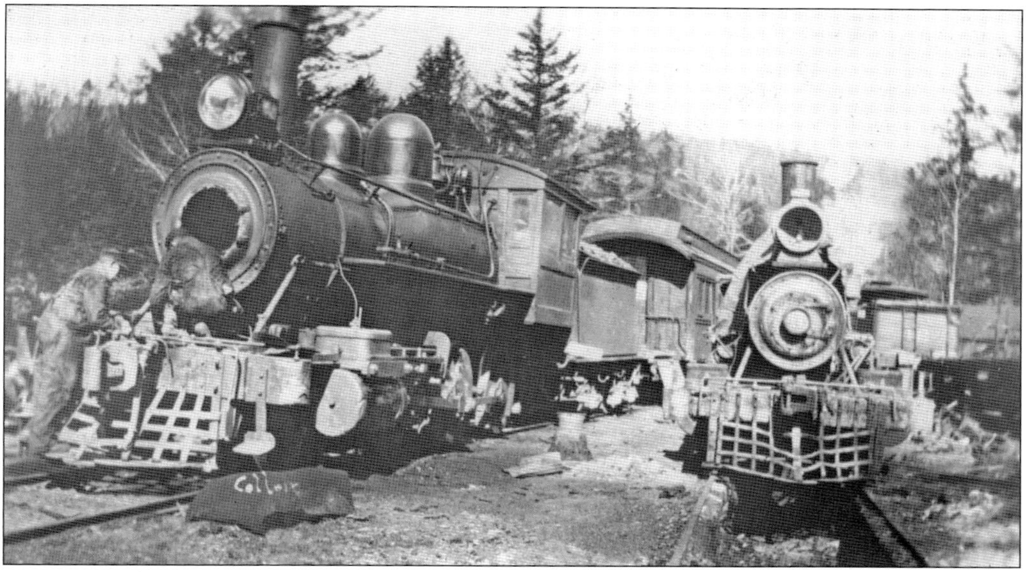

Incorporated on January 2, 1900, the Sheffield & Tionesta Railroad contained 16 miles of track spanning from Mayburg to Sheffield. These tracks ran through all the land that Teddy Collins owned but had been unable to conduct lumbering operations on due to a lack of lumber lines. Pictured is the Sheffield & Tionesta Railroad Porter engines No. 5 (left) and No. 6 in Kellettville.

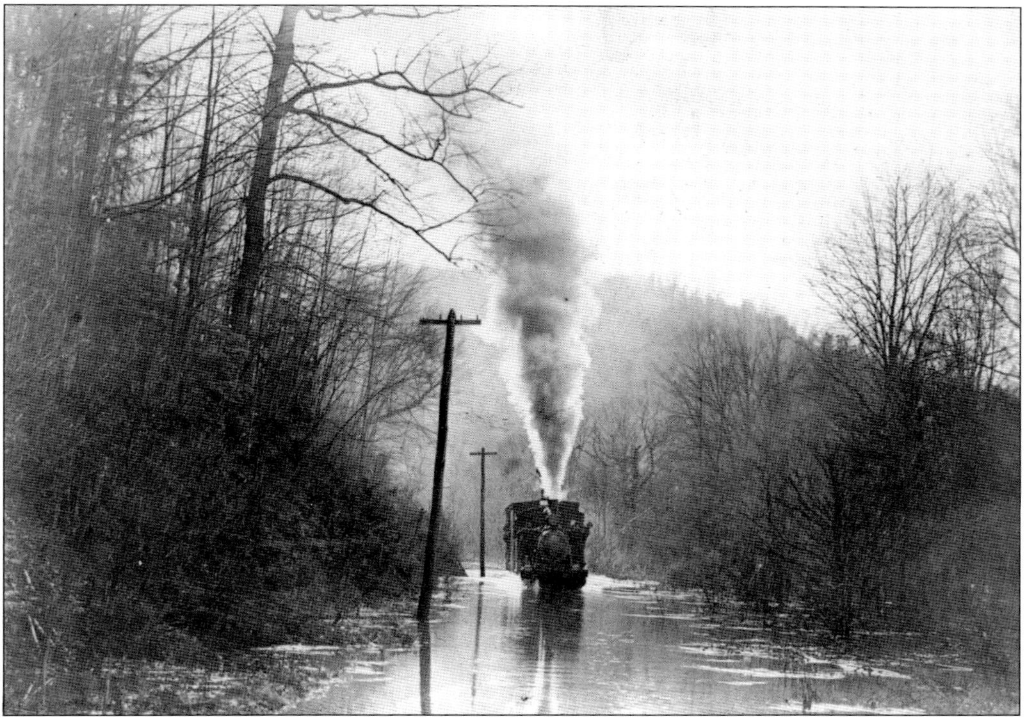

Balltown was primarily known for its oil until Isaac Ball and his partners William Manross and Luther Barnes constructed the first sawmill in 1823. Shown is the Sheffield & Tionesta Railroad Porter engine No. 5 as it travels along a flooded track near Tionesta Creek in Balltown. Crew members can be observed standing on the sides near the front of the engine looking for any signs of a washout.

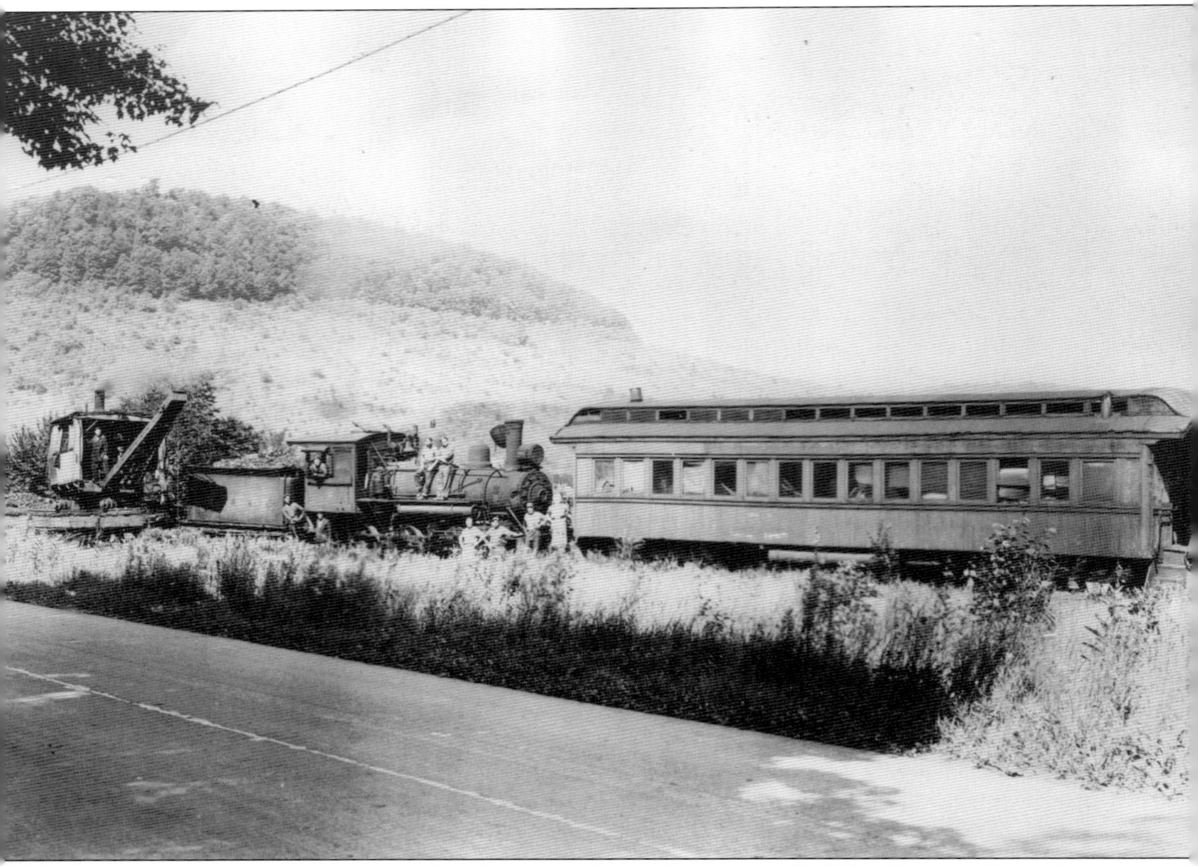

The Sheffield & Tionesta Railroad remained in operation until 1943, when track conditions became so deplorable that all operations had ceased on the railroad. By this time, only the Mayburg Chemical Company had been using the railroad. The closure of the tracks forced the chemical company out of business. Pictured is the Sheffield & Tionesta Railway engine No. 6 with a log loader to lift the track for scraps.

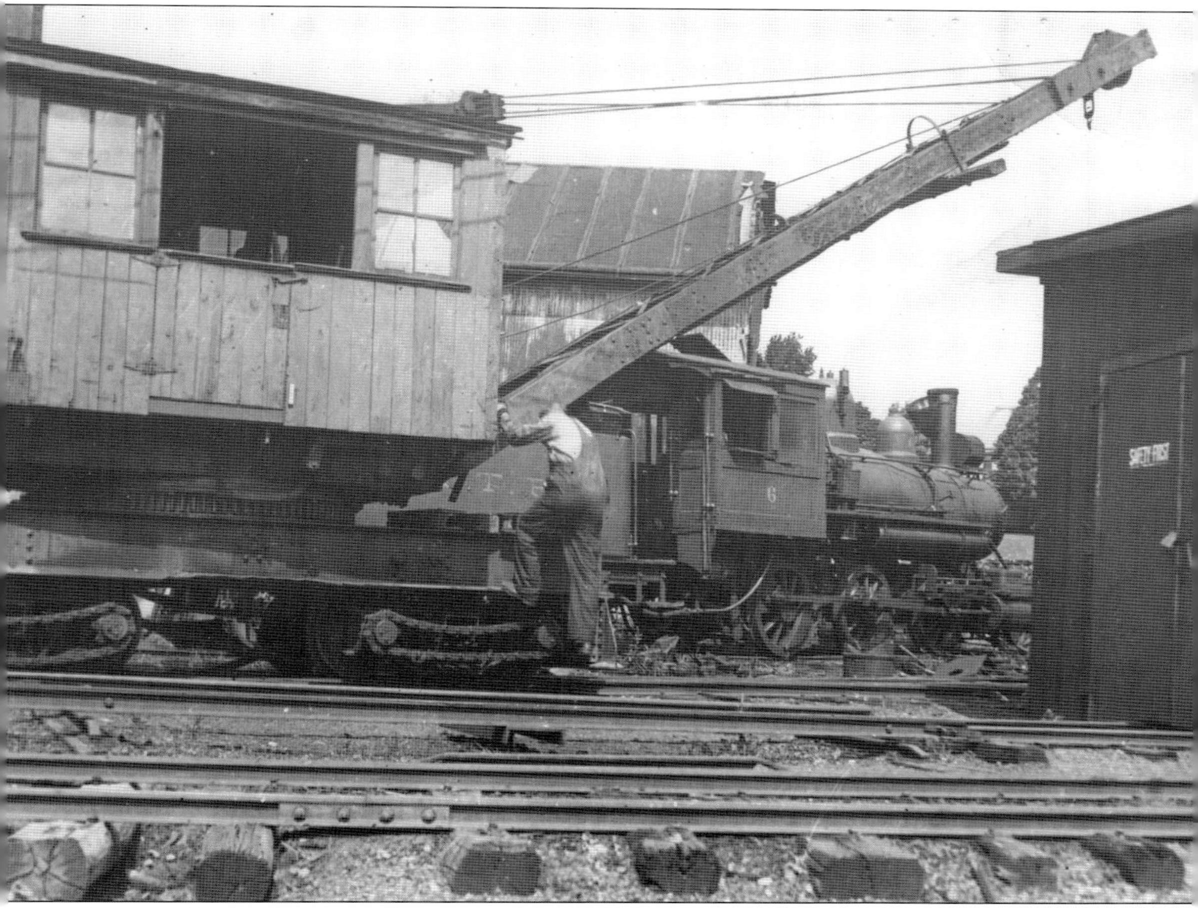

American log loaders were able to crawl from one log car to the next or operate with their own truck under them. During the logging years, very few loaders, like the one pictured, had a truck under the main compartment. Along with the loader are a railway worker and Sheffield & Tionesta Railroad engine No. 6 at a stop in Nebraska.

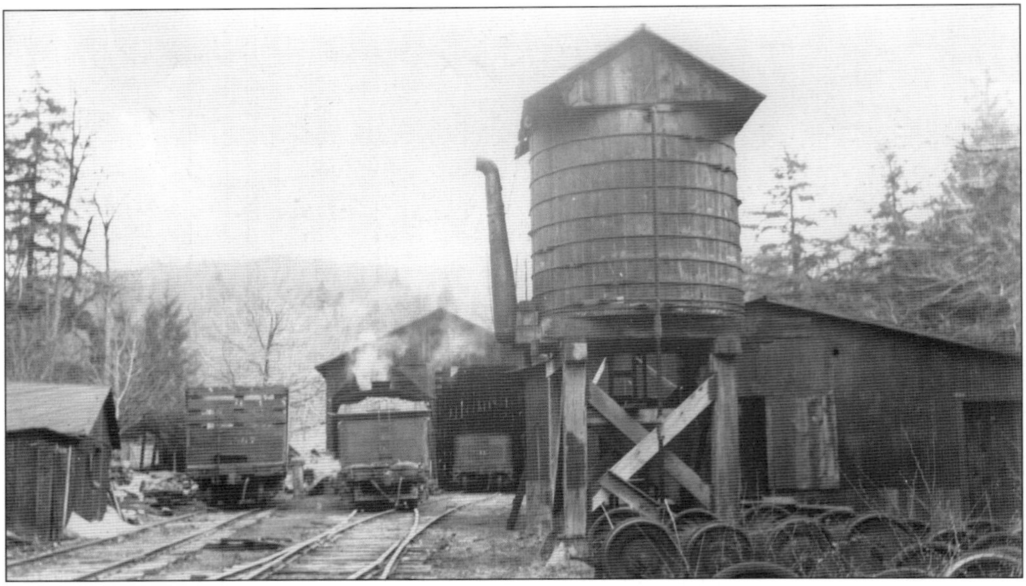

Shown in this photograph is the Sheffield & Tionesta Railway yard located in Nebraska. From left to right are the sand house, a lumber car hauling bark, two locomotives in the roundhouse, the railroad parts building, and the water tower.

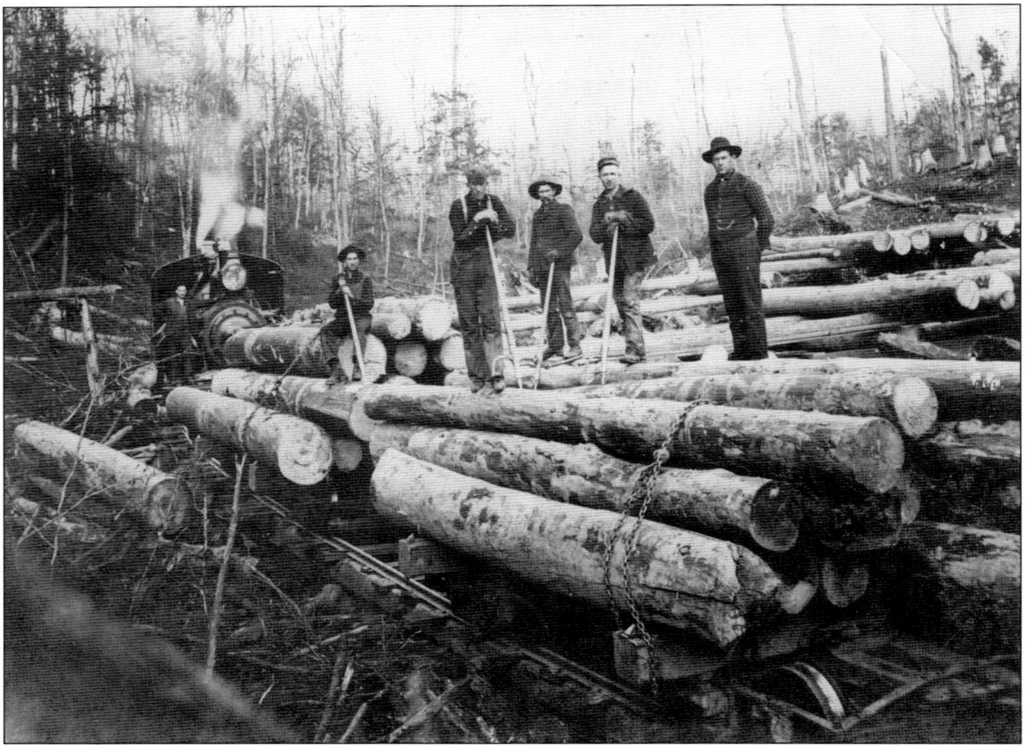

The early days of lumbering in Forest County were some of the most profitable in Pennsylvania due to the abundance of virgin old growth timber. Hemlocks (shown here) were stripped of their bark, which at that time was the primary source for tannin, used to cure leather.

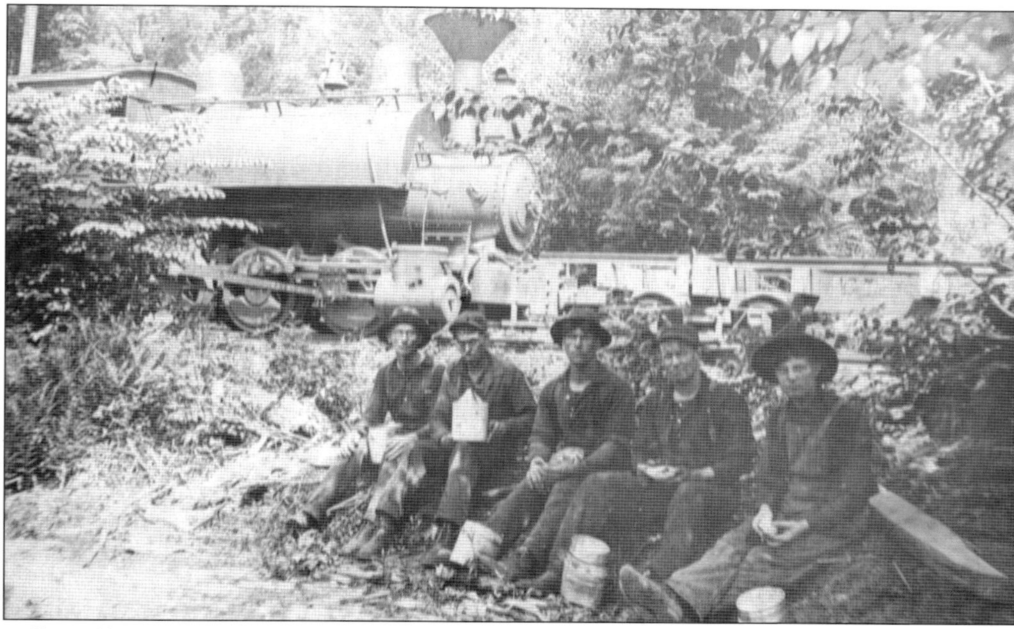

Kellettville continued to grow as Teddy Collins made massive improvements to the old and new Salmon Creek lumber mills, increasing the production of lumber immensely. Over the years, lumbering took its toll on the forested landscape, leaving only barren hillsides for miles on end. Laborers moved on, and the number of inhabitants in the town dwindled. By 1940, the decision to build Tionesta Dam caused the majority of the remaining residents to reluctantly vacate their beloved homesteads. Shown are mill workers taking a lunch break in 1909.

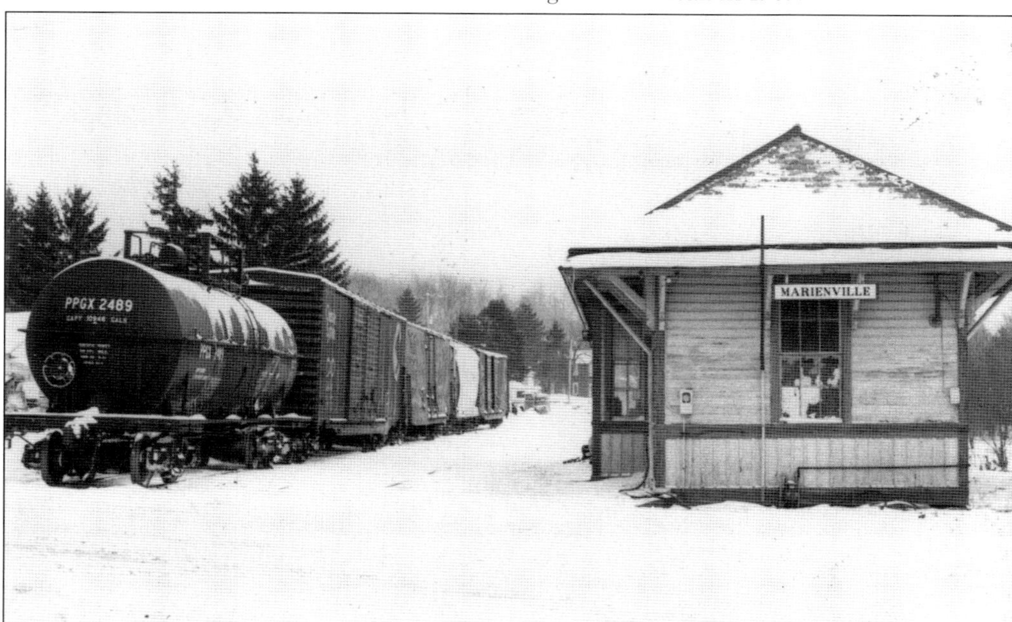

In 1881, tracks owned by the Pittsburgh, Bradford, & Buffalo Railroad were laid in Marienville to extend the lines to Kane and Mount Jewett. The Pittsburgh & Western Railroad purchased the line in 1883, and later sold it to the Baltimore & Ohio Railroad in 1890. The last passenger train rode on January 2, 1933, and the last mixed passenger train ran in 1937.

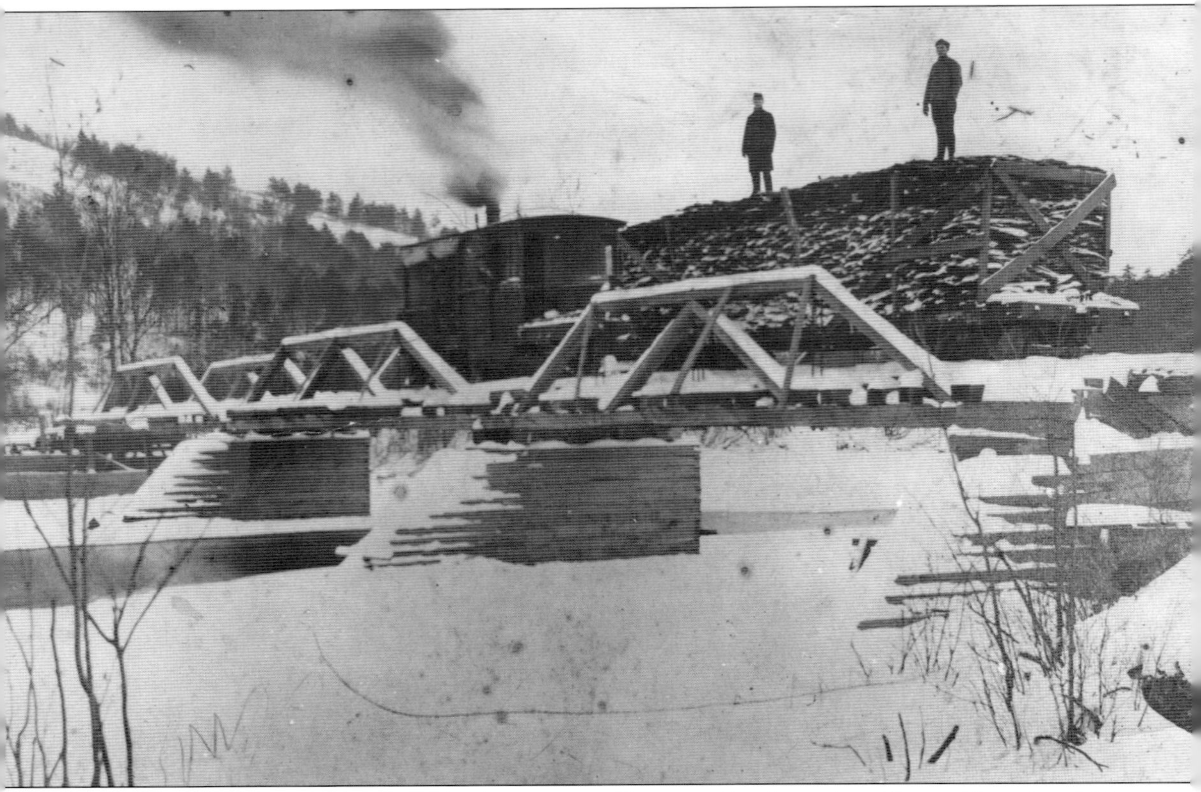

Pictured is the Lynch railroad bridge crossing Tionesta Creek in the village of Lynch, which was used extensively by the Blue Jay Lumber Company. An earlier, less stable bridge also crossed Tionesta Creek to provide transportation for vehicles and people. In 1948, a single-span Parker through truss bridge was established on Blue Jay Road and remained in place until 2010.

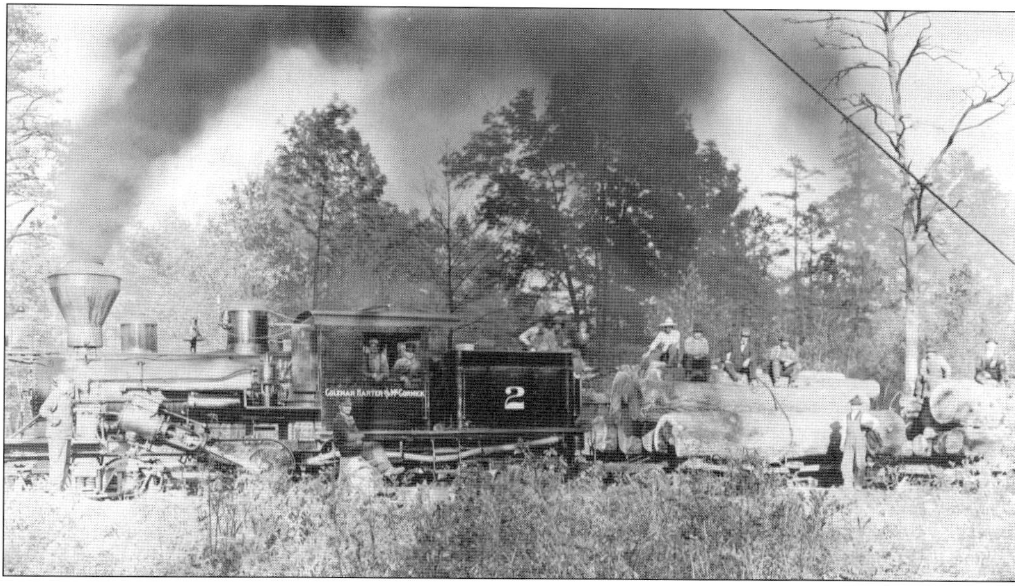

Pictured is the Coleman, Harter & McCormick train and crew around 1914 on Little Tionesta Creek. Water transportation became too slow for the flourishing lumber companies, and so many began to rely on the railroads to meet production and shipping requirements. A small tributary to the Allegheny River, Little Tionesta Creek was, and still is, a popular spot for fishing.

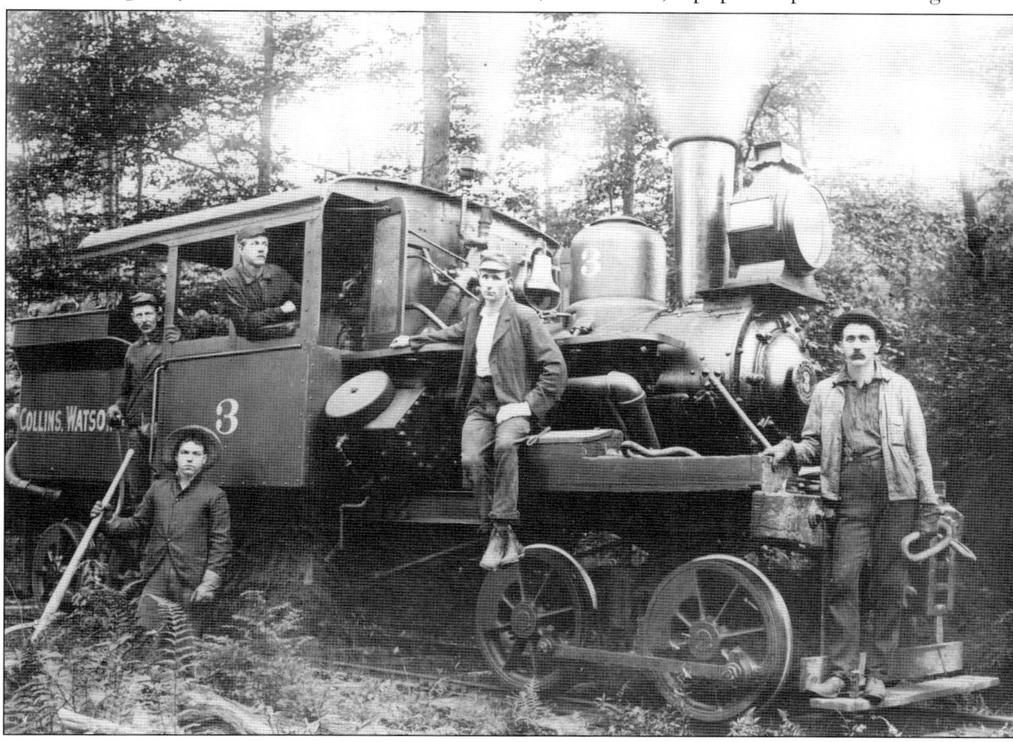

Taking a break from a long day's work in Golinza near Big Coon Creek are, from left to right, fireman James Trantman, (standing on ground) Ed Merchant, unidentified inside, J. Smith (sitting on engine), and Dan Tenstermaker. The locomotive is the Collins & Watson No. 3 and was the first of its kind in Golinza.

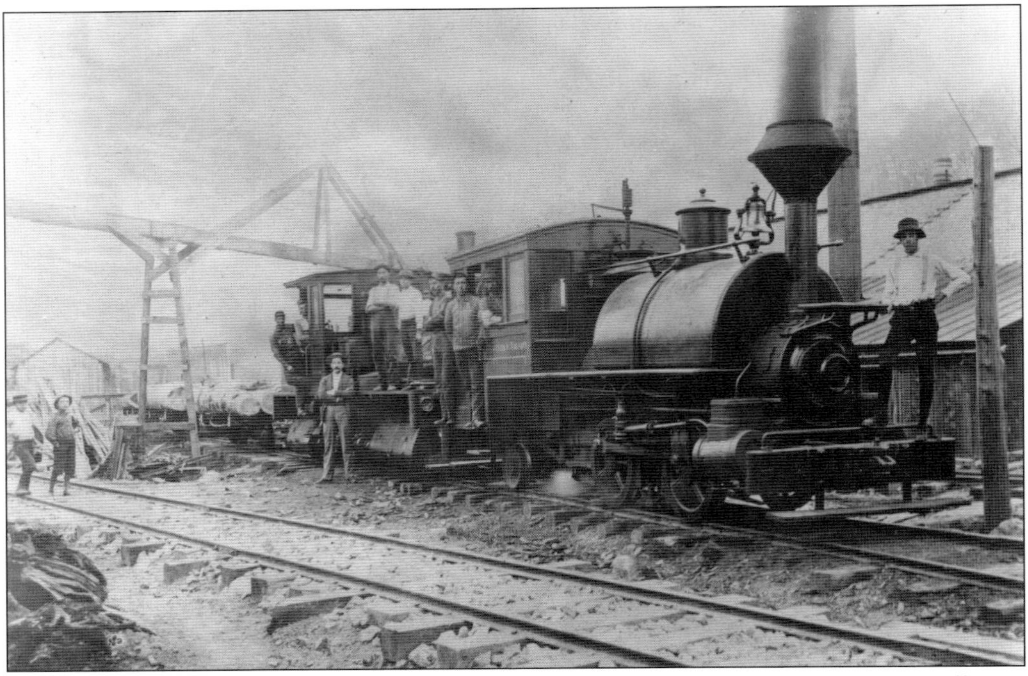

Photographed are two engines at the Wagner & Wilson Mill during the 1890s on West Millstone Creek just south of Marionville. The Porter engine is a CN 1085, and the Shay engine is a CN 447, both built around 1893. The company used three locomotives to navigate through 6,500 acres of forest during its 12 years of operation.

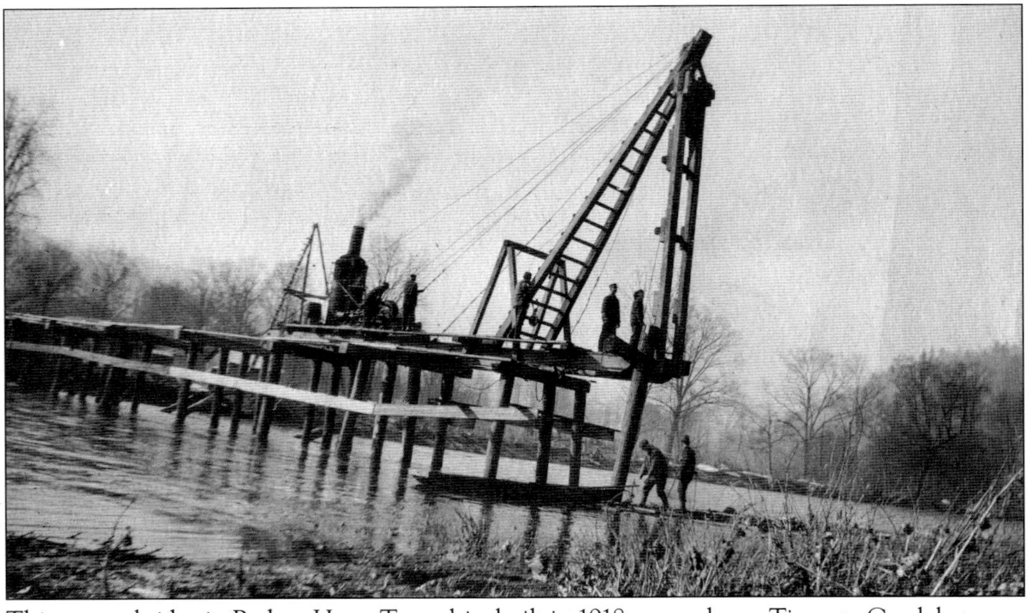

This wagon bridge in Porkey, Howe Township, built in 1918, crossed over Tionesta Creek between Balltown and Minister. The small town of Porkey is located between Balltown and Minister at the point where Porcupine Run flows into Tionesta Creek. Porkey was a small but active little town that contained three lumbering operations owned by Teddy Collins. Much of the community history was colorfully recorded by Otis Elmer Rupert (1868–1929), known as the "Porkey scribe."

Seven

Forest County Life

When the first settlers reached Forest County, whether on foot, by boat, or on horseback, these early pioneers had their work cut out for them. Some saw potential in the untouched region, while others chose to keep on moving. Those who stayed were able to tap into the potential of the land and build anything from a small family farm to a giant lumber empire. When industry began to boom, so did the population. People from all walks of life and locations came to the area for employment and a fresh start. Those savvy enough to become entrepreneurs found a wide-open socioeconomic platform to build upon. It was certainly exciting days. But with excitement also came tragedy. Without an organized law enforcement or fire department, crime and fire damage were rampant. Without proper medical facilities, the slightest ailment could become deadly. And where would food, water, and common supplies come from? Well, these rugged pioneers had a plan and quickly worked to implement a functioning society. Families and friends began organizing churches, schools, mercantile stores, factories, medical centers, governments, post offices, and anything else they found a need for. Even the children pitched in to help on the family farm or family store in hopes of one day running the business themselves. From all these aspirations and the industrial giants operating throughout the region, the rough wilds were soon transforming, or rather beginning to coexist, with a more civilized way of life.

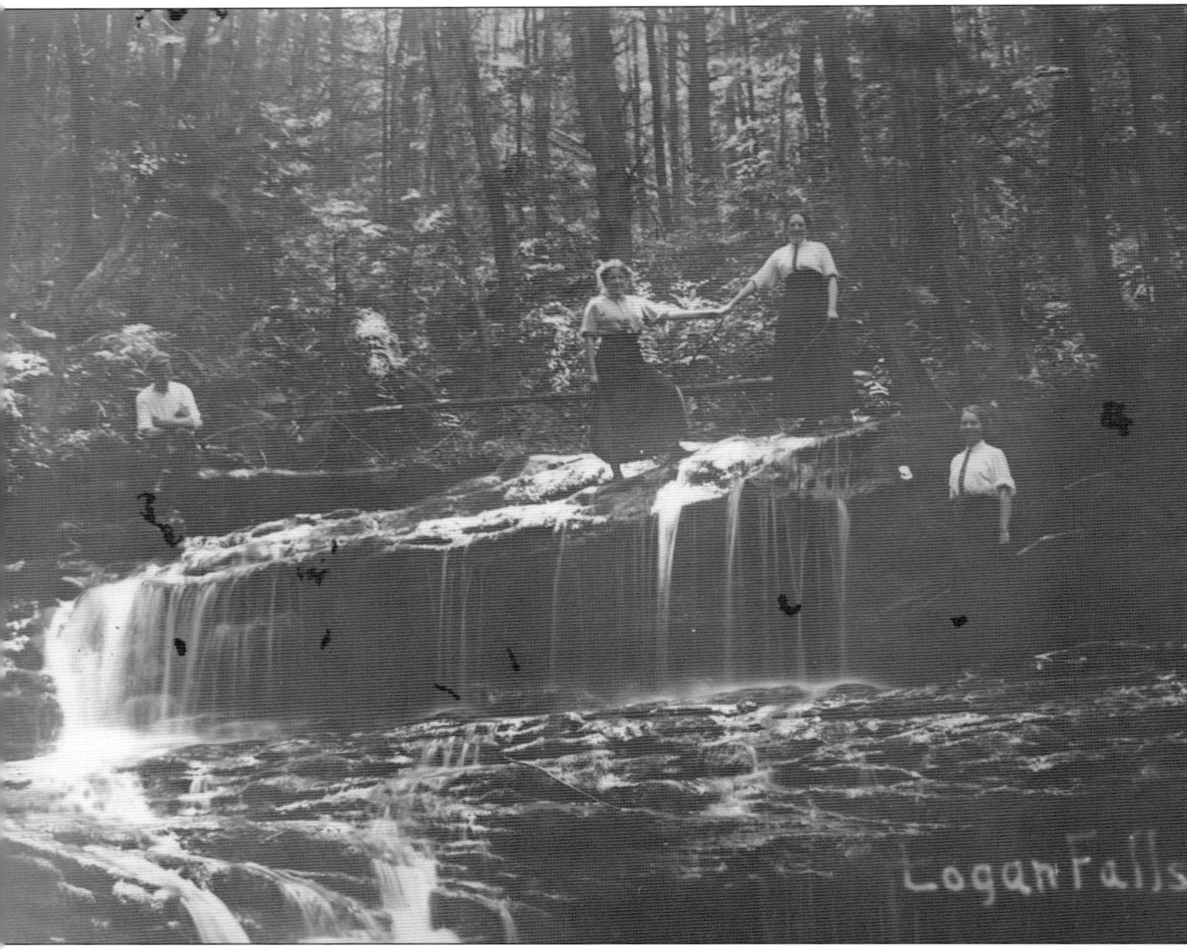

Posing for this photograph are three women and a man at Logan Falls in Balltown. Standing just nine feet tall, the falls seem to be considerably larger when seen from a distance. They were created by majestic rock formations that came to rest here thousands of years ago. Tionesta Creek flows one mile away.

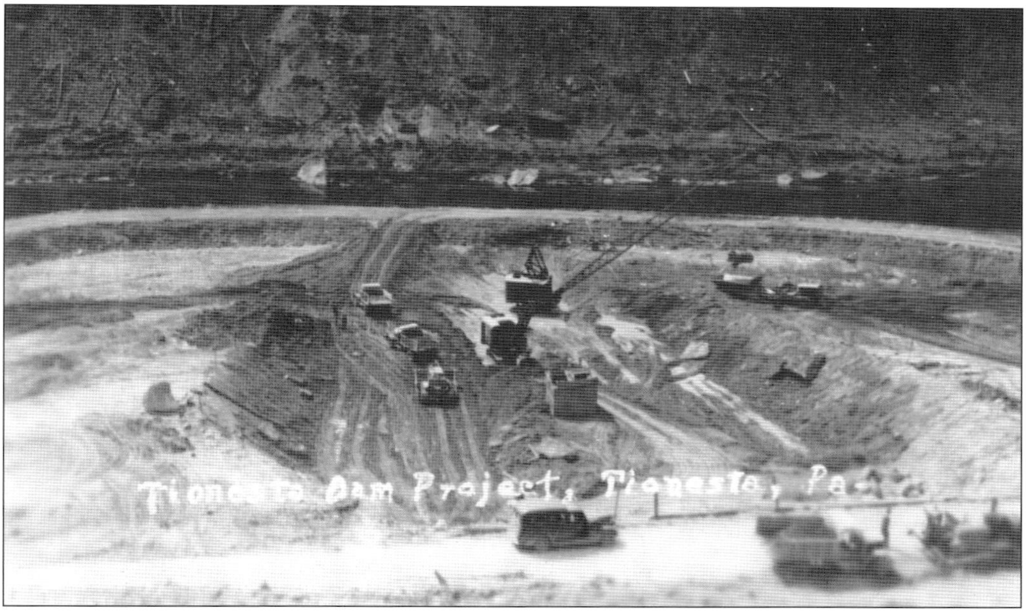

Due to the March 1936 flooding of Tionesta Creek, the US Army Corps of Engineers put together a plan in early 1938 to create a flood control system. On May 3, 1938, S.J. Goves and Sons, along with Lundin Brothers of Minnesota, began construction on the Tionesta Dam. The operation was complete on January 9, 1941, and subsequently caused the desertion of Kellettville, Newtown, Nebraska, and parts of the Sheffield & Tionesta Railroad.

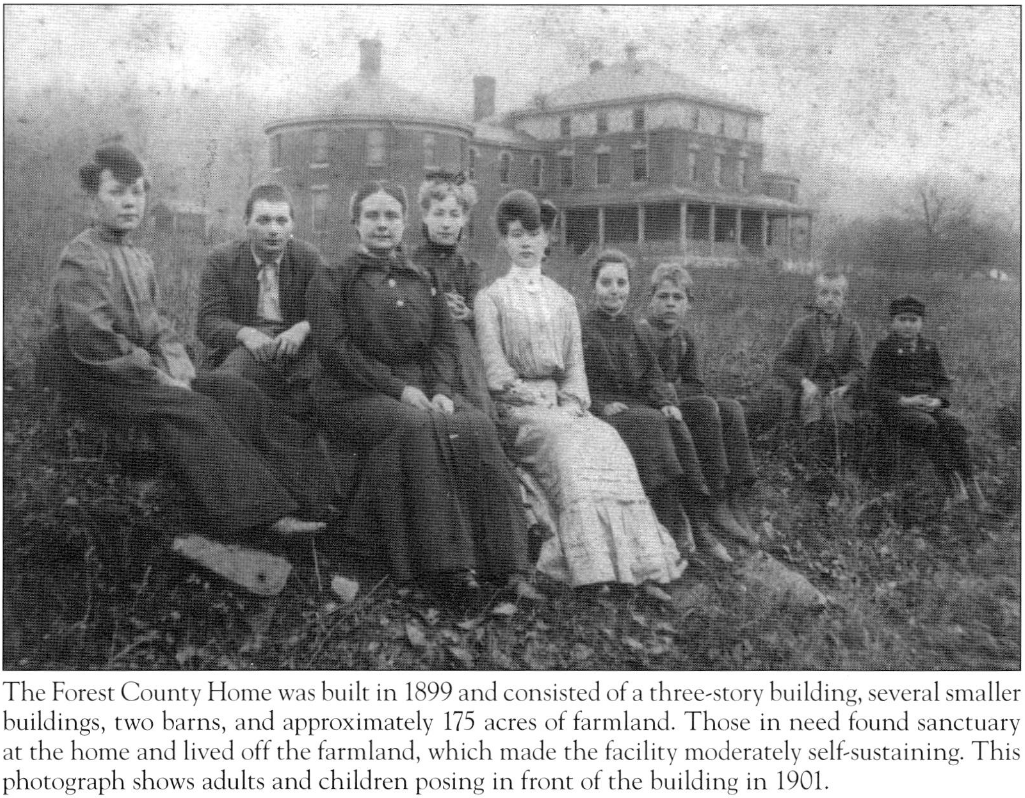

The Forest County Home was built in 1899 and consisted of a three-story building, several smaller buildings, two barns, and approximately 175 acres of farmland. Those in need found sanctuary at the home and lived off the farmland, which made the facility moderately self-sustaining. This photograph shows adults and children posing in front of the building in 1901.

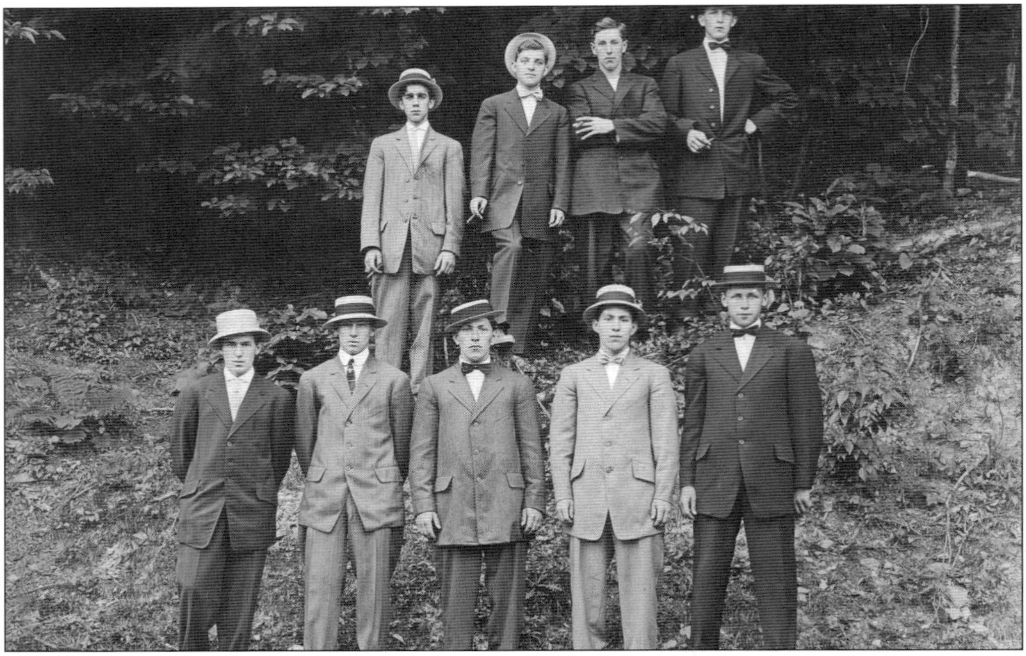

Residents of Forest County pose along the beautiful forest landscape in 1911. From left to right are (first row) Walter Wilson, Sherman Butler, Ivan Caubough, Rolland ?, and Harold Fritzgerald; (second row) Ed Barrett, Howard Watson, Glen Shaw, and Willis Dunkle.

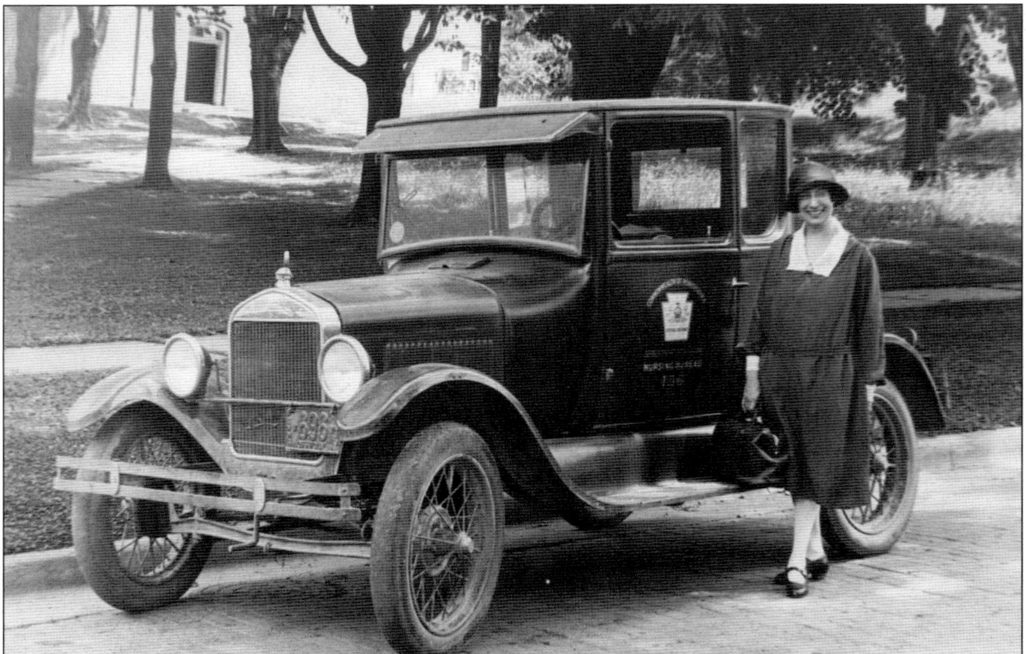

Physicians have occupied the Forest County area since the early 1800s when the logging industry began to boom. Nurses, doctors, and dentists made themselves available day and night to keep the population in good health. Posing for a photograph in 1927 is Edna Tobey, a Forest County nurse, standing next to Nursing Bureau vehicle No. 156.

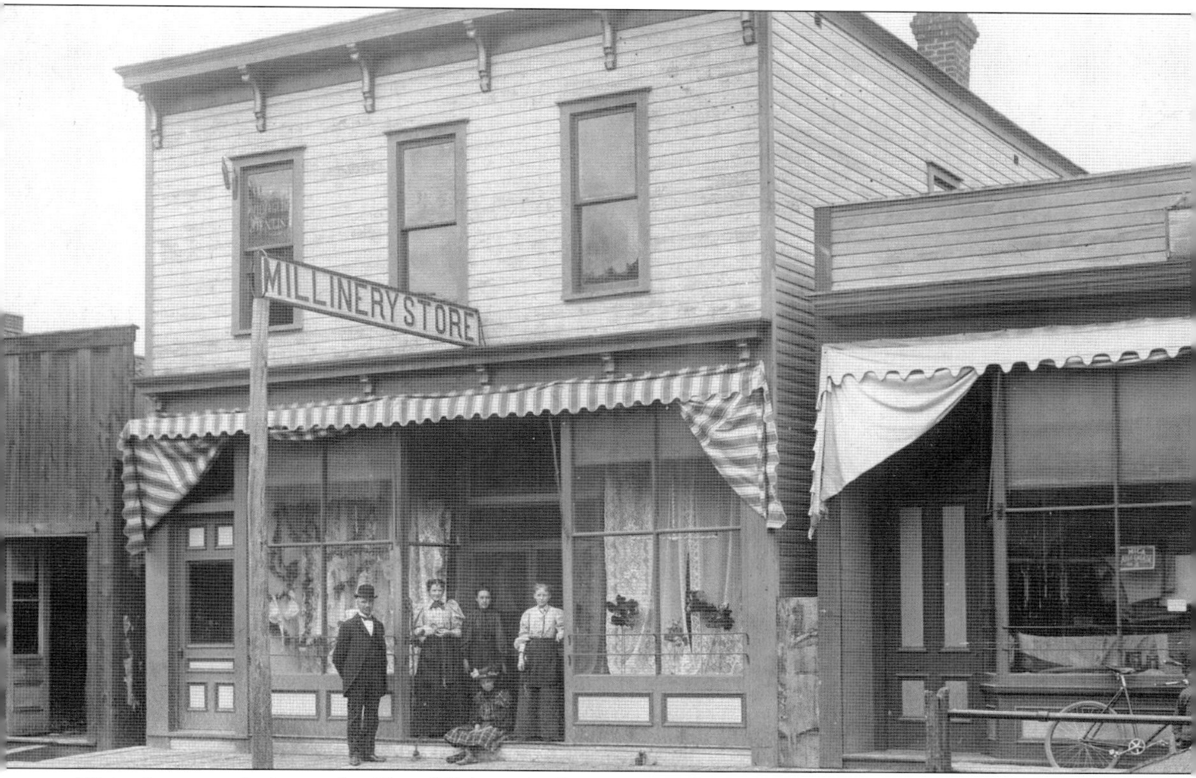

This photograph shows the Flora Walters & Company millinery & ladies furnishing goods store in October 1893. From left to right are (standing) unidentified and store owners Flora Walters, Euretta Proper, and Effa Walters. The woman sitting and the boy on the far right are unidentified. In September 1926, the building was sold and transformed into a residence on the second floor and a pool hall on the first floor.

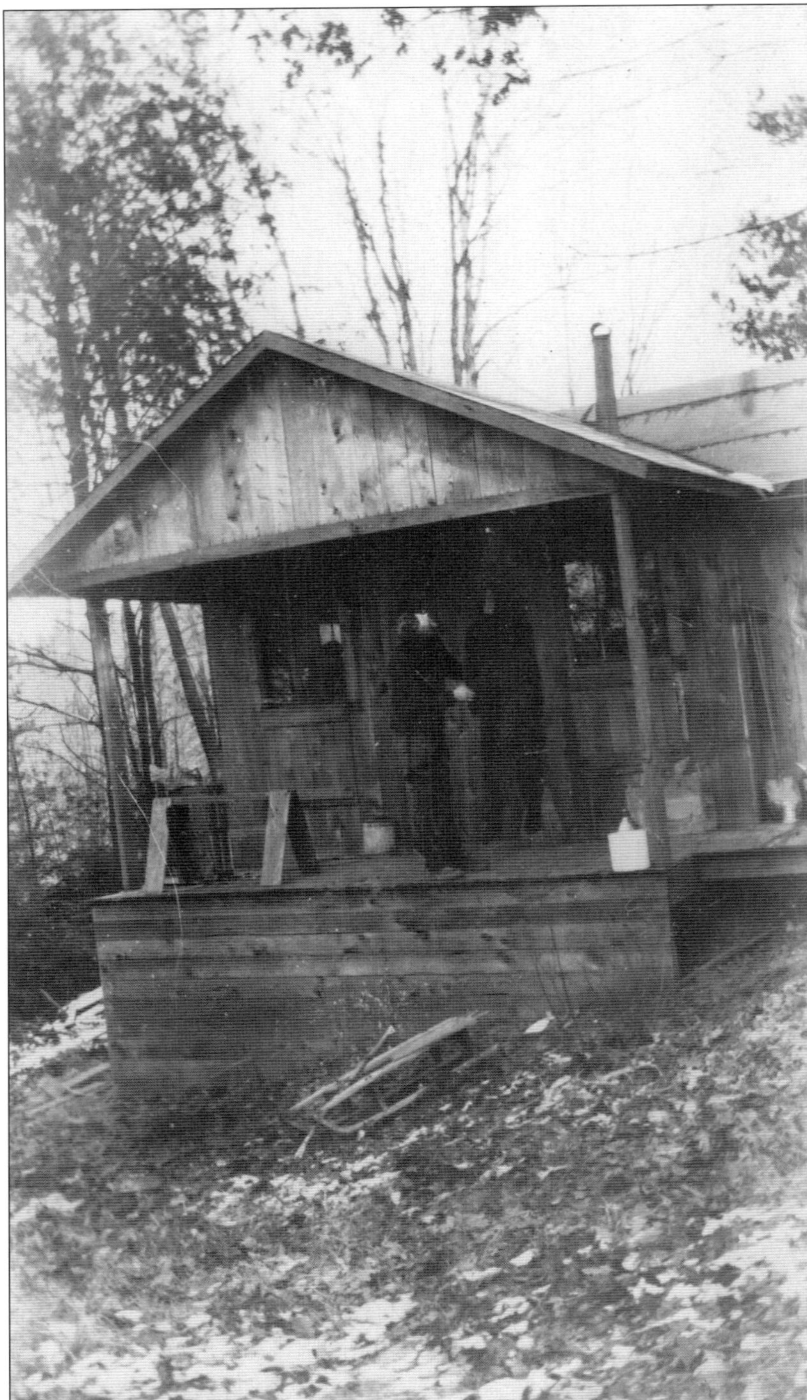

With over 430 square miles of land and water, Forest County plays host to beautiful scenery, excellent hunting locations, and unlimited year-round adventures. Although it is the third-least populated county in Pennsylvania, at one point, Forest County was dotted with many small camps, such as the Beatty camp shown here.

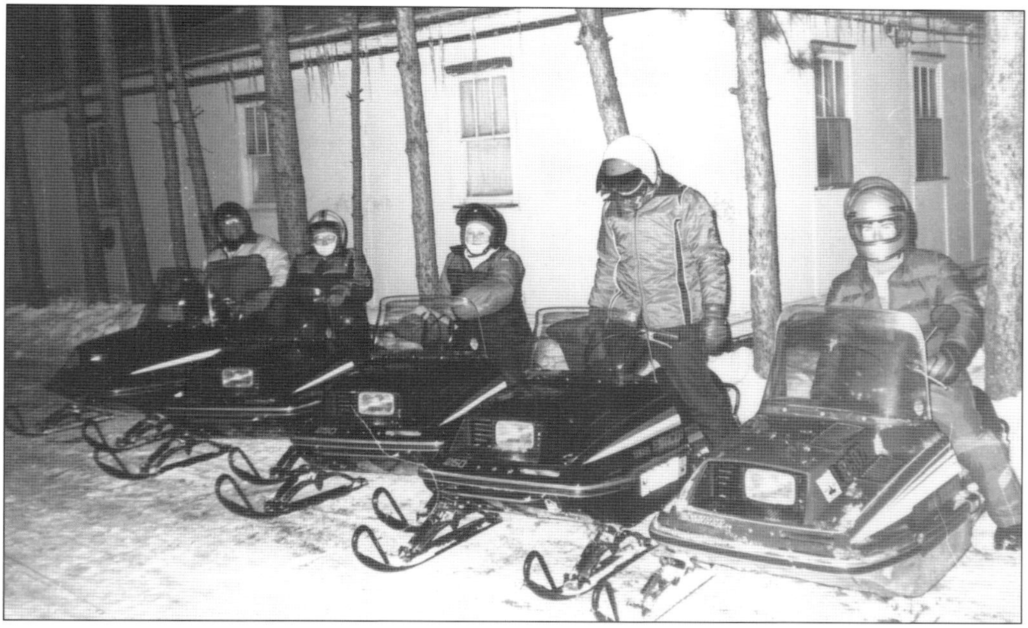

Due to the beautiful mountainous landscape found in Marienville and throughout Forest County, snowmobile riding is a popular activity during the snowy winter months. Rivaling any major sporting event, 20,000 people endured the freezing cold temperatures to watch the Marienville Area Civic Association's (MACA) third annual MACA Cup Hi Point Championship snowmobile races on January 13, 1971.

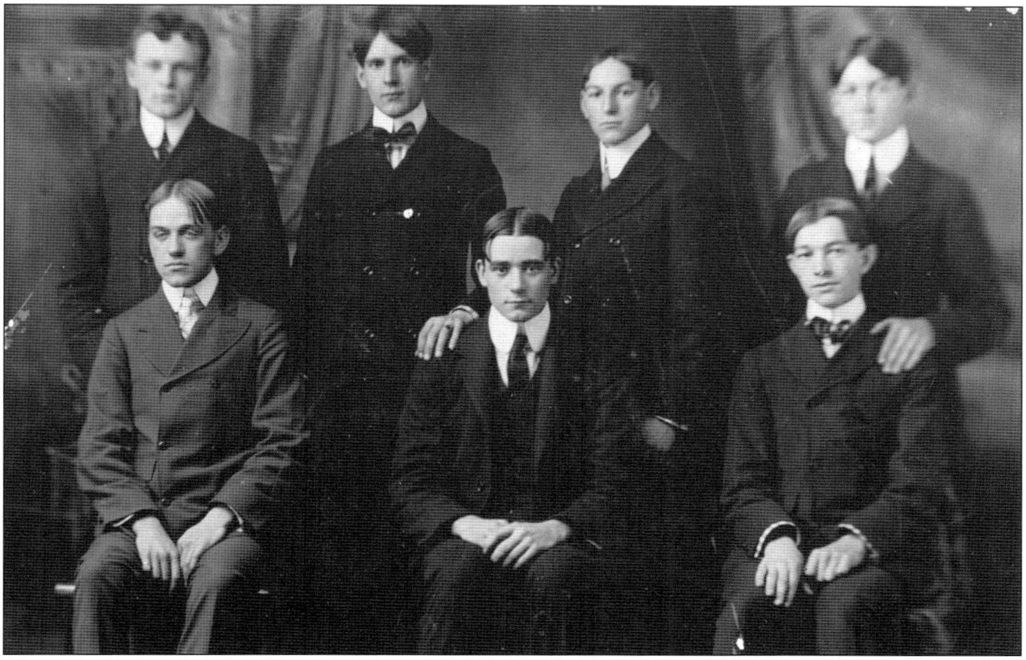

Many descendants of the first settlers remain in the county, where today some are educators, builders, and business owners. Pictured in this undated photograph are, from left to right, (seated) Paul Clark, Gordon Haslett, and Louie Swanson; (standing) Carl Neuk, Archie Holeman, Charles Jamieson, and John Lawrence.

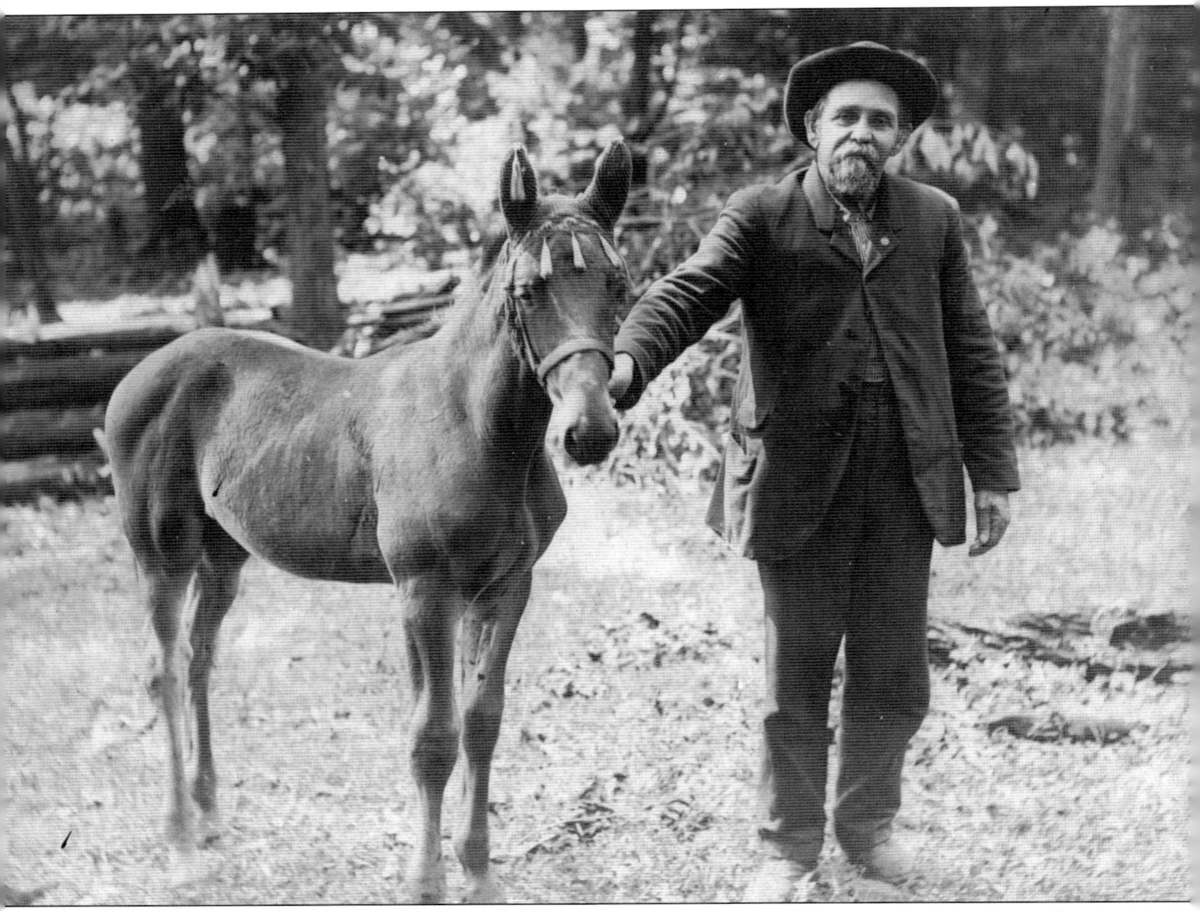

In 1862, at the age of 22, John Berlin enlisted in the 83rd Regiment, Company G of the Pennsylvania Volunteers. Private Berlin was wounded at the battle of Laurel Hill, Virginia, taken prisoner, and secured in both Libby Prison and Richmond Hospital. In 1864, he came to Forest County and worked in the lumber business, later serving as an officer inspector in Kingsley Township, where he made his home on the family farm with his wife, Lavina L. (Beck), and their five children.

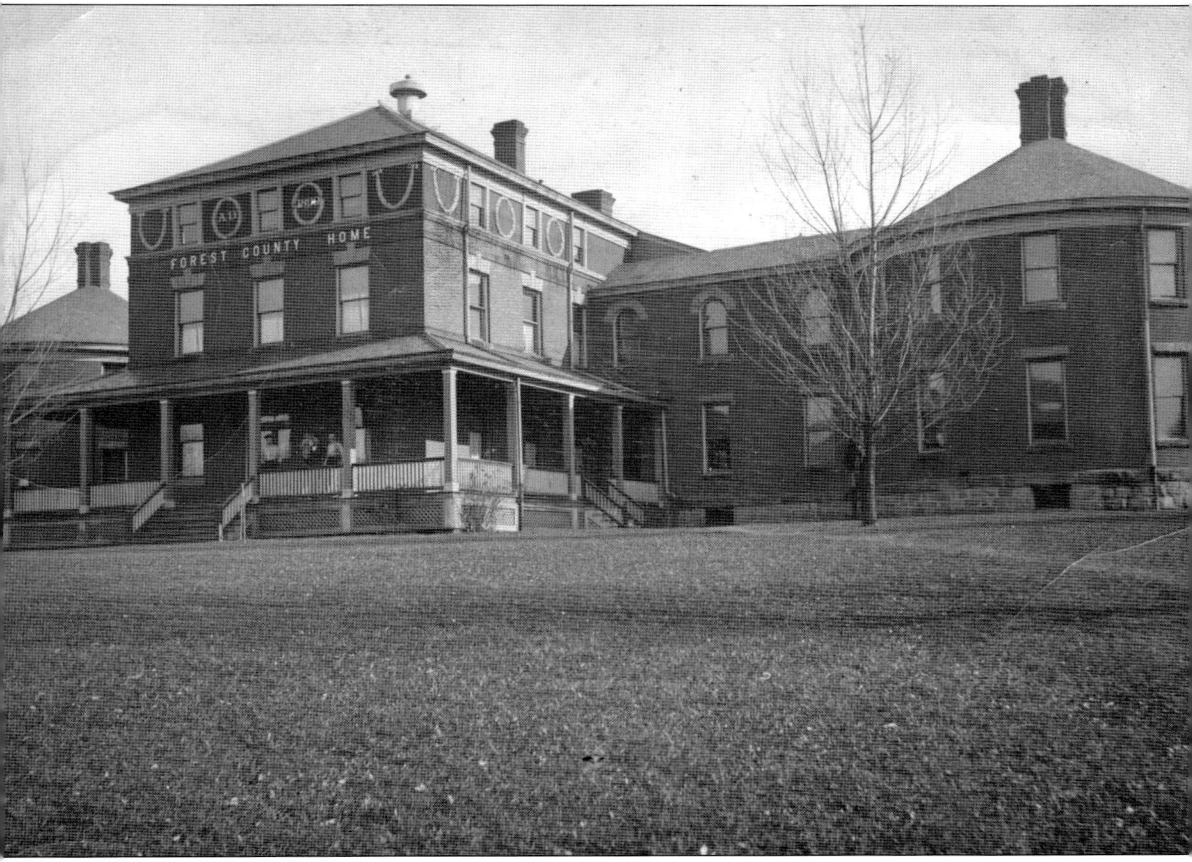

In 1956, the Forest County Home was closed due to funding issues and the increasing costs of operation. Hubert Saxon bought the property in 1959 and used it for a beef cattle business until it was sold to James Foreman in 1962 for $50,000 and remained open until being demolished in 1970. The West Forest School Board acquired 44.7 acres of the land for a new high school.

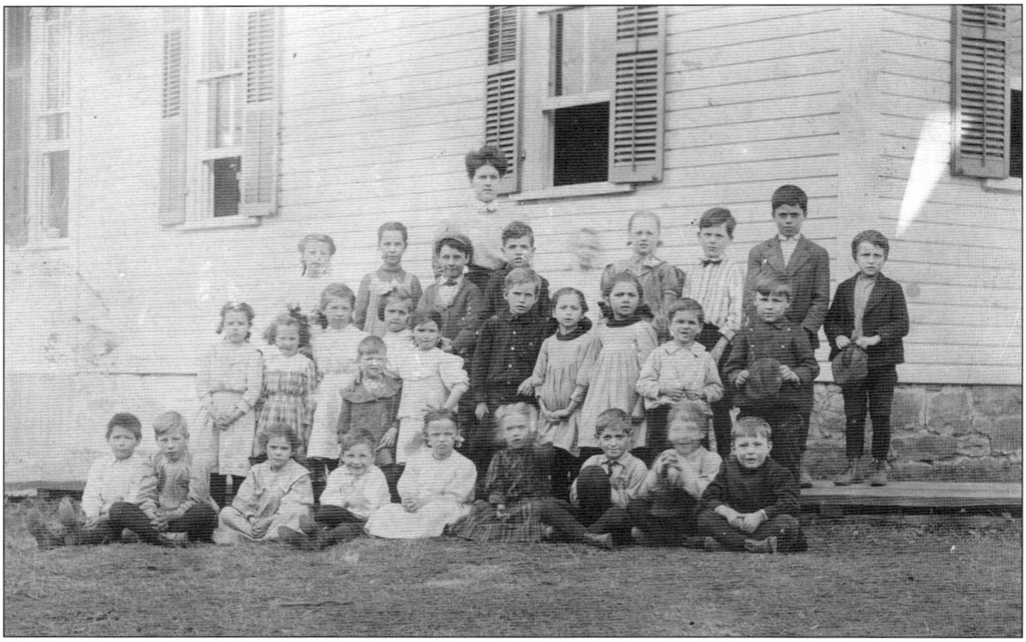

As the lumber industry continued to grow in the mid-1800s through the early 1900s, many more families found themselves settling down in the area. With society greatly expanding, schools needed to be built to accommodate the increasing population. Pictured in this undated photograph are children from the Mayburg School.

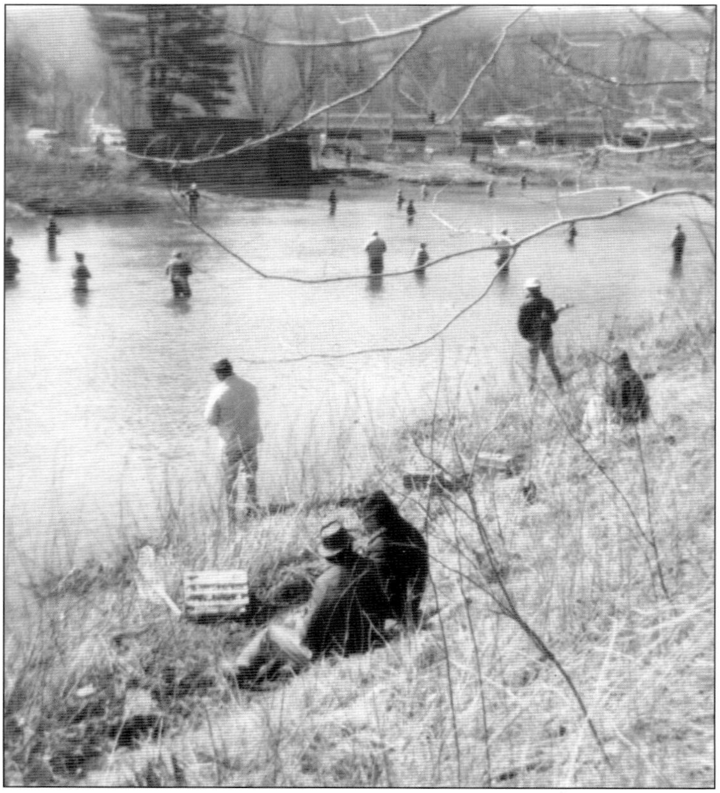

Tionesta Creek flows between the rugged terrain and into the wooded areas of Forest County while acting as the primary source to the Allegheny River. Originally named Tummeahanna by the Munsey Indians, which means Wolf Stream, the creek has also been referred to as Squirrel Creek by the Indians. From the times of the early settlers to now, the creek remains a popular recreational and fishing location.

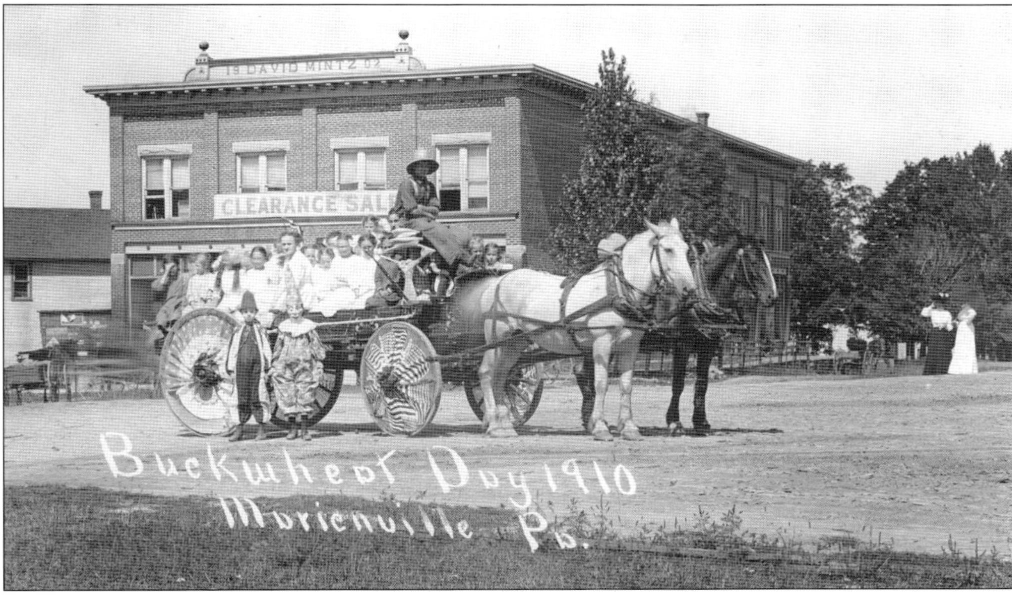

The Buckwheat Club's picnic and parade were celebrated in the early 1900s as Buckwheat Day, which brought games, sports, parades, and other exciting events. Parade participants stop for a photograph in front of the David Mintz department store in 1910.

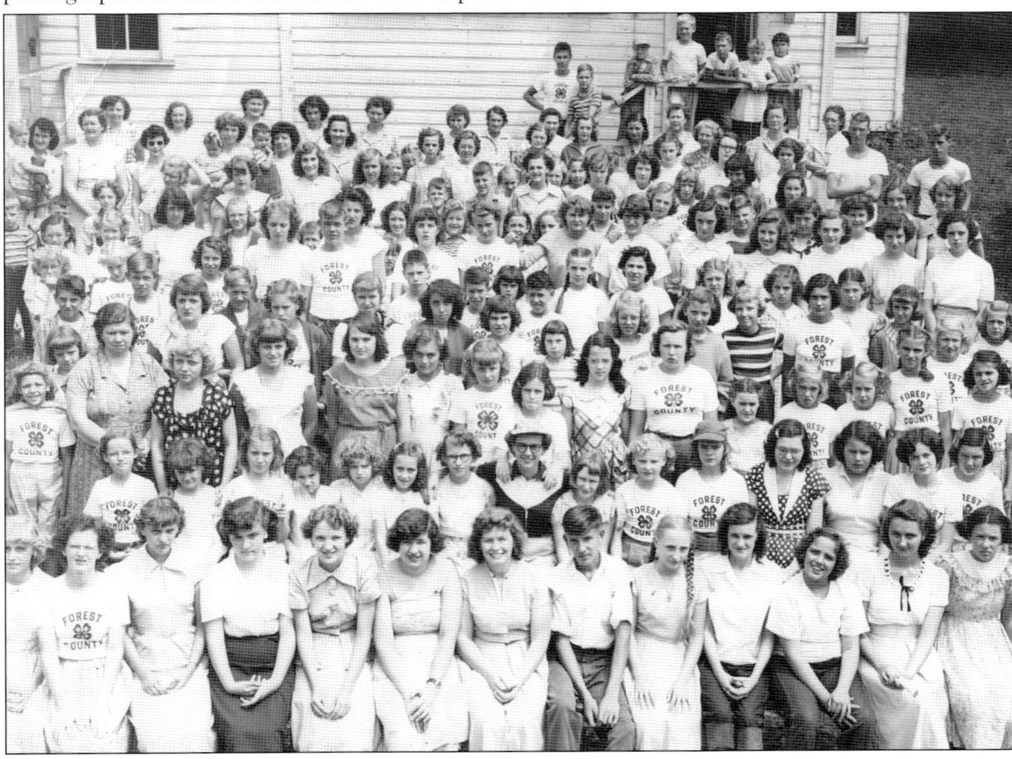

The Forest County 4-H Club began on May 8, 1946, with Pres. Faith Watson and Vice Pres. Helen Childs. Pictured is a group photograph of the club at the Duhring CCC Camp in the 1950s. The Duhring camp began in 1933 and was used as a German prisoner-of-war camp until the end of World War II.

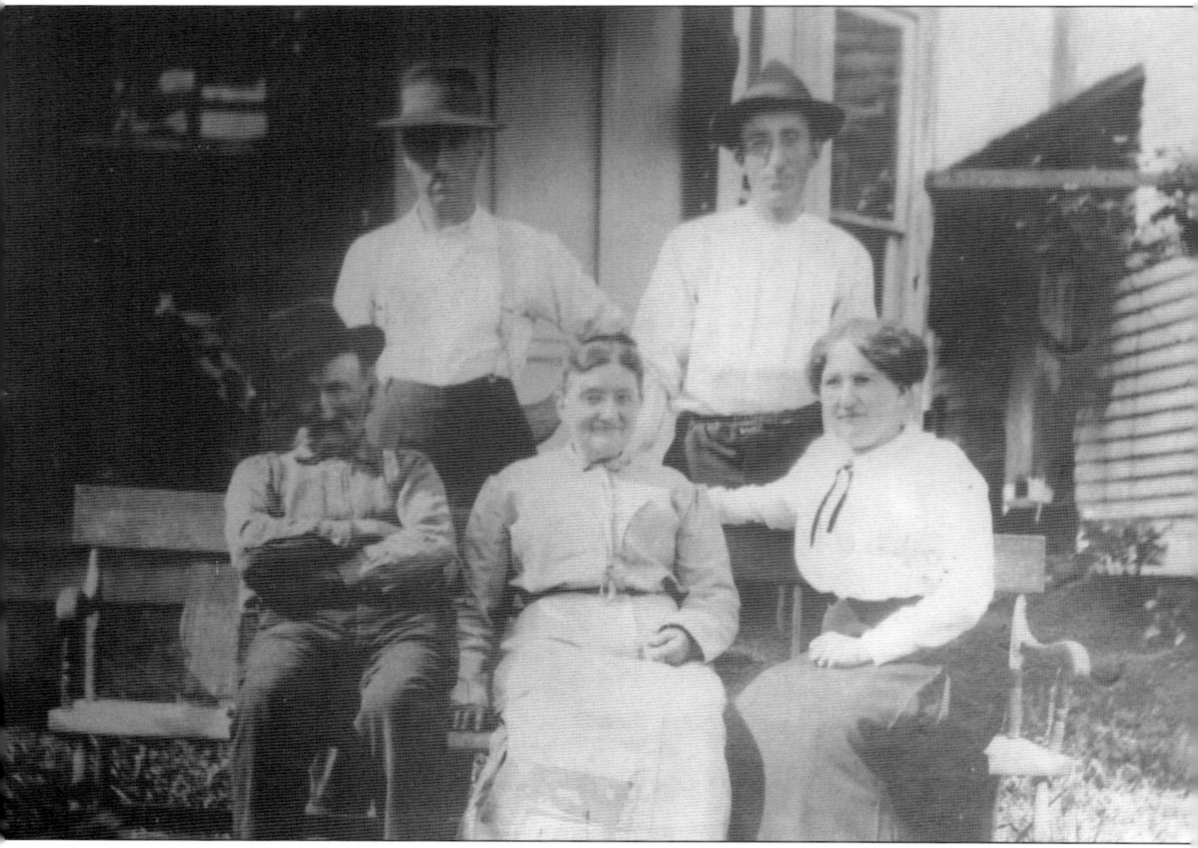

On May 17, 1785, Lt. John Range Sr. was given a generous land warrant of 285 acres on the east bank of the Allegheny as payment for his service in the Revolutionary War. This land is where Tionesta Borough stands today. Pictured here are some of his descendants, from left to right, (first row) Martin Leonard Range, Susanna (Heckman) Range, and Belle Range; (second row) Jay Range and Lawrence Range.

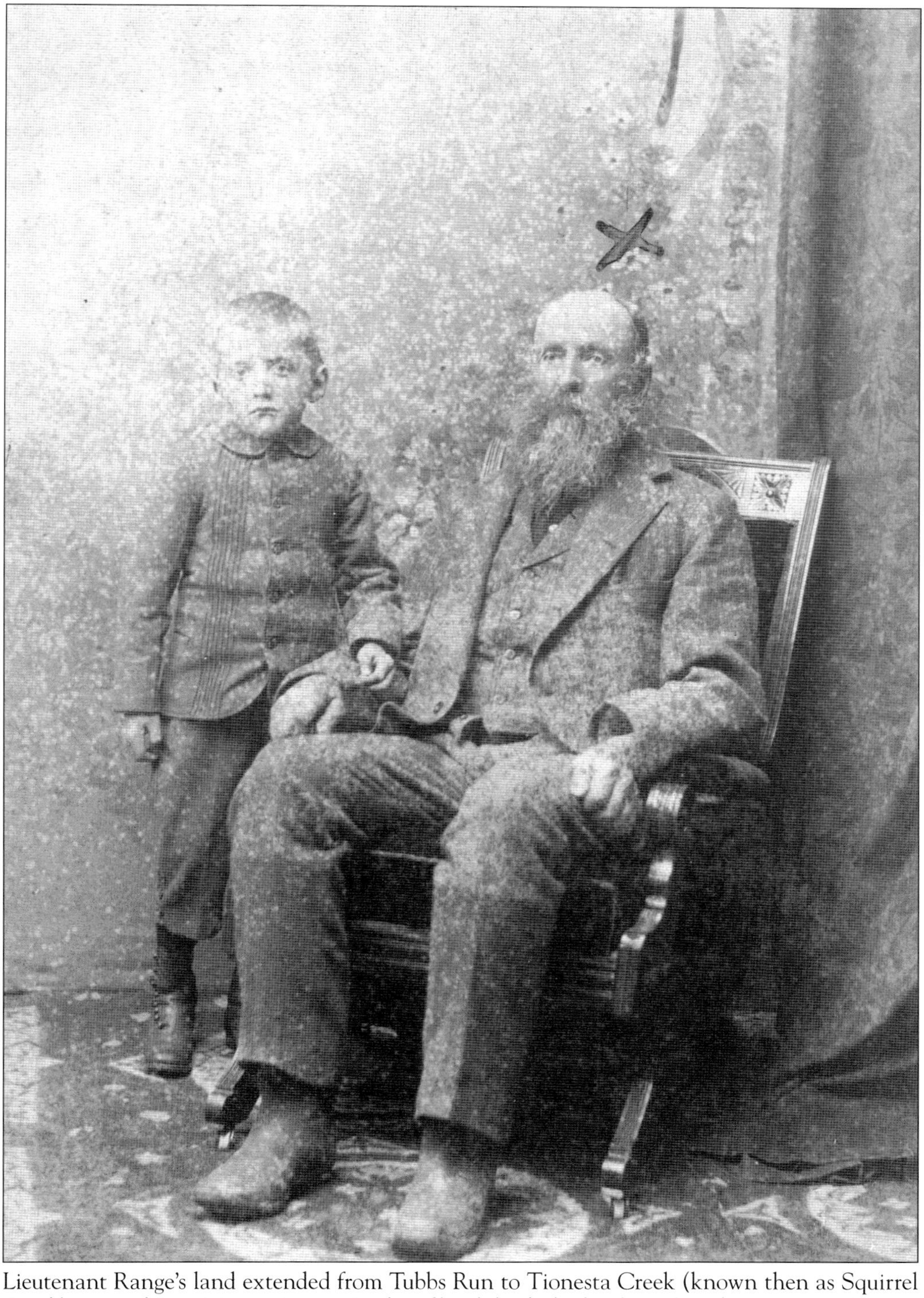

Lieutenant Range's land extended from Tubbs Run to Tionesta Creek (known then as Squirrel Creek) situated near Mount Ararat. In the official deed, the land is referred to as "Saqualinget," the Native American name meaning "Place of Council." It was known by this name until 1797. Lieutenant Range's grandson Jacob Ingersol Range and his wife, Anne, had five children. Jacob is pictured here with his son Martin Leonard Range in 1855.

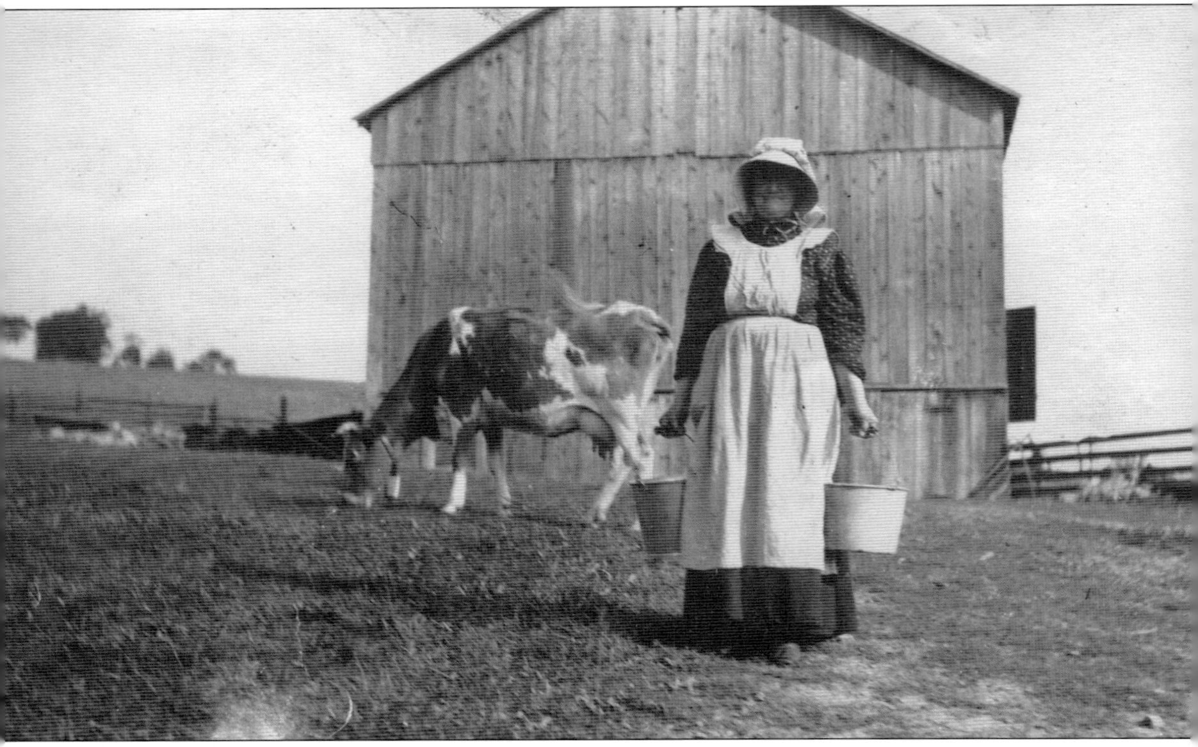

Pictured is Susanna (Heckman) Range tending to the cows at the homestead on Stewart Run. She and her husband, Martin Leonard Range, lived on a share of land called Dawson farm. In 1861, an oil well on the farm was revived using an explosive device called a torpedo. It turned out to be a modest producer. Stewart Run lies on the west bank of the Allegheny in Harmony Township.

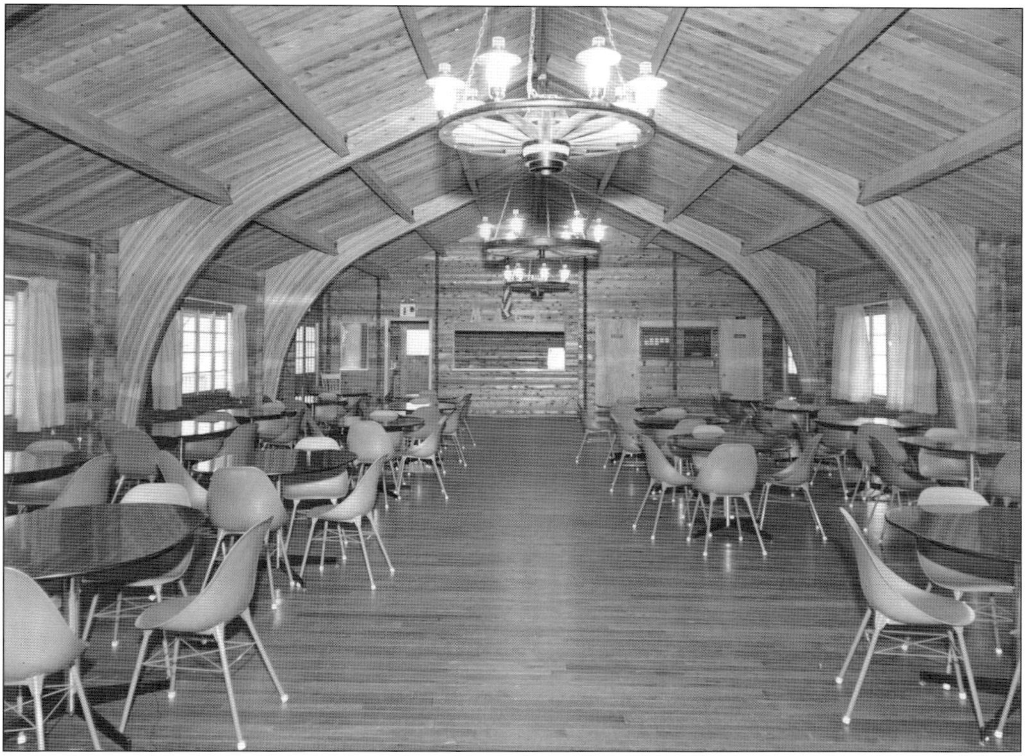

In 1967, the Marienville Area Civic Association (MACA) began through the efforts of seven local businessmen in order to provide an organization for community events. Funds were raised through this organization, which allowed for a community center, swimming pool, park, and medical center to be built. Shown is the inside of the MACA Park Building.

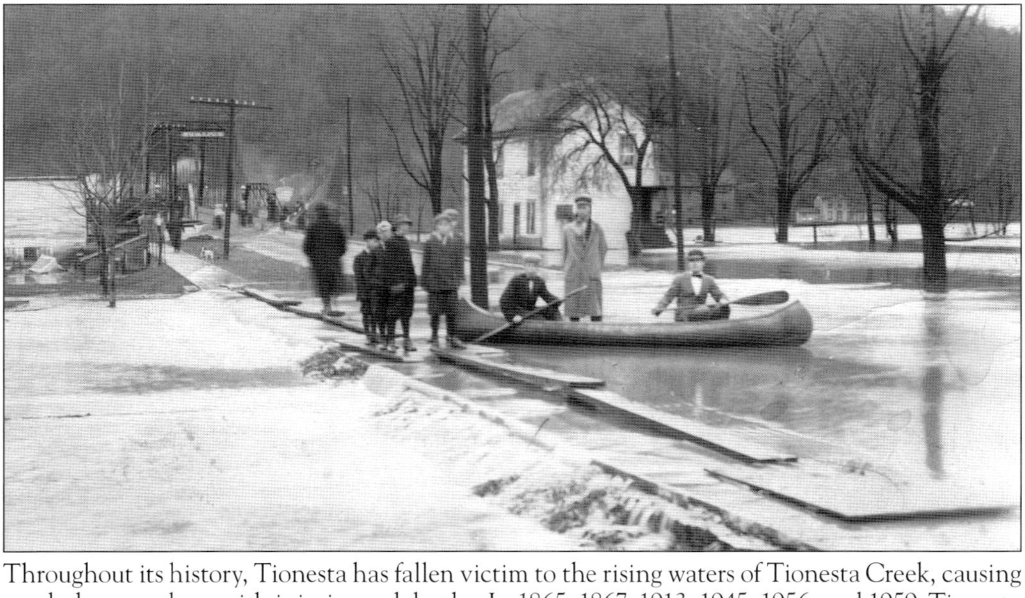

Throughout its history, Tionesta has fallen victim to the rising waters of Tionesta Creek, causing much damage along with injuries and deaths. In 1865, 1867, 1913, 1945, 1956, and 1959, Tionesta Creek rose several feet, leading many to be evacuated. This photograph from the March 25, 1913, flood shows Tionesta residents in a canoe on Bridge Street.

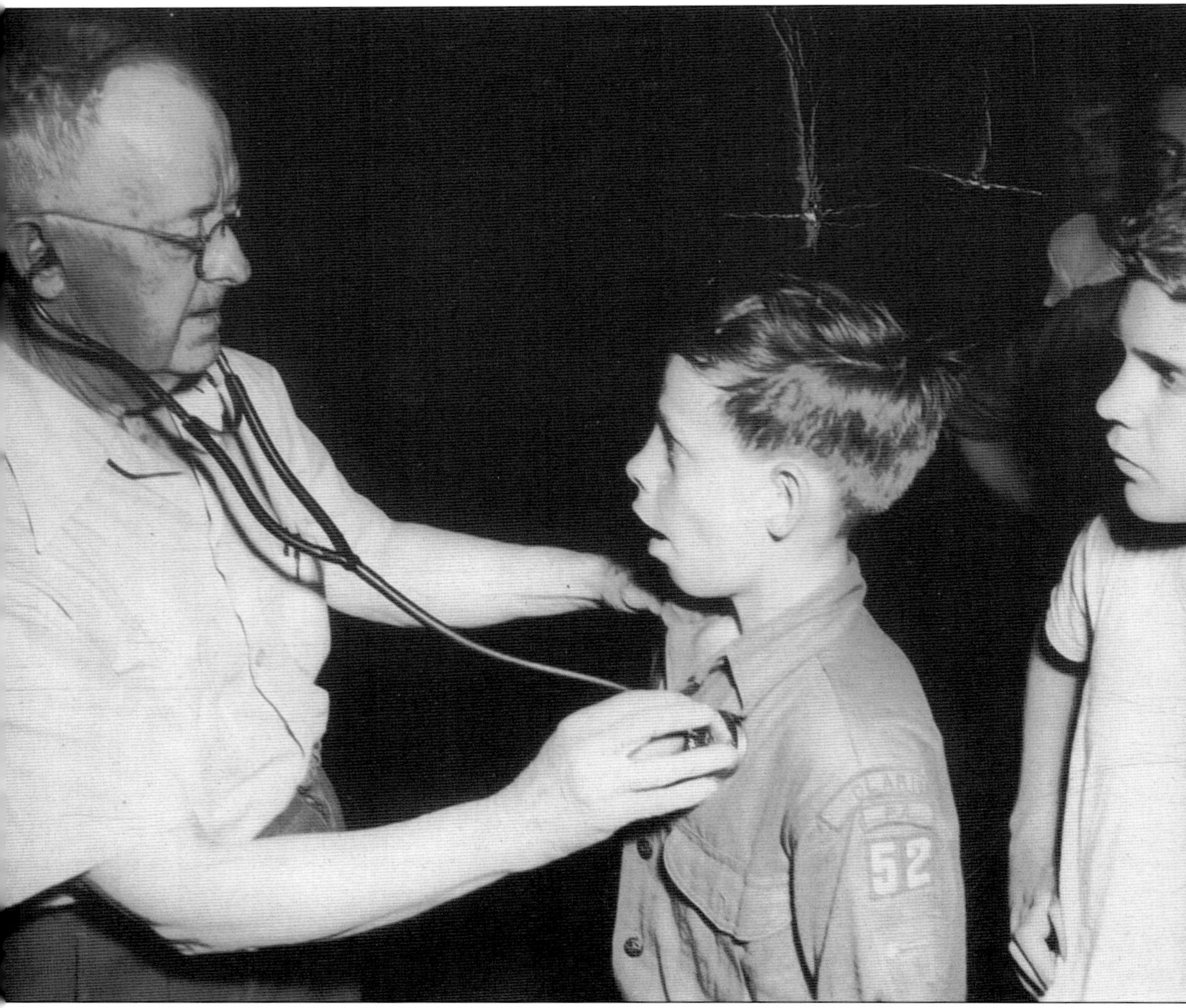

Scouting in Forest County had its beginning in Tionesta around 1932 with the formation of Troop No. 82 and Scout leaders Dr. Philip Silvis and Dr. Forrest Bovard, the "father of Scouting." Pictured are Scout members receiving a physical exam from Dr. Bovard.

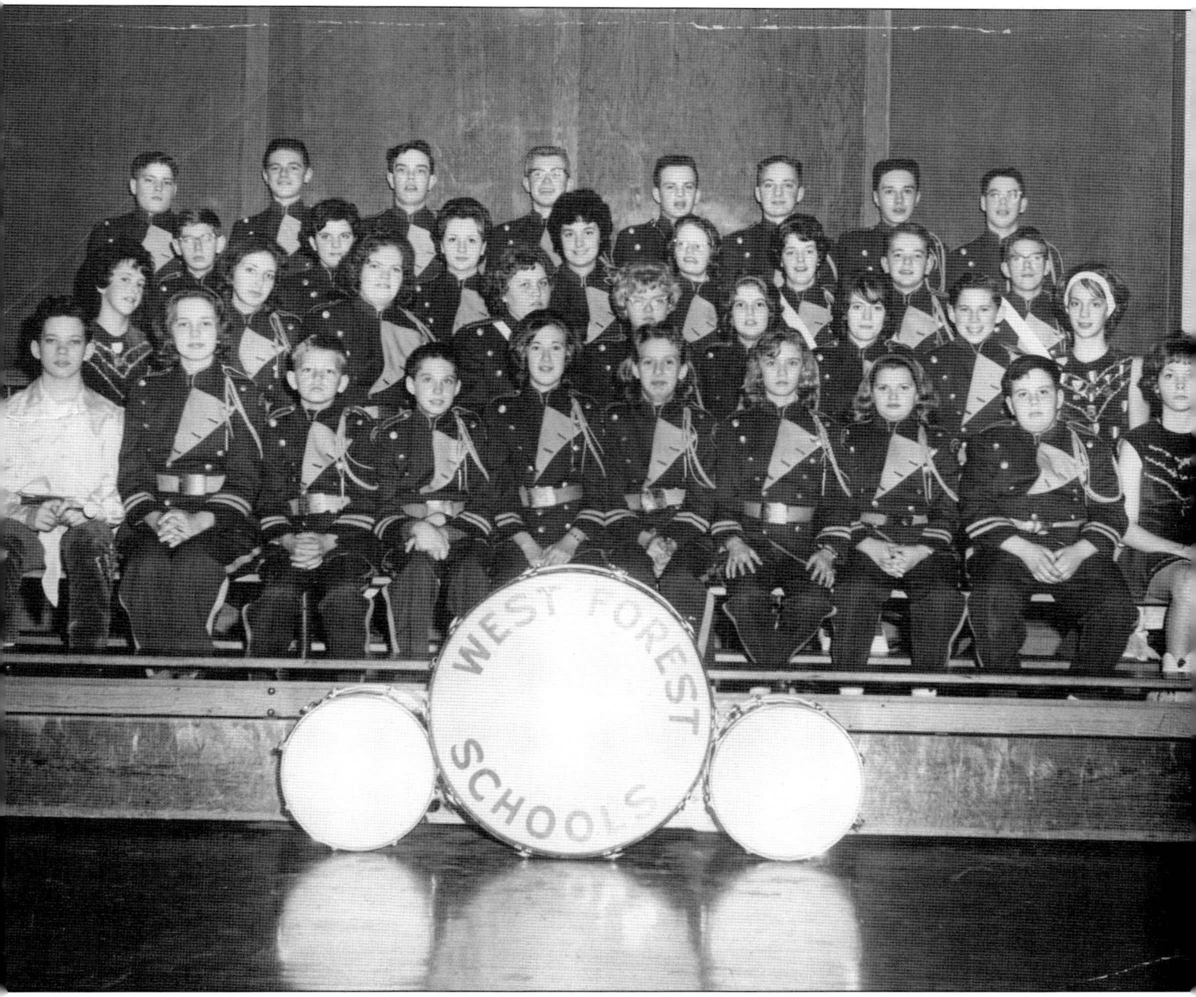

The first school to be opened in Forest County was in the Tionesta Borough around 1820; it was housed in private homes. An actual school building was not erected until about 1837, with a newer brick building being built in 1885, which was later destroyed in a fire on May 2, 1940. When reconstruction was complete, the Tionesta School remained independent until it was taken over in 1954 by the West Forest Joint School System. Shown is West Forest School's band around 1964.

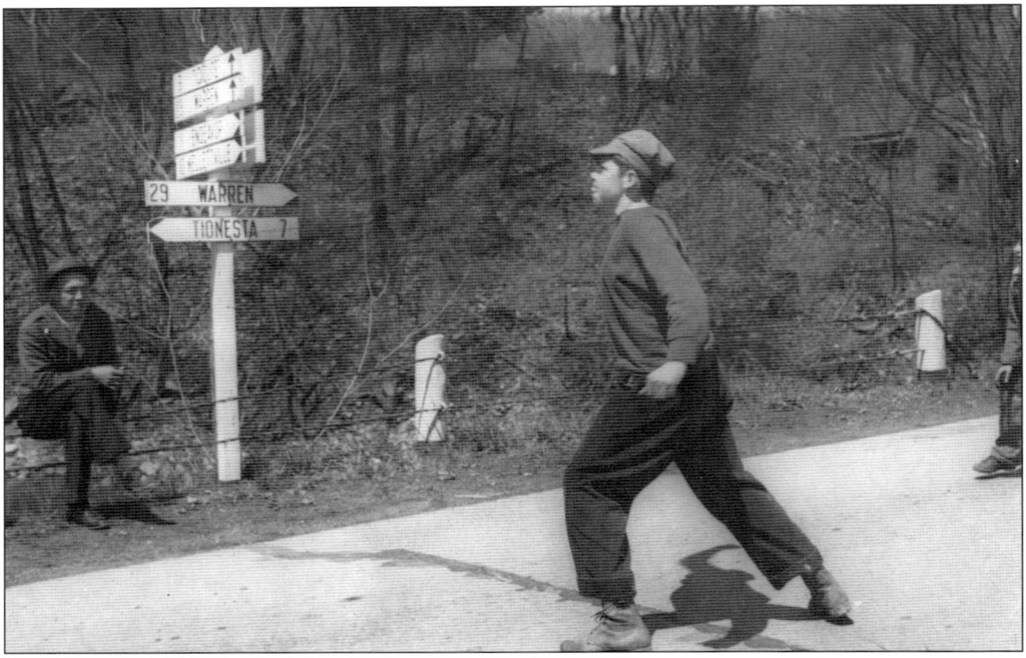

This undated photograph shows a group of boys playing in the roadway in Hickory Township near State Route 666 and US Route 62. In 1932, US Route 62 replaced State Route 65 throughout Forest County. The official name of State Route 666 is the David Zeisberger Memorial Highway.

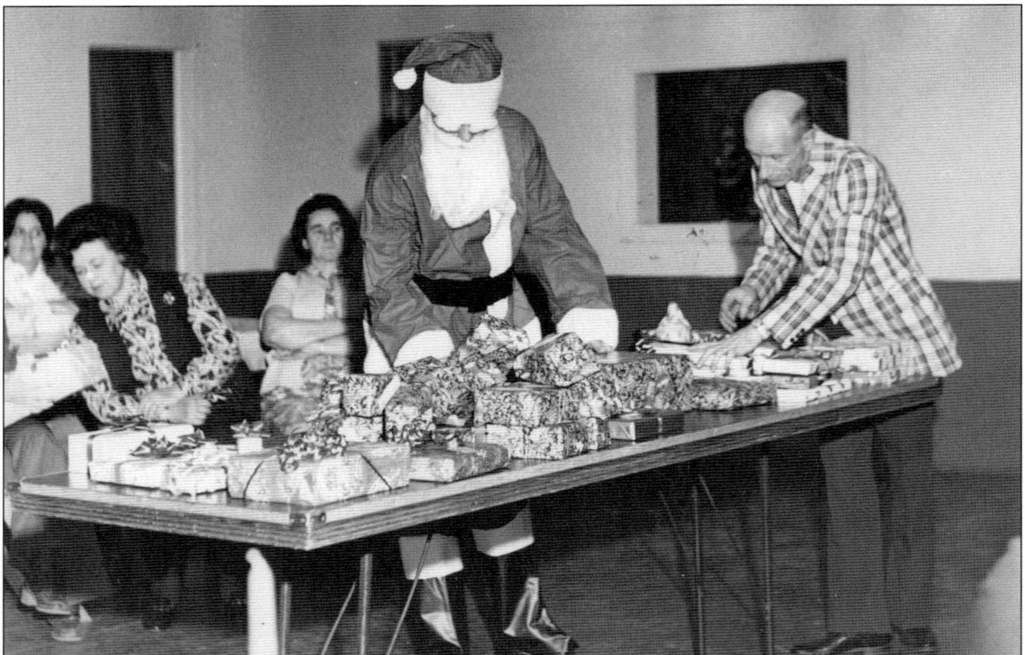

The first edition of the *Forest Press* was published on February 5, 1867, by Pete Conver in a rented room on Bridge Street in Tionesta. The slogan Conver used at the top of the paper to grab attention was "The First and Only Paper Printed in Forest County and About the Only One of the Kind Published Anywhere." Shown is a *Forest Press* Christmas party from 1974.

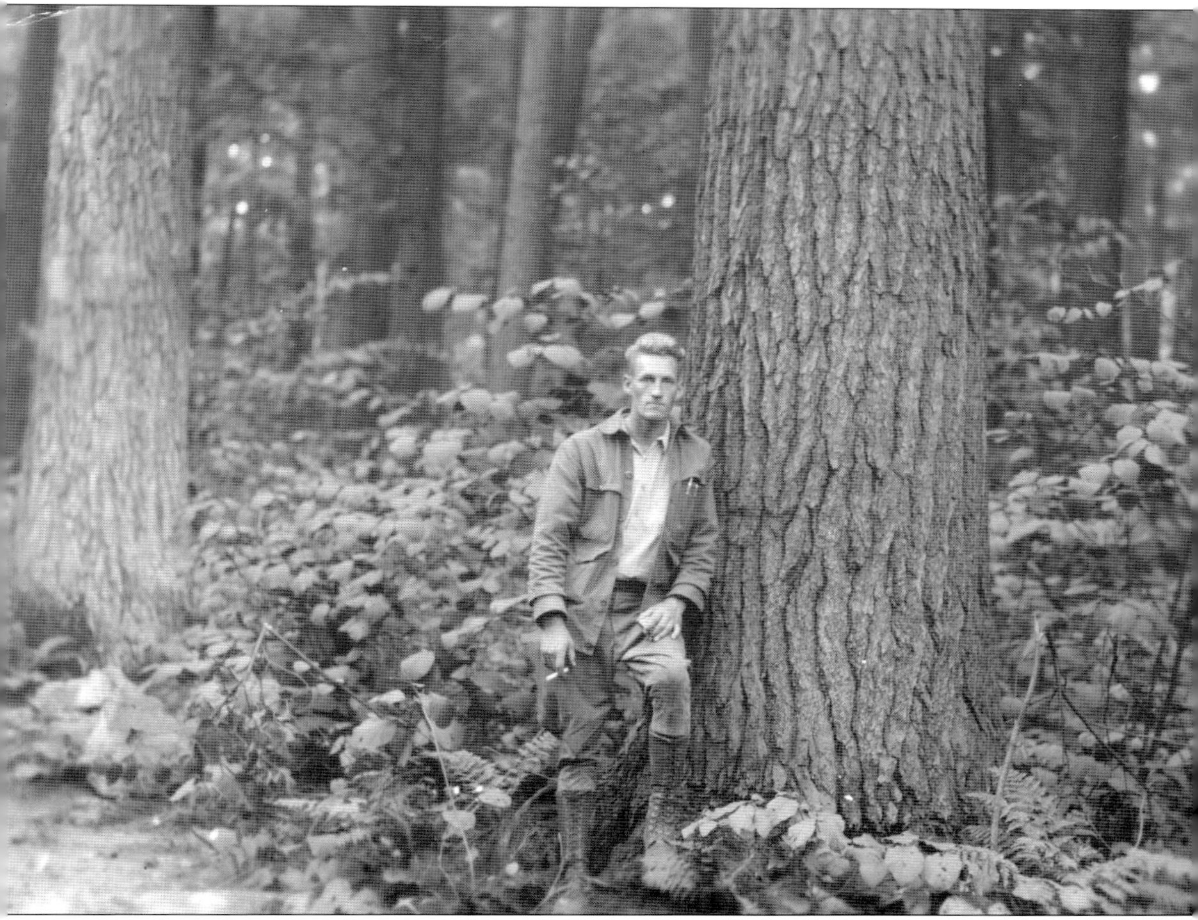

Along Pennsylvania Route 666 and Tionesta Creek is the community of Endeavor. Originally known as Stowtown, it is the location of the oldest sawmill in Pennsylvania. Constructed in the early 1830s by William Wheeler, Henry Van Bergan, Ezra May, Henry Dusenbury, and Edgar Gregory of the Wheeler & Dusenbury Lumber Company, the sawmill was the first successfully managed band-saw mill in the United States. Hamilton Stowe also bought into the sawmill and moved his family to the area, where they made their home.

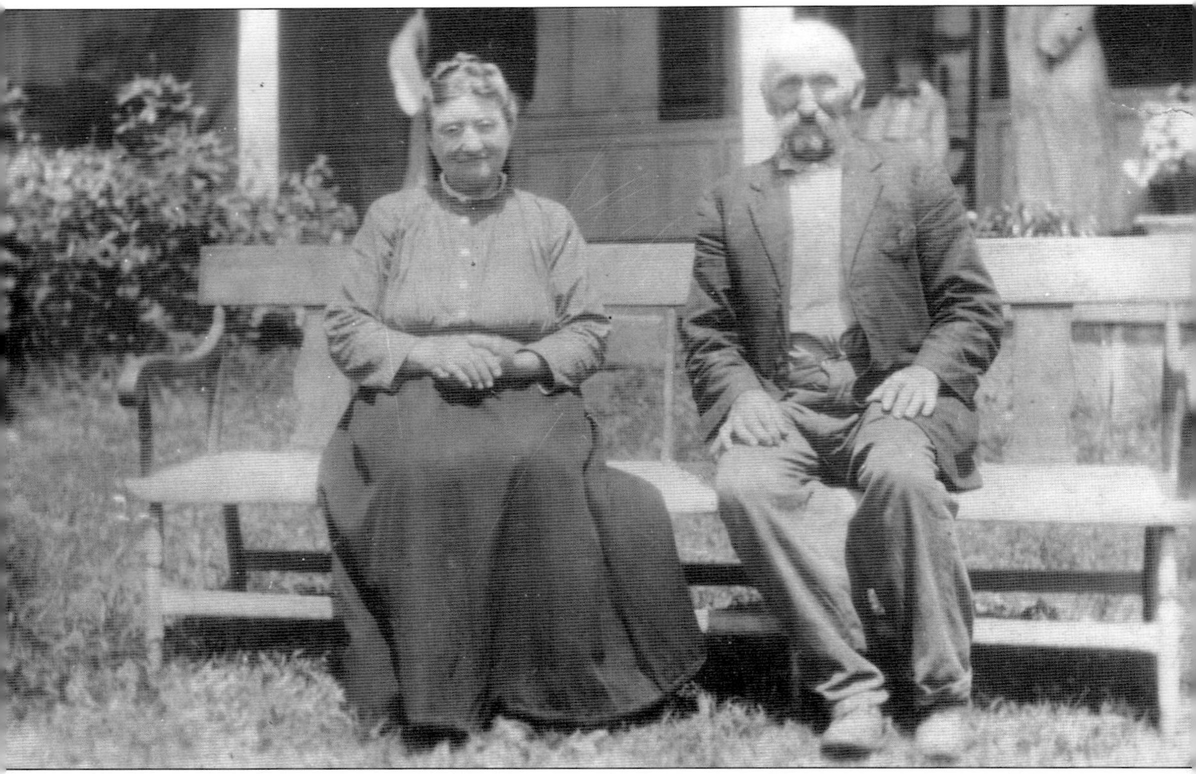

Martin Leonard Range, great-grandson of early settler Lt. John Range Sr., married Susanna (Heckman) Range in 1874. They resided on a farm located next to his parents' home on the north side of the borough. Martin and Susanna had four children. Several generations of the Range family members, beginning with Lt. John Range Sr., are buried in Riverside Cemetery in Tionesta.

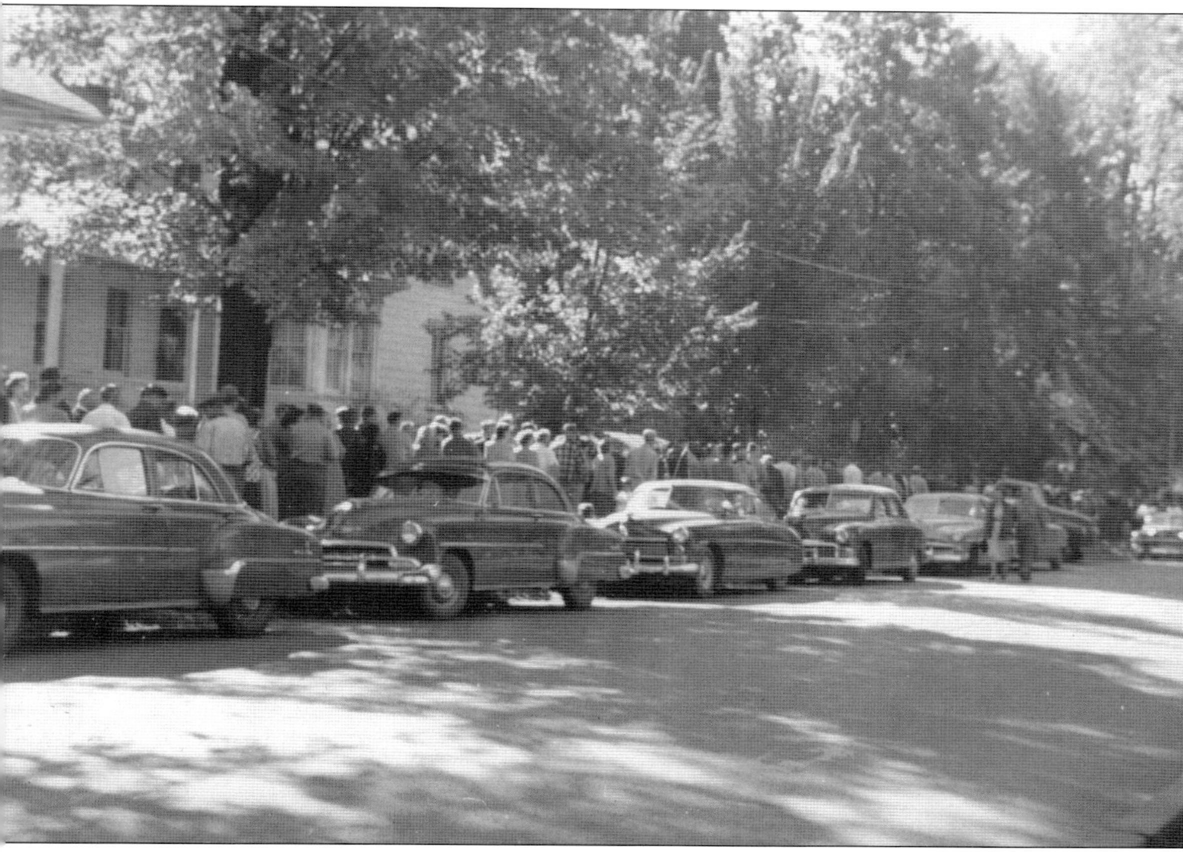

Due to its sparse population and mostly untouched wilds, the Allegheny National Forest is a fisherman's and hunter's paradise. Hunters line up as far as the eye can see on the Elm Street sidewalk to obtain their doe licenses at the Tionesta Courthouse on October 1, 1953.

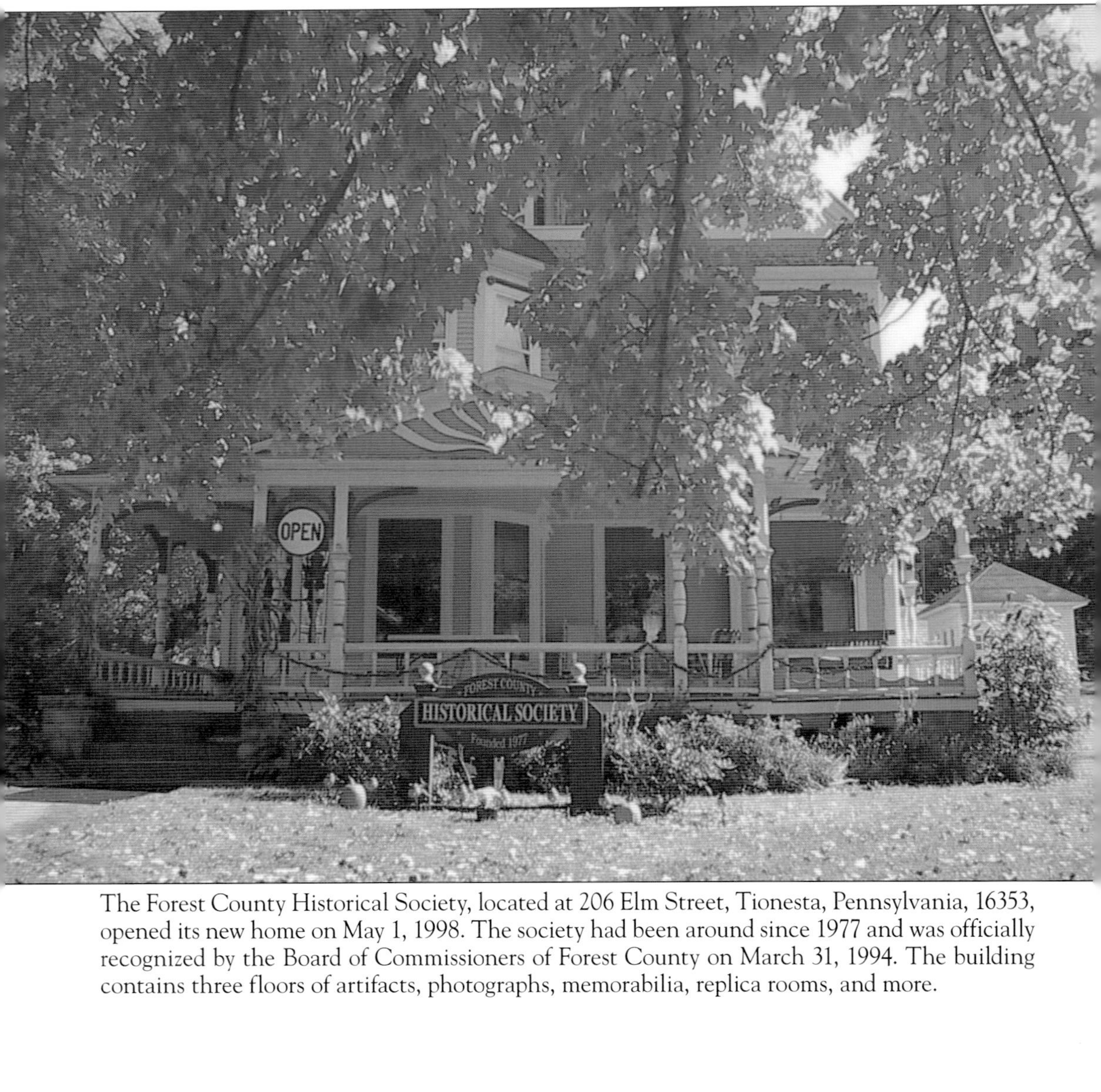

The Forest County Historical Society, located at 206 Elm Street, Tionesta, Pennsylvania, 16353, opened its new home on May 1, 1998. The society had been around since 1977 and was officially recognized by the Board of Commissioners of Forest County on March 31, 1994. The building contains three floors of artifacts, photographs, memorabilia, replica rooms, and more.

Bibliography

Badenoch, A. *Past and Present: Place Names and Post Offices of Forest County, Pennsylvania.* Tionesta, PA: Forest Press Inc., 1976.

Beers, J.H. *History of the Counties of McKean, Elk, and Forest, Pennsylvania.* Chicago, IL: J.H. Beers and Company, 1890.

Casler, W.C. *Teddy Collins Empire.* Williamsport, PA: Lycoming Printing Company Inc., 1976.

Childs, R. *History of Forest County, 1867–1967.* Tionesta, PA: Forest Press Inc., 1989.

Patrick, E.R. *History of Tionesta, 1856–2006.* Tionesta, PA: Forest Press Inc.

Small, E.C. *Nebraska, Forest County: A Lumber Town of 250 People, 1828–1940.* Tionesta, PA: Forest Press Inc., 2000.

Woman's Club of Marienville. *Marienville, 1833–1976.* Tionesta, PA: Forest Press Inc., 1976.